National Standards for History

Basic Edition

NATIONAL CENTER FOR HISTORY IN THE SCHOOLS

The development of the History Standards was administered by the National Center for History in the Schools at the University of California, Los Angeles under the guidance of the National Council for History Standards. The standards were developed with funding from the National Endowment for the Humanities and the U.S. Department of Education. This publication does not necessarily represent positions or policies of the United States government, and no official endorsement should be inferred. This publication may be freely reproduced and distributed for educational and research purposes.

Project Co-directors:	Gary B. Nash
	Charlotte Crabtree
Project Assistant Director:	Linda Symcox
Coordinating Editor World History Standards:	Ross E. Dunn
Assistant Editor U.S. History Standards:	David Vigilante
Book and cover design:	Robin Weisz
Production planning:	Chris Coniglio
Document control:	Marta Hill

Published 1996, National Center for History in the Schools

Ordering Information

National Standards for History
ISBN 09633218-4-6

Write to:

> National Center for History in the Schools
> University of California, Los Angeles
> 1100 Glendon Avenue, Suite 927
> Box 951588
> Los Angeles, CA 90095-1588
> FAX: (310) 794-6740

TABLE OF CONTENTS

PREFACE

The *National Standards for History* address one of the major goals for national education reform developed within the past decade. First envisioned by President George Bush and the nation's governors in their historic summit meeting in Charlottesville, Virginia in 1989, this reform agenda took shape in the National Education Goals jointly adopted by the National Governors' Association and President Bush a year later. These Goals were subsequently incorporated into legislation by the Congress and signed into law by President Bill Clinton in the GOALS 2000, Educate America Act of March 1994. Broadly supported by the American people, their state governors, their legislators in the United States Congress, and two successive presidential administrations, these National Education Goals have represented a genuine bipartisan approach to education reform.

The vision behind this reform agenda was initially expressed by the Bush Administration with the 1990 launching of the National Education Goals: " A new standard for an educated citizenry is required, one suitable for the next century. Our people must be as knowledgeable, as well-trained, as competent, and as inventive as those in any other nation. . . . America can meet this challenge if our society is dedicated to a renaissance in education." Central to this reform agenda was Goal 3, affirming that "by the year 2000, American students will leave grades four, eight, and twelve having demonstrated competency in challenging subject matter including English, mathematics, science, history, and geography; and every school in America will ensure that all students learn to use their minds well, so they may be prepared for responsible citizenship, further learning, and productive employment in our modern economy."

To move the nation toward this goal, President Bush announced on April 18, 1991 the launching of AMERICA 2000, a comprehensive reform strategy calling for the development of "world class" standards in the five subjects identified in the National Education Goals and the development of voluntary "American Achievement Tests" to assess progress toward this goal. Both proposals were strongly supported by the American public.

On January 24, 1992, the National Council on Education Standards and Testing, appointed by the Congress to advise on these matters and co-chaired by Governors Roy Romer (D-Colorado) and Carroll A. Campbell (R-South Carolina), released its report to the Congress and the American people. That report, *Raising Standards for American Education*, affirmed the importance of both national content standards and a national system of assessments. Nine months later, in October 1992, presidential candidate Bill Clinton committed himself, too, to the "establishment of world class standards [specifically to include history] and development of a meaningful national examination system. . . to increase expectations, and to give schools incentives and structures to improve student performance." It was a goal advanced by the passage of the GOALS 2000 legislation two years later and heralded by the Clinton Administration with the words, "Final passage of [this] legislation moves us one step closer to the day when we can assure every parent in America that their children. . . are receiving an education that is up to world class standards."

It was in this robust climate of bipartisan support for a national program of education reform that the National History Standards Project was born. Initially co-funded in the spring of 1992 by the National Endowment for the Humanities, chaired by Lynne Cheney, and by the United States Department of Education, headed by Secretary of Education Lamar Alexander, this project sought to develop broad national consensus for what constitutes excellence in the teaching and learning of history in the nation's schools. Developed through a broad-based national consensus-building process, this task has involved working toward agreement both on the larger purposes of history in the school curriculum and on the more specific history understandings and thinking processes all students should have equal opportunity to acquire over twelve years of precollegiate education.

This present publication, *National Standards for History*, is the result of nearly four years of intensive work by hundreds of gifted classroom teachers of history; of supervisors, state social studies specialists, and chief state school officers responsible for history in the schools; of dozens of talented and active academic historians in the nation; and of representatives of a broad array of professional and scholarly organizations, civic and public interest groups, parents and individual citizens with a stake in the teaching of history in the schools.

The National Council for History Standards, the policy-setting body responsible for providing policy direction and oversight of the Project, consisted of 30 members, including the present or immediate past presidents of such large-membership organizations directly responsible for the content and teaching of history as the Council of Chief State School Officers, the Association for Supervision and Curriculum Development, the Council of State Social Studies Specialists, the National Council for the Social Studies, the American Historical Association, the Organization of American Historians, the National Council for History Education, and the Organization of History Teachers. In addition, members included the Director and Associate Director of the Social Studies Development Center, supervisory and curriculum development staff of county and city school districts, experienced classroom teachers, and distinguished historians in the fields of United States and World History. To foster correspondence in the development of these standards with the work under development for the 1994 National Assessment of Educational Progress (NAEP) in United States History, several participants in the NAEP Planning and Steering Committees were included in the National Council for History Standards. For similar reasons two members of the Congressionally-mandated National Council for Education Standards and Testing also served on this Council. Finally, the two directors of the National Center for History in the Schools, responsible for administering this Project, served as co-chairs of the Council.

The National Forum for History Standards was composed of representatives from major education, public interest, parent-teacher, and other organizations concerned with history in the schools. Advisory in its function, the Forum provided important counsel and feedback for this Project as well as access to the larger public through the membership of the organizations represented in the Forum.

Nine Organizational Focus Groups of between 15 and 29 members each, chosen by the leadership of their respective organizations, were contracted with to provide important advisory, review, and consulting services to the Project. Organizations providing this special service included the Council of Chief State School Officers, the Association for Supervision and Curriculum Development, the American Historical Association, the World History Association, the National Council for the Social Studies, the Organization of American Historians, the National Council for History Education, the Council of State Social Studies Specialists, and the Organization of History Teachers.

Three Curriculum Task Forces were formed, totaling more than 50 members, with responsibility for developing the standards for students in grades kindergarten through four, and for students in grades five through twelve in the fields of United States and World History. Composed of veteran classroom teachers from throughout the United States who had been recommended by the many organizations participating in this Project, and of recognized scholars of United States and World History with deep commitments to history education in schools, these groups have worked for many months in grade-alike writing teams and in meetings of the whole to ensure continuity of standards across all levels of schooling, elementary through high school.

In particular we express the special appreciation due the team of editorial - writers—John Pyne, Gloria Sesso, Kirk Ankeney, and David Vigilante—who over the closing months of the Project addressed the final changes requested in the third national review of the United States History Standards and helped bring the Project to completion.

We also express deep appreciation to Sara Shoob, Cub Run Elementary School, Centreville, Virginia, who chaired the Curriculum Task Force for the K-4 History Standards; and to Helen Debelak, Birchwood Elementary and Junior High School, Cleveland, Ohio, and John M. Fisher, Fifth Avenue Elementary School, Columbus, Ohio, who served with Shoob as the editorial team who responded to the recommendations of all the review groups and worked long hours throughout the late spring and summer months of 1994 to refine the standards and bring them to completion.

The drafting of the World History Standards required more than the usual collaborative effort that any standards project must mount. Acknowledgements and appreciation are therefore especially apt. The National Council for History Standards Project established an *ad hoc* World History Committee of experienced teachers and historians with expertise in various eras and areas of World History to draft a scaffolding for the writing of the standards. This devoted group, which met for four work sessions over a period of six months, was chaired by Michael Winston, Howard University and the Alfred Harcourt Foundation. The other members of the committee were: Joan Arno, George Washington High School, Philadelphia, PA; David Baumbach, Woolsair Elementary Gifted Center, Pittsburgh, PA; Richard Bulliet, Columbia University; Ainslee T. Embree, Columbia University; Carol Gluck, Columbia University; Akira Iriye, Harvard University; Henry G. Kiernan, Director of Curriculum, West Morris Regional High School District, Chester, NJ; Colin Palmer, University of North Carolina, Chapel Hill; Richard Saller, University of Chicago; and Theodore Rabb, Princeton University.

Working from the Winston Committee's report were a group of experienced, knowledgeable, and dedicated classroom teachers and historians who have been in the forefront of efforts to teach and write a more balanced and inclusive World History. This group—the World History Curriculum Task Force—worked over two summers and in week-long sessions throughout these two academic years. They included: Joann Alberghini, Lake View Junior High School, Santa Maria, CA; John Arevalo, Harlandale High School, San Antonio TX; Joan Arno, George Washington High School, Philadelphia, PA; David Baumbach, Woolsair Elementary Gifted Center, Pittsburgh, PA; Edward Berenson, University of California, Los Angeles; Margaret Binnaker, St. Andrews-Swanee School, St. Andrews, TN; Jacqueline Brown-Frierson, Lemmel Middle

School, Baltimore, MD; Richard Bulliet, Columbia University; Stanley Burstein, California State University, Los Angeles; Anne Chapman, Western Reserve Academy, Hudson, OH; Peter Cheoros, Lynwood High School, Lynwood, CA; Sammy Crawford, Soldotna High School, Soldotna, AK; Ross Dunn, San Diego State University; Benjamin Elman, University of California, Los Angeles; Jean Fleet, Riverside University High School, Milwaukee, WI; Jana Flores, Pine Grove Elementary School, Santa Maria, CA; Michele Forman, Middlebury High School, Middlebury, VT; Charles Frazee, California State University, Fullerton; Marilynn Jo Hitchens, Wheat Ridge High School, Wheat Ridge, CO; Jean Johnson, Friends Seminary, New York, NY.; Henry G. Kiernan, West Morris Regional High School District, Chester, NJ; Carrie McIver, Santee Summit High School, Santee, CA; Susan Meisler, Vernon Center Middle School, Vernon, CT; Joe Palumbo, Long Beach Unified School District, Long Beach, CA; Sue Rosenthal, High School for Creative and Performing Arts, Philadelphia, PA; Heidi Roupp, Aspen High School, Aspen, CO; Irene Segade, San Diego High School, San Diego, CA; Geoffrey Symcox, University of California, Los Angeles; David Vigilante, Gompers Secondary School, San Diego, CA; Scott Waugh, University of California, Los Angeles; Julia Werner, Nicolet High School, Glendale, WI; and Donald Woodruff, Fredericksburg Academy, Fredericksburg, VA.

To all of these precollegiate and university members of the World History Curriculum Task Force we express great respect and admiration for their tireless efforts and good spirits in negotiating the choppy waters of World History. None of their efforts would have reached fruition without the very special involvement of Ross Dunn, who played a leading and indispensable role in coordinating the work of the World History Curriculum Task Force, led two of the drafting sessions, and acted as a gentle intellectual *padrone* in negotiating the many cross-currents that necessarily attend the writing of anything as ambitious as a framework for the study of humankind's entire history.

In the final drafting of National Standards for World History, a small group of people worked with Dunn in the summer and early fall of 1994: Joann Alberghini, Roger Beck, Anne Chapman, Jean Fleet, Jana Flores, Jean Johnson, Henry Kiernan, David Vigilante, and Donald Woodruff. The East Asian Curriculum Project at the East Asian Institute, Columbia University, and the Council on Islamic Education greatly assisted this group. The co-directors of this project believe that only rarely in the history of American education has such a group of good-spirited, gifted, and devoted teachers—from across the country and teaching at every level of education from elementary schools to baccalaureate institutions—accomplished so much for the teaching of history in the schools.

Our thanks go also to the many members of the National Council for History Standards, the National Forum for History Standards, and the Organizational Focus Groups who gave unfailingly and selflessly of their time and professional expertise during the more than two years of intensive work that went into the development of the standards. The Appendix presents the rosters of all these working groups. In particular, we salute those who read draft after draft under difficult deadlines throughout the spring and summer of 1994, and submitted substantive recommendations for revisions that have contributed importantly to the completion of this volume.

Special appreciation is due also to the many school districts and administrators who time and again agreed to the release time that allowed the gifted teachers who served on the History Curriculum Task Forces to meet at UCLA for week-long working sessions throughout the school year in order to complete the development of the standards and of the grade-appropriate examples of student achievement.

As co-directors of this project, we express special appreciation, also, to the many thousands of teachers, curriculum leaders, assessment experts, historians, parents, textbook publishers, and others too numerous to mention who sought review copies of the standards and turned out for public hearings and information sessions scheduled at regional and national conferences throughout these several years, and who provided their independent assessments and recommendations for making these standards historically sound, workable in classrooms, and responsive to the needs and interests of students in the schools.

Finally, we note with appreciation the funding provided by the National Endowment for the Humanities and by the Office of Educational Research and Improvement of the United States Department of Education to conduct this complex and broadly inclusive enterprise.

The United States and World History Standards were revised in early 1996. The revisions are responsive to the recommendations of two panels of distinguished educators and public figures that were organized by the Council for Basic Education and funded by the Pew Charitable Trusts, the John D. and Catherine T. MacArthur Foundation, the Ford Foundation, and the Spencer Foundation. The panelists are listed in the Appendix. In making these revisions, we are grateful for the participation and advice of the following history educators: Richard del Rio, Muirlands Middle School, La Jolla, CA; Gerald Holton, Harvard University; Daniel Kevles, California Institute of Technology; Richard Steele, San Diego State University, CA; David Vigilante, San Diego; Bob Bain, Beachwood High School, Cleveland Heights, OH; Joanne Ferraro, San Diego State University, CA; Craig Lockard, University of Wisconsin, Green Bay; Bullitt Lowry, University of North Texas; Robert Rittner, Hasting High School, Spring Valley, NY; and Peter Stearns, Carnegie-Mellon University.

A newly-formed Advisory Board to the National Center for History in the Schools appraised the revisions and made important contributions to the final version. Their names are also listed in the Appendix. Their work, like that of the panelists convened by the Council for Basic Education, should be seen—and appreciated—as a part of the effort to achieve a participatory and wide-reaching consensus on what constitutes historical literacy in this nation.

In this most contentious field of the curriculum, there have been many who have wondered if a national consensus could be forged concerning what all students should have opportunity to learn about the history of the world and of the peoples of all racial, religious, ethnic, and national backgrounds who have been a part of that story. The responsiveness, enormous good will, and dogged determination of so many to meet this challenge has reinforced our confidence in the inherent strength and capabilities of this nation to undertake the steps necessary for bringing to all students the benefits of this endeavor. The stakes are high. It is the challenge that must now be undertaken.

Gary B. Nash and Charlotte Crabtree
Co-directors

National Standards for History K-4

PART ONE

1

Developing Standards in History for Students in Grades K-4

Significance of History for the Educated Citizen

Setting standards for history in the schools requires a clear vision of the place and importance of history in the general education of all students. The widespread and growing support for more and better history in the schools, beginning in the early grades of elementary education, is one of the encouraging signs of this decade. The reasons are many, but none more important to a democratic society than this: *knowledge of history is the precondition of political intelligence*. Without history, a society shares no common memory of where it has been, of what its core values are, or of what decisions of the past account for present circumstances. Without history, one cannot undertake any sensible inquiry into the political, social, or moral issues in society. And without historical knowledge and the inquiry it supports, one cannot move to the informed, discriminating citizenship essential to effective participation in the democratic processes of governance and the fulfillment for all our citizens of the nation's democratic ideals.

Today's students, more than ever before, need also a comprehensive understanding of the history of the world, and of the peoples of many cultures and civilizations who have developed ideas, institutions, and ways of life different from students' own. From a balanced and inclusive world history students may gain an appreciation both of the world's many cultures and of their shared humanity and common problems. Students may acquire the habit of seeing matters through others' eyes and come to realize that by studying others, they can also better understand themselves. Historical understanding based on such comparative studies in World History does not require approval or forgiveness for the tragedies either of one's own society or of others'; nor does it negate the importance of critically examining alternative value systems and their effects in supporting or denying the basic human rights and aspirations of all peoples. Especially important, an understanding of the history of the world's many cultures can contribute to fostering the kind of mutual patience, respect, and civic courage required in our increasingly pluralistic society and our increasingly interdependent world.

These learnings directly contribute to the education of the *public citizen*, but they uniquely contribute to nurturing the *private individual* as well. Historical memory is the key to self-identity, to seeing one's place in the stream of time, and one's connectedness with all of humankind. We are part of an ancient chain, and the long hand of the past is upon us—for good and for ill—just as our hands will rest on our descendants for years to come.

Denied knowledge of one's roots and of one's place in the great stream of human history, the individual is deprived of the fullest sense of self and of shared community on which one's fullest personal development as well as responsible citizenship depends. For these purposes, history and the humanities must occupy an indispensable role in the school curriculum, beginning in the earliest years of school.

The Case for History in Grades K-4

For young children, history—along with literature and the arts—provides one of the most enriching studies in which they can be engaged. "What children of this age need," Bruno Bettelheim has written, "is rich food for their imagination, a sense of history, how the present situation came about." History enlarges children's experience, providing, in the words of Philip Phenix, "a sense of personal involvement in exemplary lives and significant events, an appreciation of values and a vision of greatness." History connects each child with his or her roots and develops a sense of personal belonging in the great sweep of human experience.

Fortunately, the nation's educators are increasingly recognizing the importance of history in these early years of schooling, and of the interests and capabilities history fosters in young children. If students are to enjoy these immediate benefits of historical studies which Bettelheim, Phenix, and others have observed, and to lay the foundations on which their continuing development of the major goals addressed above depend, then schools must broaden the curriculum to include historical studies from the earliest school years onward.

Definition of Standards

Standards in history make explicit the goals that all students should have opportunity to acquire, if the purposes just considered are to be achieved. In history, standards are of two types:

1. *Historical thinking skills* that enable children to differentiate past, present, and future time; raise questions; seek and evaluate evidence; compare and analyze historical stories, illustrations, and records from the past; interpret the historical record; and construct historical narratives of their own.

2. *Historical understandings* that define what students should *know* about the history of families, their communities, states, nation, and world. These understandings are drawn from the record of human aspirations, strivings, accomplishments, and failures in at least five spheres of human activity: the social, political, scientific/technological, economic, and cultural (the philosophical/religious/aesthetic), as appropriate for children.

Historical thinking and understanding do not, of course, develop independently of one another. Higher levels of historical thinking depend upon and are linked to the attainment of higher levels of historical understanding. For these reasons, the standards presented in Chapter 3 of Part One provide an integration of historical thinking and understanding.

Basic Principles Guiding the Development of Standards for K-4

History Standards for elementary school children, grades K-4, have been developed with the following principles in mind:

1. Children can, from the earliest elementary grades, begin to build historical understandings and perspectives and to think historically. An important responsibility of schooling in these years is to support the conditions which foster children's natural curiosity and imagination, to provide them opportunities to reach out in time and space, and to expand their world of understanding far beyond the "here and now."

2. Although young children are only in the early stages of acquiring concepts of chronology and time, they easily learn to differentiate time present, time past, and time "long, long ago"—skills on which good programs in historical thinking can then build over grades K-4.

3. To bring history alive, an important part of children's historical studies should be centered in people—the history of families and of people, ordinary and extraordinary, who have lived in children's own community, state, nation, and the world.

4. History becomes especially accessible and interesting to children when approached through stories, myths, legends, and biographies that capture children's imaginations and immerse them in times and cultures of the recent and long-ago past.

5. In addition to stories, children should be introduced to a wide variety of historical artifacts, illustrations, and records that open to them first-hand glimpses into the lives of people in the past: family photos; letters, diaries, and other accounts of the past obtained from family records, local newspapers, libraries, and museums; field trips to historical sites in their neighborhood and community; and visits to "living museums" where actors reenact life long ago.

6. All these resources should be used imaginatively to help children formulate questions for study and to support historical thinking, such as the ability to marshal information; create sound hypotheses; locate events in time and place; compare and contrast past and present; explain historical causes and consequences; analyze historical fiction and illustrations for their accuracy and perspectives, and compare with primary sources that accurately portray life, attitudes, and values in the past; compare different stories about an era or event in the past and the interpretations or perspectives of each; and create historical narratives of their own in the form of stories, letters such as a child long ago might have written, and descriptive accounts of events.

Developing Standards in History for Grades K-4

Topical Organization

Determining the organization by which standards for grades K-4 would be presented involved something of a dilemma, given the variety of curriculum approaches teachers can adopt in developing engaging historical studies for children. In addressing this problem in 1988, the Bradley Commission on History in Schools identified three curricular options for grades K-4:

(1) **A "here—there—then" approach:** This approach first centers instruction in each of these grades in the child's immediate present and then each year reaches out in space and back in time to enlarge children's breadth of geographic and historical understandings to distant places and times long ago. From kindergarten onward, this model introduces children to peoples and cultures throughout the world, and to historical times as distant as the earliest human memories, contained in myths, legends, and heroic tales, which are part of the cultural heritage of the world.

(2) **A modification of the "expanding environments" approach to social studies:** This approach includes, each year, rich studies in history and literature that connect with grade 1 studies of the family, grade 2 studies of the neighborhood, grade 3 studies of the community, and grade 4 studies of the state, but that expand and deepen these studies far beyond their traditional emphasis on the "here and now." Thus, this modified model compares family, community, and state today with family life long ago, and with the people and events of earlier times in the historical development of their community and state. Fully expanded, this model also compares family and community life in the United States with life in the many cultures from which our increasingly diverse population has come, and with the historical experiences and traditions that are part of those cultures.

(3) **A "literature-centered" approach:** This approach focuses instruction each year on compelling selections of literature appropriate for children from many historical periods, and then expands those studies to explore more deeply the historical times they bring to life. This pattern is, essentially, a child's version of the humanities-centered "Great Books" approach to curriculum-making, with literature used to take children into adventurous and deeply engaging excursions through a variety of historical eras and cultures.

In developing standards for history in grades K-4, the Curriculum Task Force sought an organizational structure flexible enough to support improved programs in history under any of these curriculum approaches, rather than assuming a single national curriculum for the schools. The topics believed to meet this need and under which the eight standards in history have been organized are as follows:

Topic 1:   Living and Working Together in Families and Communities, Now and Long Ago

Topic 2:   The History of Students' Own State or Region

Topic 3:   The History of the United States: Democratic Principles and Values and the Peoples from Many Cultures Who Contributed to Its Cultural, Economic, and Political Heritage

Topic 4:   The History of Peoples of Many Cultures around the World

Although organized geographically from "near to far," these topics reach far beyond the traditional content of the "expanding environments" curriculum model for grades K-4 by including at all grade levels studies of the nation and the world, and of the ancient as well as more recent past. How teachers draw upon these standards and how they sequence their programs of instruction should be determined by the particular curriculum approach they have adopted. For example:

(1) **Teachers adopting the "here—there—then" model of curriculum-making** will find standards that connect the child's present world with the long-ago past and with distant cultures at every grade level, K-2 as well as 3-4. Thus, teachers of grades K-2 are not limited to comparative studies of family and community life (Topic 1). They may also select standards from Topics 2-4 that deepen young children's understanding of people, ordinary and extraordinary, who have contributed to the betterment of others' lives in their state, nation, and the world at various times in history; and they can engage children in analyses of compelling stories of individual heroism and epic events from ancient times until today by adopting standards from Topics 2-4, as well.

(2) **Teachers adopting the modified "expanding environments" approach** will find Topics 1 and 2 easily incorporated in their present curriculum and find in Topics 3 and 4 rich opportunities for expanding children's understandings beyond the immediate "here and now."

(3) **Teachers adopting the "literature-centered" approach to history** will find throughout the standards rich inclusions of literature and of associated historical studies of the era or context in which the literary selections were developed. Visiting museums and "living history" sites to observe the clothing, houses, furnishings, tools, and other artifacts referenced in a particular selection of historical fiction or biography; observing the geographic site in which historic events in the story occurred; comparing the characters and descriptions in the story and its illustrations with diaries, documents, photos, and other records of the time to judge the historical authenticity of the work; placing events in their chronological and geographic place on time lines and maps; reenacting episodes in the story through dramatizations; and writing their own narrative accounts are all examples of student achievement of standards on which teachers choosing a literature-centered approach to history can draw.

The standards, in short, define outcomes of instruction. They assume no one curriculum design. Teachers must be free to enter these standards and use them appropriately to meet the interests and instructional needs of the students they are teaching.

Historical Understanding for Grades K-4

History for grades K-4 is a broadly integrative field, recounting and analyzing human aspirations and strivings in at least five spheres of human activity: social, scientific/technological, economic, political, and cultural (the religious/philosophical/ aesthetic). Introducing young children to history—the history of families, their communities, their state, nation, and various cultures of the world—at once engages them in the lives, aspirations, struggles, accomplishments, and failures of real people, in all these aspects of their lives.

> ♦ Through history, children come to deeper understandings of society: of different and changing patterns of family structures, of men's and women's roles, of childhood

and of children's roles, of various groups in society, and of relationships among all these individuals and groups.

▶ Through history, children come to deeper understandings of the scientific quest to understand the world we live in and the quest to do better, or more efficiently, everything from producing food to caring for the ill, to transporting goods, to advancing economic security and the well-being of the group. Understandings of the work people have done, the exchange relationships they have developed with others, and the scientific/technological developments that have propelled change are all central to the study of history and of great interest to children.

▶ Through history, children come to a beginning understanding of the political sphere of activity as it has developed in their local community, their state, and their nation. Particularly important are understandings of the core principles and values of American democracy that unite us as a people; of the people and events that have exemplified these principles in local, state, and national history; and of the struggles to bring the rights guaranteed by these principles to all Americans.

▶ Ideas, beliefs, and values have profoundly influenced human actions throughout history. Religion, philosophy, art, and popular culture have all been central to the aspirations and achievements of all societies, and have been a mainspring of historical change from earliest times. Children's explorations of this sphere of human activity, through delving into the literature, sacred writings and oral traditions, drama, art, architecture, music, and dance of a people, bring history to life for children, foster empathy, and deepen their understandings of the human experience.

Historical Thinking

History, properly developed for children in the early years of schooling, can open important opportunities to analyze and develop appreciation for all these spheres of human activity and of the interactions among them. To do so requires that children be engaged in *active* questioning and learning, and not merely in the passive absorption of facts, names, and dates. Real historical understanding requires that students engage in historical reasoning; listen to and read historical stories, narratives, and literature with meaning; think through cause-effect relationships; interview "old-timers" in their communities; analyze documents, photos, historical newspapers, and the records of the past available in local museums and historical sites; and construct time lines and historical narratives of their own. Essential to developing historical insights and lasting learning, these skills are also the processes of *active* learning.

Tailored to the capabilities of young students, these activities are capable of developing skills in the following five types of historical thinking:

▶ **Chronological thinking,** developing a beginning sense of historical time—past, present, and future—in order to identify the temporal sequence in which events occurred, measure calendar time, interpret and create time lines, and explain patterns of historical continuity and change.

▶ **Historical comprehension,** including the ability to listen to and read historical stories and narratives with understanding, to identify the basic elements of the narrative or story structure (the characters, situation, sequence of events, their causes, and their outcome); and to develop the ability to describe the past through the eyes and experiences of those who were there, as revealed through their literature, art, artifacts, and other records of their time.

▶ **Historical analysis and interpretation,** including the ability to compare and contrast different experiences, beliefs, motives, traditions, hopes, and fears of people from various groups and backgrounds, and at various times in the past and present; to analyze how these differing motives, interests, beliefs, hopes, and fears influenced people's behaviors; to compare the different perspectives included in different stories about historical people and events; to compare historical fiction and documentary sources about a particular era or event; and to analyze the historical accuracy of fictional accounts.

▶ **Historical research capabilities,** including the ability to formulate historical questions from encounters with historical documents, artifacts, photos, visits to historical sites, and eyewitness accounts; to acquire information concerning the historical time and place where the artifact, document, or other record was created; and to construct a historical narrative or story concerning it.

▶ **Historical issues-analysis and decision-making,** including the ability to identify problems that people confronted in historical literature, the local community, and the state; to analyze the various interests and points of view of people caught up in these situations; to evaluate alternative proposals for dealing with the problem(s); and to analyze whether the decisions reached or the actions taken were good ones and why.

Integrating Standards in Historical Understanding and Thinking

Chapter 2 presents the K-4 Standards in Historical Thinking, largely independent of historical content in order to specify the quality of thinking desired for each. None of these skills in historical thinking, however, can be developed or even expressed in a vacuum. Every one of them requires historical content in order to function—a relationship clarified in Chapter 3, in which the standards integrating historical understandings and thinking are presented for all four topics in history for grades K-4.

Figure 1 illustrates the approach taken to integrate historical thinking and understandings in the standards. The example is drawn from Topic 2, *The History of Students' Own State or Region.* As illustrated, the five skills in historical thinking (the left side of the diagram) and the three historical understandings students should acquire concerning the history of their state (the right side of the diagram) are integrated in the central area of overlap in the diagram in order to define (immediately below) Standard 3B: What students should be able to do to demonstrate their understanding of the first European, African, and/or Asian/Pacific explorers and settlers in their state or region.

Figure 2 provides a further illustration of this same standard, presented this time in the format in which the standards are stated (Chapter 3). The selection is again drawn from Topic 2, *The History of Students' Own State or Region.* As illustrated, the standard first presents a statement defining what students should understand: "The people, events, problems, and ideas that were significant in creating the history of their state."

Directly below the standard is <u>standard component</u> 3A, a statement which zooms in on part of the full standard: "The history of indigenous peoples who first lived in his or her state or region." This statement is followed by three <u>elaborated standards</u> which specify what students should be able to do to demonstrate their understanding of the history of indigenous peoples who first lived in their state or region. Each elaborated standard illustrates the integration of historical thinking and understanding by marrying a particular thinking skill (e.g., read historical narratives imaginatively) to a specific historical understanding (e.g., legends and myths of the Native Americans or Hawaiians). One thinking skill appears highlighted in brackets following each statement. The particular thinking skill was selected to serve as an example of the integration of historical thinking and historical understanding, and it is by no means the only one that can be employed. In fact, the standards encourage teachers to approach content through a wide variety of thinking skills.

Finally, each elaborated standard is coded to indicate in which grades the standard can appropriately be developed.

K-4   indicates the standard is appropriate for grades K-2, as well as for grades 3-4

3-4   indicates the standard is appropriate for grades 3-4

However, the order in which the elaborated standards are presented is driven by the logical unfolding of the particular topic rather than by grade level.

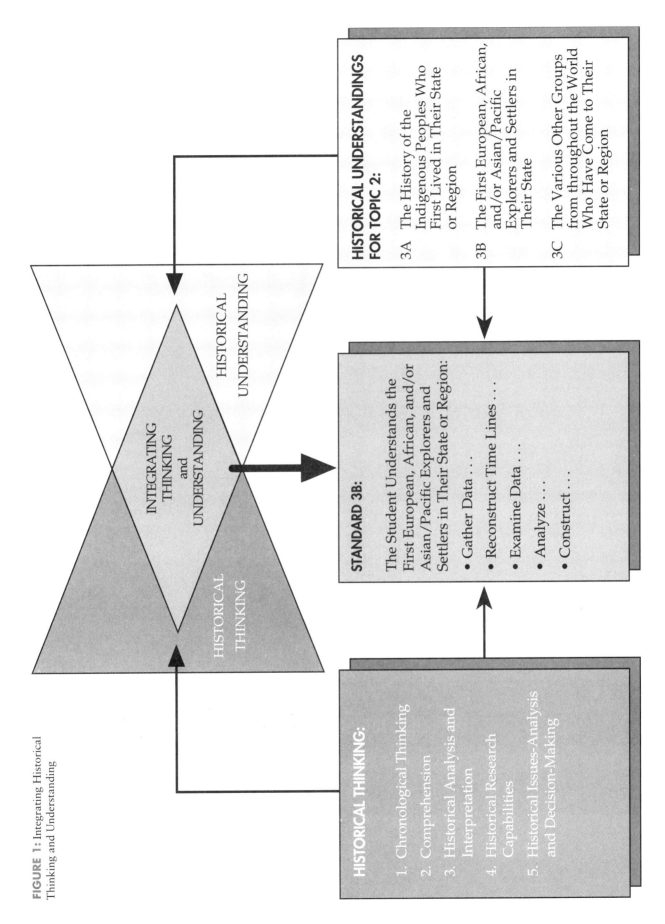

FIGURE 1: Integrating Historical Thinking and Understanding

FIGURE 2: Elements of a History Standard

STANDARD:

Statement of the historical understanding that students should acquire

STANDARD COMPONENT:

Statement identifying the first part of Standard 3 (3A)

ELABORATED STANDARD:

Standard 3A elaborations with recommendations of grade-level appropriateness

THINKING SKILL:

One of several appropriate thinking skills

TOPIC 2: THE HISTORY OF STUDENTS' OWN STATE OR REGION

TOPIC 2

The History of Students' Own State or Region

STANDARD 3   The people, events, problems, and ideas that were significant in creating the history of their state.

3A   **The student understands the history of indigenous peoples who first lived in his or her state or region.**

Therefore, the student is able to:

K-4   Draw upon data in paintings and artifacts to hypothesize about the culture of the early Hawaiians or Native Americans who are known to have lived in the state or region, e.g., the Anasazi of the Southwest, the Makah of the Northwest coast, the Eskimos/Inupiat of Alaska, the Creeks of the Southeast, the Mississippians (Cahokia), or the Mound Builders. [**Formulate historical questions**]

K-4   Draw upon legends and myths of the Native Americans or Hawaiians who lived in students' state or region in order to describe personal accounts of their history. [**Read historical narratives imaginatively**]

3-4   Compare and contrast how Native American or Hawaiian life today differs from the life of these same groups over 100 years ago. [**Compare and contrast differing sets of ideas**]

Questions Concerning These Standards

Q: Do these Standards require that Topic 2, The History of Students' Own State or Region, be taught at all grades, K-2 and 3-4?

A: No. The local school curriculum and the approach it takes to history for young children will determine when the standards included in Topic 2 are taught, whether partially in grades K-3, exclusively in grade 4, or in some other curriculum arrangement. Once that curriculum decision is made, teachers can enter these standards to determine which ones are appropriate for their students.

Q: Are teachers of grades 3-4 expected to teach all the standards coded K-4 in the shaded boxes?

A: No. These standards assume that teachers at all grades of early schooling, K-4, will include history in their programs. In that case, standards coded as appropriate for grades K-4 will probably have been studied to some degree during grades K-2, and emphasis can be turned in grades 3 and 4 to those standards that are coded 3-4 and that are better reserved for these later years. Again, these are matters of well-designed, articulated curriculum planning within the jurisdiction of local schools.

Q: Does the thinking skill incorporated in a particular standard limit teachers to that one skill?

A: No. Decidedly not. Each elaborated standard highlights one important thinking skill. However, it is understood that good teaching will incorporate several, or even many, thinking skills to develop these understandings. In fact, as students mature, they will draw on a widening range of skills.

Three Policy Issues

Ensuring Equity for All Students

The purposes of the national standards developed in this document are threefold: (1) to establish high expectations for what all students should know and be able to do; (2) to clarify what constitutes successful achievement; and (3) *most significantly, to promote equity in the learning opportunities and resources to be provided all students in the nation's schools.*

Standards in and of themselves cannot ensure remediation of the pervasive inequalities in the educational opportunities currently available to students. The roots of these problems are deep and widely manifested in gross inequities in school financing, in resource allocations, and in practices of discriminatory "lower tracks" and "dumbed down" curricula that continue to deny large sectors of the nation's children equal educational opportunity.

What the national commitment to high achievement standards for all students can do is to serve as an engine of change: (1) defining for all students the goals essential to success in a rapidly changing global economy and in a society undergoing wrenching social, technological, and economic change; and (2) establishing the moral obligation to provide equity in the educational resources required to help all students attain these goals.

As for resources, if students are to achieve the understandings and thinking skills specified in these Standards, they must have equal access to well-prepared history teachers and to engaging, balanced, accurate, and challenging curricular materials. For these reasons the success of Goals 2000 and of the systemic educational reform program it has launched requires the provision of high quality professional development in history and in pedagogy for teachers who are not prepared to teach the content or thinking skills presented in this document. Equally important, all students must be provided with the best available curricular materials needed to support these standards.

As Robert Hutchins said many years ago: "The best education for the best should be the best education for all." Every child is entitled to and must have equal access to excellence in the goals their teachers strive to help them achieve and in the instructional resources and opportunities required to reach those ends. Nothing less is acceptable in a democratic society; no commitment is more essential to meeting the challenges—economic, social, and ethical—confronting this nation in the years ahead.

Providing Adequate Instructional Time for History

One of the major commitments called for in Goals 2000 and in the reform movement supported by this legislation is the need to allocate considerably more time in the school day to the core academic subjects, history among them. The "drill the skills" and "minimum competencies" approaches of the 1970s virtually extinguished content studies in elementary schools, with the result that not only did content languish, so too did the higher-order thinking and reading skills that are dependent upon rich subject-matter content, if students are to have something to "think about."

The schools today are in the process of remediating those lacks and the high costs they exacted in students' intellectual development. In doing so, it is especially important that schools provide adequate time for history in all grades, K-4. Linking these historical studies to related studies in geography, civics, literature, and the arts is one important way to do so, and is considered below.

Linking History to Related Studies in Geography, Civics, Literature, and the Arts in an Integrated or Interdisciplinary Curriculum for Grades K-4

Two factors encourage linking history to related studies in the social studies, literature, and the arts in grades K-4:

(1) **History itself is a highly integrative field,** engaging children in studies not only of the people and events in the history of their community, state, nation, and world, but opening as well the study of the geographic places in which these events occurred; the ideas, beliefs, and values that influenced how people acted in their daily lives; the rules, laws, and institutions they established and lived by; the oral traditions and literature, music, art, architecture, and dance they created; and the technological and scientific developments they invented, or adopted, in their quest to improve daily life. In short, studies in history necessarily include geographic, economic, political, social, and scientific studies, as well as studies in the arts.

(2) Teachers of grades K-4 normally are responsible for the entire curriculum and therefore are uniquely able to schedule activities that cut across subject lines and develop standards from two or more fields in a single lesson. Thus, lessons in literature can include literary selections from historical fiction, biography, and other readings important to the history curriculum as well as to the language arts. In turn, activities in creating group stories in history (K-1) and individual historical narratives, letters, journals, and so on (grades 2-4) in children's studies of history are important in furthering standards in English as well as in history. So, too, can lessons simultaneously develop certain standards in history and in civics, in geography, in economics, in the arts, and—to some degree—in mathematics and science.

Developing the interdisciplinary or integrated curriculum is not without pitfalls. Teachers should be aware of some of the problems that led to the widespread withdrawal from these approaches in the curriculum reform movement of the 1960s. One safeguard is to keep clearly in mind the unique characteristics of each field, and to respect those characteristics in any curriculum plan that seeks to capitalize upon the natural affinities among these fields. The National Standards being separately developed in these various fields as well as in history provide an important contribution to that end.

2

Standards in Historical Thinking

Children's study of history rests on knowledge of facts, names, dates, and places. In addition, real historical understanding requires students to engage in historical thinking: to raise questions and to marshal evidence in support of their answers; to read historical narratives and fiction; to consult historical documents, journals, diaries, artifacts, historic sites, and other records from the past; and to do so imaginatively—taking into account the time and places in which these records were created and comparing the multiple points of view of those on the scene at the time.

Real historical understanding also requires that children have opportunities to create historical narratives of their own. Such narratives may take many forms: group stories dictated to the teacher in grades K-1, and individual stories, letters such as a child of the time may have written, journals, and reports in grades 2-4, for example.

Historical understanding also requires that students thoughtfully listen to and read the historical narratives created by others. Well-written historical narratives are interpretative, revealing conditions, changes, and consequences, and explaining why things happened as they did. Following such narratives, and analyzing the events they describe and the explanations they offer, promote important skills in historical thinking.

Because of the importance of historical fiction in opening the past to children and engaging their interests in the people and events of long ago, it is especially important for children to learn to analyze these stories for their historical accuracy, to compare these stories and their illustrations with primary sources—historical artifacts, photos, diaries, and other records of the past—and to differentiate fact and fiction. Children should also have opportunities to compare different stories about a historical figure or event in order to analyze the facts each author includes or omits, and the interpretations or point-of-view communicated by each—important early steps in the development of students' abilities to compare competing historical interpretations of events.

Students engaged in activities of the kinds just considered will draw upon skills in the following five types of historical thinking:

1. Chronological Thinking
2. Historical Comprehension
3. Historical Analysis and Interpretation
4. Historical Research Capabilities
5. Historical Issues-Analysis and Decision-Making

These skills, while presented in five separate categories, are nonetheless interactive and mutually supportive. In conducting historical research or creating a historical story of their own, for example, students must be able to draw upon skills in all five categories. Beyond the skills of conducting their research, students must, for example, be able to comprehend historical artifacts and records consulted in their search, analyze their purpose and importance, and demonstrate a grasp of the historical time (e.g., long, long ago) and geographic place in which the problem or events developed.

In short, these five sets of skills, developed in the following pages as the five Standards in Historical Thinking, are statements of the outcomes we desire students to achieve. They are not mutually exclusive when put into practice, nor do they prescribe a particular teaching sequence to be followed. Teachers will draw upon all these Thinking Standards, as appropriate, to develop their teaching plans and to guide students through challenging programs of study in history.

Finally, it is important to point out that these five sets of Standards in Historical Thinking are defined in the following pages largely independent of historical content in order to specify the quality of thinking desired for each. It is essential to understand, however, that these skills do not develop, nor can they be practiced, in a vacuum. Every one of these skills requires historical content in order to function—a relationship that is made explicit in Chapter 3, which presents the standards integrating historical understandings and thinking.

Overview of Standards in Historical Thinking

Standard 1. Chronological Thinking

A. Distinguish between past, present, and future time.

B. Identify the temporal structure of a historical narrative or story.

C. Establish temporal order in constructing students' own historical narratives.

D. Measure and calculate calendar time.

E. Interpret data presented in time lines.

F. Create time lines.

G. Explain change and continuity over time.

Standard 2. Historical Comprehension

A. Identify the author or source of the historical document or narrative.

B. Reconstruct the literal meaning of a historical passage.

C. Identify the central question(s) the historical narrative addresses.

D. Read historical narratives imaginatively.

E. Appreciate historical perspectives.

F. Draw upon data in historical maps.

G. Draw upon visual and mathematical data presented in graphs.

H. Draw upon the visual data presented in photographs, paintings, cartoons, and architectural drawings.

Standard 3. Historical Analysis and Interpretation

A. Formulate questions to focus their inquiry or analysis.

B. Compare and contrast differing sets of ideas, values, personalities, behaviors, and institutions.

C. Analyze historical fiction.

D. Distinguish between fact and fiction.

E. Compare different stories about a historical figure, era, or event.

F. Analyze illustrations in historical stories

G. Consider multiple perspectives.

H. Explain causes in analyzing historical actions.

I. Challenge arguments of historical inevitability.

J. Hypothesize influences of the past.

Standard 4. Historical Research Capabilities

A. Formulate historical questions.

B. Obtain historical data.

C. Interrogate historical data.

D. Marshal needed knowledge of the time and place, and construct a story, explanation, or historical narrative.

Standard 5. Historical Issues-Analysis and Decision-Making

A. Identify problems and dilemmas in the past.

B. Analyze the interests and values of the various people involved.

C. Identify causes of the problem or dilemma.

D. Propose alternative choices for addressing the problem.

E. Formulate a position or course of action on an issue.

F. Identify the solution chosen.

G. Evaluate the consequences of a decision.

STANDARD 1

Chronological Thinking

Chronological thinking is at the heart of historical reasoning. Without a clear sense of historical time—time past, present, and future—students are bound to see events as one great tangled mess. Without a strong sense of chronology—of when events occurred and in what temporal order—it is impossible for students to examine relationships among them or to explain historical causality. Chronology provides the mental scaffolding for organizing historical thought.

In developing students' chronological thinking, an important share of instructional time should be given to the use of well-constructed *historical narratives*: literary narratives including biographies and historical literature, and well-written narrative histories that have the quality of "stories well told." Well-crafted narratives such as these have the power to grip and hold students' attention. Thus engaged, the reader (or young listener) is able to focus on what the narrator discloses: the temporal structure of events unfolding over time, the actions and intentions of those who were there, the temporal connections between antecedents and their consequences.

It is these characteristics of well-structured historical narratives that probably account for the relationships that have been observed between the use of narratives and young students' developing concepts of time and temporal causation. Responding to well-chosen historical narratives, myths, stories, and fables read by the teacher, young children can determine their temporal structure—their "beginning," "middle," and "end"—and retell, reenact, or illustrate the story to put its important developments into correct temporal sequence. They might illustrate, too, the different ending that might have come about, had one of the characters chosen a different course of action—the beginnings of causal and contingency thinking in the elementary years.

Long before young children are ready to calculate calendar time, they are able to use such concepts as "long, long ago," "long ago," "yesterday," "today," and "tomorrow," and to put historical developments they have learned about in correct temporal relationships according to broad categories such as these. Children should also be developing their ability to identify examples of changes and continuity over time.

Children by grade 4 have been observed to use more precise historical eras, such as the "time of empires" or the "American Revolution." By this time, mathematical understandings should be sufficiently developed to support students' meaningful use of years, decades, and centuries to calculate historical time, and to create more elaborate systems of "chronological scaffolding" on which more challenging analyses can be undertaken.

STANDARD 1	The student thinks chronologically:

Therefore, the student is able to:

A. **Distinguish between past, present, and future time.**

B. **Identify the temporal structure of a historical narrative or story:** its beginning, middle, and end (the latter defined as the outcome of a particular beginning).

C. **Establish temporal order in constructing their [students'] own historical narratives:** working *forward* from some beginning through its development, to some end or outcome; working *backward* from some issue, problem, or event to explain its origins and its development over time.

D. **Measure and calculate calendar time** by days, weeks, months, years, decades, centuries.

E. **Interpret data presented in timelines.**

F. **Create timelines** by designating appropriate equidistant intervals of time and recording events according to the temporal order in which they occurred.

G. **Explain change and continuity over time.**

STANDARD 2

Historical Comprehension

One of the defining features of historical narratives is their believable recounting of human events. To read such accounts with understanding, students must learn to recognize the chronological structure through which the narrative develops—its beginning, middle, and end—and to identify such basic elements of the narrative structure as the characters involved, the situation or setting in which the narrative takes place, the sequence of events through which the story unfolds, the initiating or causal event(s) that led to these developments, and the results or consequences of these actions.

Beyond providing a believable recounting of human events, historical narratives also have the power to disclose the intentions of the characters involved, the difficulties they encountered, and, as Jerome Bruner has observed, the "psychological and cultural reality in which the participants in history actually lived." To read historical stories, biographies, autobiographies, and narratives with comprehension, therefore, students must develop the ability to read imaginatively, to take into account what the narrative reveals of the humanity of the individuals involved—their probable motives and intentions, their hopes, doubts, fears, strengths, and weaknesses. Comprehending historical narratives requires, also, that students develop the ability to describe the past on its own terms, through the eyes and experiences of those who were there, as revealed through their literature, diaries, letters, arts, artifacts, and the like; and to avoid "present-mindedness," not judging the past solely in terms of the norms and values of today, but taking into account the historical context in which the event unfolded—the values, outlook, crises, options, and contingencies of that time and place.

Acquiring these skills begins in the early years of childhood through the use of superbly written stories and biographies that capture children's imagination, evoke the ethos and perspectives of the past, and provide an important foundation for students' continuing historical study.

Beyond these important outcomes, students in grades 3 and 4 should also develop the skills needed to comprehend historical narratives that *explain* as well as *recount* the course of events. These skills include: (1) identifying the central question the historical narrative seeks to answer; (2) defining the purpose or point of view from which the narrative has been constructed; (3) following the historical explanation with meaning; and (4) recognizing the cues that signal how the author has organized the text.

Comprehending these historical narratives will also be facilitated if students are able to draw upon the data presented in historical maps, graphics, and a variety of visual sources such as historical photographs, political cartoons, paintings, and architecture in order to clarify, illustrate, or elaborate upon the information presented in the text.

STANDARD 2	**The student comprehends a variety of historical sources:**

Therefore, the student is able to:

A. **Identify the author or source of the historical document or narrative.**

B. **Reconstruct the literal meaning of a historical passage** by identifying who was involved, what happened, where it happened, what events led to these developments, and what consequences or outcomes followed.

C. **Identify the central question(s)** the historical narrative addresses and the purpose, perspective, or point of view from which it has been constructed.

D. **Read historical narratives imaginatively,** taking into account (a) the historical context in which the event unfolded—the values, outlook, crises, options, and contingencies of that time and place; and (b) what the narrative reveals of the humanity of the individuals involved—their probable motives, hopes, fears, strengths, and weaknesses.

E. **Appreciate historical perspectives**—the ability (a) to describe the past on its own terms, through the eyes and experiences of those who were there, as revealed through their literature, diaries, letters, arts, artifacts, and the like; and (b) to avoid "present-mindedness," judging the past solely in terms of present-day norms and values.

F. **Draw upon data in historical maps** in order to obtain or clarify information on the geographic setting in which the historical event occurred, its relative and absolute location, the distances and directions involved, the natural and man-made features of the place, and critical relationships in the spatial distributions of those features and the historical event occurring there.

G. **Draw upon the visual and mathematical data presented in graphs,** including charts, tables, pie and bar graphs, flow charts, Venn diagrams, and other graphic organizers to clarify, illustrate, or elaborate upon information presented in the historical narrative.

H. **Draw upon the visual data presented in photographs, paintings, cartoons, and architectural drawings** in order to clarify, illustrate, or elaborate upon information presented in the historical narrative.

STANDARD 3

Historical Analysis and Interpretation

One of the important tasks teachers face in helping children become critical, analytical thinkers as well as thoughtful readers of historical narratives is fostering their intellectual independence and overcoming tendencies to look to teachers for cues, to seek the one "right answer," and to accept without question the printed word as authoritative and true. Young children come to school curious, filled with imagination, eager to reach out, discover, and learn, unless home or prior school experiences have thwarted their development of these natural powers in early childhood. The good teacher of young children will work to create the classroom climate and learning opportunities rich in inviting materials that capture children's interest, fuel their imagination, and pose issues and problems for thinking and resolution.

Teachers will find in history many resources to foster these ends: lively, compelling stories and biographies that catch children up in the real problems, issues, and dilemmas encountered by people at various times in history, and that disclose the variety of perspectives, feelings, motivations, and responses of different people involved in the situation; field trips and visits to historic sites and museums; and a rich variety of historical documents, photos, artifacts, and other records of the past that present alternative voices and accounts of events, and that confront students with more than one interpretation of the past.

Many of these resources will be found in local libraries and in the historical collections or files of local newspapers, local museums, and in the collections or personal experiences of parents, and other people in the community. Teachers should cultivate the professional ties and support librarians are eager to offer them, and not hesitate to ask the assistance of historians and geographers in a local college, many of whom are pleased to assist.

In such a classroom setting, children as young as kindergartners can become enthusiastically involved in real historical issues and events, engage actively in examining such data, and analyze and interpret the data for themselves. As has often been noted, thinking cannot occur in a vacuum. Classrooms rich in the historical resources proposed here support even the youngest children with compelling opportunities for active thinking.

Among the analytic thinking skills children should be developing through inviting experiences such as these are the ability to examine a situation and raise questions or define problems for themselves; compare differing ideas, interests, perspectives, actions, and institutions represented in these sources; and elaborate upon what they read and see to develop interpretations, explanations, or solutions to the questions they have raised.

STANDARD 3	The student engages in historical analysis and interpretation:

Therefore, the student is able to:

A. **Formulate questions to focus their inquiry and analysis.**

B. **Compare and contrast differing sets of ideas,** values, personalities, behaviors, and institutions by identifying likenesses and differences.

C. **Analyze historical fiction** on such criteria as the accuracy of the story's historical details and sequence of events; and the point of view or interpretation presented by the author through the words, actions, and descriptions of the characters and events in the story.

D. **Distinguish fact and fiction** by comparing documentary sources on historical figures and events with the fictional characters and events included in the story and its illustrations.

E. **Compare different stories about a historical figure, era, or event** and analyze the different portrayals or perspectives they present.

F. **Analyze illustrations in historical stories** for the information they reveal and compare with historic sites, museum artifacts, historical photos, and other documents to judge their accuracy.

G. **Consider multiple perspectives** in the records of human experience by demonstrating how their differing motives, beliefs, interests, hopes, and fears influenced individual and group behaviors.

H. **Explain causes in analyzing historical actions,** including (a) the importance of the individual in history, of human will, intellect, and character; (b) the influence of ideas, human interests, and beliefs; and (c) the role of chance, the accidental, and the irrational.

I. **Challenge arguments of historical inevitability** by giving examples of how different choices could have led to different consequences.

J. **Hypothesize the influence of the past,** including both the limitations and opportunities made possible by past decisions.

STANDARD 4

Historical Research Capabilities

Perhaps no aspect of historical thinking is as exciting to students or as productive of their growth in historical thinking as "doing history." Such inquiries can be generated by encounters with historical documents, eyewitness accounts, letters, diaries, artifacts, photos, a visit to a historic site, a record of oral history, or other evidence of the past.

Worthy inquiries are especially likely to develop if the documents students encounter are rich with the voices of people caught up in the event and sufficiently diverse to bring alive to students the interests, beliefs, and concerns of people with differing backgrounds and opposing viewpoints or perspectives of the events.

Meaningful historical inquiry proceeds with the formulation of a problem or set of questions worth pursuing. In the most direct approach, students might be encouraged to analyze the document, record, or site itself. Who produced it, when, how, and why? What is the evidence of its authenticity, authority, and credibility? What does it tell them of the point of view, background, and interests of its author or creator? What else must they discover in order to construct a story, explanation, or narrative of the event of which this document or artifact is a part?

Obtaining needed background information can send students on a search for additional resources. Providing students access to a school library, history books, interviews with experts in the community, knowledgeable parents and community residents, or other documents will sometimes be required. In this process the teacher, too, can join in the search and share in the process of discovery, thereby communicating to students that historical inquiry is a search in which answers are not known in advance, and that finding and interpreting the results is a genuine process of knowledge-building.

STANDARD 4	The student conducts historical research:

Therefore, the student is able to:

A. **Formulate historical questions** from encounters with historical documents, eyewitness accounts, letters, diaries, artifacts, photos, historical sites, art, architecture, and other records from the past.

B. **Obtain historical data** from a variety of sources, including: library and museum collections, historic sites, historical photos, journals, diaries, eyewitness accounts, newspapers, and the like; documentary films; and so on.

C. **Interrogate historical data** by determining by whom and when it was created; testing the data source for its credibility, authority and authenticity; and detecting and evaluating bias, distortion, and propaganda by omission, suppression, or invention of facts.

D. **Marshal needed information of the time and place** in order to construct a story, explanation, or historical narrative.

STANDARD 5

Historical Issues-Analysis and Decision-Making

Issue-centered analysis and problem solving activities place students squarely in the center of historical dilemmas with which people have coped at critical moments in the past and near-present. Providing children in grades K-4 opportunity to examine such issues in historical literature and in the history of their local community, state, and nation fosters their personal involvement in these events. If well chosen, these activities promote the development of skills and attitudes essential to citizenship in a democratic society.

Among those skills appropriate for grades K-4 are the ability to analyze a situation; define the issue, problem, or dilemma confronting people in that situation; suggest alternative choices for addressing the problem; evaluate the possible consequences—costs as well as benefits—of each; propose an action; and judge its consequences.

Because the problems confronting people in well written historical fiction, fables, legends, and myths as well as in historical records of the past are usually value-laden, examining these dilemmas, the choices before the people who confronted them, and the consequences of the decisions they made provide opportunities for children to consider the values and beliefs that have influenced human decisions both for good and for ill. They provide opportunities, as well, for students to deepen their understanding and appreciation of such democratic principles and values as individual responsibility, concern for the rights and welfare of others, truth, justice, freedom, and equality of opportunity.

STANDARD 5	The student engages in historical issues-analysis and decision-making:

Therefore, the student is able to:

    A.   **Identify problems and dilemmas** confronting people in historical stories, myths, legends, and fables, and in the history of their school, community, state, nation, and the world.

    B.   **Analyze the interests, values, and points of view** of those involved in the dilemma or problem situation.

    C.   **Identify causes of the problem or dilemma.**

    D.   **Propose alternative ways of resolving the problem or dilemma** and evaluate each in terms of ethical consideration (is it fair? just?), the interest of the different people involved, and the likely consequences of each proposal.

    E.   **Formulate a position or course of action on an issue** by identifying the nature of the problem, analyzing the underlying factors contributing to the problem, and choosing a plausible solution from a choice of carefully evaluated options.

F.   **Identify the solution** chosen by characters in the story or in the historical situation; *or*, recommend a course of action themselves.

G.   **Evaluate the consequences of the actions taken.**

3

Standards in History for Grades K-4

Overview

Topic 1: Living and Working Together in Families and Communities, Now and Long Ago

Standard 1: Family Life Now and in the Recent Past; Family Life in Various Places Long Ago

Standard 2: History of Students' Local Community and How Communities in North America Varied Long Ago

Topic 2: The History of the Students' Own State or Region

Standard 3: The People, Events, Problems, and Ideas that Created the History of Their State

Topic 3: The History of the United States: Democratic Principles and Values and the Peoples from Many Cultures Who Contributed to Its Cultural, Economic and Political Heritage

Standard 4: How Democratic Values Came to Be, and How They Have Been Exemplified by People, Events, and Symbols

Standard 5: The Causes and Nature of Various Movements of Large Groups of People into and within the United States, Now and Long Ago

Standard 6: Regional Folklore and Cultural Contributions That Helped to Form Our National Heritage

Topic 4: The History of Peoples of Many Cultures around the World

Standard 7: Selected Attributes and Historical Developments of Various Societies in Africa, the Americas, Asia, and Europe

Standard 8: Major Discoveries in Science and Technology, Their Social and Economic Effects, and the Scientists and Inventors Responsible for Them

TOPIC 1

Living and Working Together in Families and Communities, Now and Long Ago

STANDARD 1   **Family life now and in the recent past; family life in various places long ago.**

1A The student understands family life now and in the recent past; family life in various places long ago.

Therefore, the student is able to:

K-4   Investigate a family history for at least two generations, identifying various members and their connections in order to construct a timeline. *(Teachers should help students understand that families are people from whom they receive love and support. Understanding that many students are raised in nontraditional family structures—i.e., single-parent families, foster homes, guardians raising children—teachers must be sensitive and protect family privacy.)* [**Establish temporal order**]

K-4   From data gathered through family artifacts, photos, and interviews with older relatives and/or other people who play a significant part in a student's life, draw possible conclusions about roles, jobs, schooling experiences, and other aspects of family life in the recent past. [**Draw upon historical and visual data**]

K-4   For various cultures represented in the classroom, compare and contrast family life now with family life over time and between various cultures and consider such things as communication, technology, homes, transportation, recreation, school and cultural traditions. [**Distinguish between past and present**]

K-4   Examine and formulate questions about early records, diaries, family photographs, artifacts, and architectural drawings obtained through a local newspaper or historical society in order to describe family life in their local community or state long ago. [**Formulate historical questions**]

K-4   Compare and contrast family life now with family life in the local community or state long ago by considering such things as roles, jobs, communication, technology, style of homes, transportation, schools, religious observances, and cultural traditions. [**Compare and contrast**]

1B   **The student understands the different ways people of diverse racial, religious, and ethnic groups, and of various national origins have transmitted their beliefs and values.**

Therefore, the student is able to:

K-4   Explain the ways that families long ago expressed and transmitted their beliefs and values through oral traditions, literature, songs, art, religion, community celebrations, mementos, food, and language. [**Obtain historical data**]

3-4   Compare the dreams and ideals that people from various groups have sought, some of the problems they encountered in realizing their dreams, and the sources of strength and determination that families drew upon and shared. [**Compare and contrast**]

STANDARD 2	**The history of students' own local community and how communities in North America varied long ago.**

2A   **The student understands the history of his or her local community.**

Therefore, the student is able to:

K-4   Create a historical narrative about the history of his or her local community from data gathered from local residents, records found in early newspapers, historical documents and photographs, and artifacts and other data found in local museums and historical societies. [**Construct a historical narrative**]

K-4   From resources that are available in the local community, record changes that have occurred in goods and services over time. [**Establish temporal order**]

K-4   Describe local community life long ago, including jobs, schooling, transportation, communication, religious observances, and recreation. [**Obtain historical data**]

3-4   Interpret population data from historical and current maps, charts, graphs, and census tables in order to make generalizations about the changing size and makeup of the local community. [**Interrogate the data**]

K-4   Examine local architecture and landscape to compare changes in function and appearance over time. [**Draw upon visual data**]

K-4   Identify historical figures in the local community and explain their contributions and significance. [**Assess the importance of the individual in history**]

3-4   Identify a problem in the community's past, analyzing the different perspectives of those involved, and evaluate choices people had and the solution they chose. [**Identify issues and problems in the past**]

2B **The student understands how communities in North America varied long ago.**

Therefore, the student is able to:

> *K-4* Compare and contrast the different ways in which early Hawaiian and Native American peoples such as the Iroquois, the Sioux, the Hopi, the Nez Perce, the Inuit, and the Cherokee adapted to their various environments and created their patterns of community life long ago. [**Compare and contrast differing sets of ideas**]

> *K-4* Draw upon written and visual sources and describe the historical development and daily life of a colonial community such as Plymouth, Williamsburg, St. Augustine, San Antonio, and Fort Vincennes, in order to create a historical narrative, mural, or dramatization of daily life in that place long ago. [**Construct a historical narrative**]

> *K-4* Describe the challenges and difficulties encountered by people in a pioneer farming community such as those found in the Old Northwest (e.g., Ohio), the prairies, the Southwest (e.g., Santa Fe), eastern Canada (e.g., Quebec), and the Far West (e.g., Salt Lake City). [**Read historical narratives imaginatively**]

> *3-4* Draw upon maps and stories in order to identify geographical factors that led to the establishment and growth of communities such as mining towns (Sacramento) and trading settlements (New Orleans, Vincennes, and Astoria). [**Draw upon historical maps and read historical narratives imaginatively**]

> *3-4* Describe and compare daily life in ethnically diverse urban communities long ago, such as a free African American community in Philadelphia, an Italian community in New York, or a Chinese community in San Francisco. [**Draw upon visual data and read historical narratives imaginatively**]

TOPIC 2

The History of Students' Own State or Region

STANDARD 3	The people, events, problems, and ideas that created the history of their state.

3A **The student understands the history of indigenous peoples who first lived in his or her state or region.**

Therefore, the student is able to:

K-4 Draw upon data in paintings and artifacts to hypothesize about the culture of the early Hawaiians or Native Americans who are known to have lived in the state or region, e.g., the Anasazi of the Southwest, the Makah of the Northwest coast, the Eskimos/Inupiat of Alaska, the Creeks of the Southeast, the Mississippians (Cahokia), or the Mound Builders. [**Formulate historical questions**]

K-4 Draw upon legends and myths of the Native Americans or Hawaiians who lived in students' state or region in order to describe personal accounts of their history. [**Read historical narratives imaginatively**]

3-4 Compare and contrast how Native American or Hawaiian life today differs from the life of these same groups over 100 years ago. [**Compare and contrast differing sets of ideas**]

3B **The student understands the history of the first European, African, and/or Asian-Pacific explorers and settlers who came to his or her state or region.**

Therefore, the student is able to:

3-4 Gather data in order to analyze geographic, economic, and religious reasons that brought the first explorers and settlers to the state or region. [**Obtain historical data**]

3-4 Reconstruct in timelines the order of early explorations and settlements including explorers, early settlements, and cities. [**Establish temporal order**]

K-4 Examine visual data in order to describe ways in which early settlers adapted to, utilized, and changed the environment. [**Draw upon visual data**]

3-4 Analyze some of the interactions that occurred between the Native Americans or Hawaiians and the first European, African, and Asian-Pacific explorers and settlers in the students' state or region. [**Read historical narratives imaginatively**]

K-4 Use a variety of sources to construct a historical narrative about daily life in the early settlements of the student's state or region. [**Obtain historical data**]

3C   **The student understands the various other groups from regions throughout the world who came into the his or her own state or region over the long-ago and recent past.**

Therefore, the student is able to:

3-4   Develop a timeline on their state or region and identify the first inhabitants who lived there, each successive group of arrivals, and significant changes that developed over the history of their state or region. [**Establish temporal order**]

K-4   Use a variety of visual data, fiction and nonfiction sources, and speakers to identify the groups that have come into the state or region and to generate ideas about why they came. [**Obtain historical data**]

K-4   Examine photographs and pictures of people from the various racial and ethnic groups of varying socioeconomic status who lived in the state 100-200 years ago in order to hypothesize about their lives, feelings, plans, and dreams, and to compare ways in which their experiences were similar and different. [**Formulate historical questions**]

3-4   Examine newspaper and magazine accounts and construct interview questions for a written, telephone, or in-person interview with a recent immigrant in order to discover why they came, what their life was like, and to describe some of the experiences that they have had in adjusting to the state or region. [**Obtain historical data**]

3-4   Draw upon census data and historical accounts in order to describe patterns and changes in population over a period of time in a particular city or town in the students' state or region. [**Draw upon historical data**]

3-4   Describe the problems, including prejudice and intolerance, as well as the opportunities that various groups who have lived in their state or region have experienced in housing, the workplace, and the community. [**Appreciate historical perspectives**]

3-4   Draw upon historical narratives to examine the sources of strength and determination, such as family, church, synagogue, community, or fraternal organizations that various groups drew upon in attempts to overcome problems during this period. [**Consider multiple perspectives**]

3D   **The student understands the interactions among all these groups throughout the history of his or her state.**

Therefore, the student is able to:

3-4   List in chronological order the major historical events that are part of the state's history. [**Establish temporal order**]

3-4   Analyze the significance of major events in the state's history, their impact on people then and now, and their relationship to the history of the nation. [**Analyze cause-and-effect relationships**]

3-4   Read historical narratives to describe how the territory or region attained its statehood. [**Reconstruct the literal meaning of a historical passage**]

3-4   Identify historical problems or events in the state and analyze the way they were solved and/or the ways that they continue to be addressed. [**Identify issues and problems in the past**]

3-4   Examine various written accounts in order to identify and describe regional or state examples of major historical events and developments that involved interaction among various groups (e.g., the Alamo, the Underground Railroad, the building of the Transcontinental Railroad, and the California Gold Rush). [**Consider multiple perspectives**]

3-4   Investigate the influence of geography on the history of the state or region and identify issues and approaches to problems such as land use and environmental problems. [**Reconstruct the literal meaning of a historical passage**]

3E   **The student understands the ideas that were significant in the development of the state and that helped to forge its unique identity.**

Therefore, the student is able to:

K-4   Draw upon visual and other data to identify symbols, slogans, or mottoes, and research why they represent the state. [**Draw upon visual data**]

3-4   Analyze how the ideas of significant people affected the history of their state. [**Assess the importance of the individual in history**]

K-4   Research in order to explain why important buildings, statues, monuments, and place names are associated with the state's history. [**Obtain historical data**]

3-4   Draw upon a variety of sources to describe the unique historical conditions that influenced the formation of the state. [**Obtain historical data**]

TOPIC 3

The History of the United States: Democratic Principles and Values and the People from Many Cultures Who Contributed to Its Cultural, Economic, and Political Heritage

STANDARD 4 | How democratic values came to be, and how they have been exemplified by people, events, and symbols.

4A **The student understands how the United States government was formed and the nation's basic democratic principles set forth in the Declaration of Independence and the Constitution.**

Therefore, the student is able to:

K-4   Explain that the U.S. government was formed by English colonists who fought for independence from England. [**Explain causes and consequences**]

3-4   Identify and explain the basic principles that Americans set forth in the documents that declared the nation's independence from England (the Declaration of Independence) and that created the new nation's government (U.S. Constitution). [**Demonstrate and explain the influence of ideas**]

K-4   Explain the importance of the basic principles of American democracy that unify us as a nation: our individual rights to life, liberty, and the pursuit of happiness; responsibility for the common good; equality of opportunity and equal protection of the law; freedom of speech and religion; majority rule with protection for minority rights; and limitations on government, with power held by the people and delegated by them to their elected officials who are responsible to those who elected them to office. [**Demonstrate and explain the influence of ideas**]

K-4   Analyze how over the last 200 years individuals and groups in American society have struggled to achieve the liberties and equality promised in the principles of American democracy. [**Analyze continuity and change**]

4B **The student understands ordinary people who have exemplified values and principles of American democracy.**

Therefore, the student is able to:

K-4   Identify ordinary people who have believed in the fundamental democratic values such as justice, truth, equality, the rights of the individual, and responsibility for the common good, and explain their significance. [**Assess the importance of the individual in history**]

32

K-4 Analyze in their historical context the accomplishments of ordinary people in the local community now and long ago who have done something beyond the ordinary that displays particular courage or a sense of responsibility in helping the common good. [**Assess the importance of the individual in history**]

4C **The student understands historic figures who have exemplified values and principles of American democracy.**

Therefore, the student is able to:

K-4 Identify historical figures who believed in the fundamental democratic values such as justice, truth, equality, the rights of the individual, and responsibility for the common good, and explain their significance in their historical context and today. [**Assess the importance of the individual in history**]

K-4 Describe how historical figures in the United States and other parts of the world have advanced the rights of individuals and promoted the common good, and identify character traits such as persistence, problem solving, moral responsibility, and respect for others that made them successful. [**Assess the importance of the individual in history**]

3-4 Compare historical biographies or fictionalized accounts of historical figures with primary documents in order to analyze inconsistencies and disagreements in these accounts, and assess their reliability. [**Compare competing historical narratives**]

4D **The student understands events that celebrate and exemplify fundamental values and principles of American democracy.**

Therefore, the student is able to:

K-4 Describe the history of holidays, such as the birthday of Martin Luther King Jr., Presidents' Day, Memorial Day, the Fourth of July, Labor Day, Veterans' Day and Thanksgiving, that celebrate the core democratic values and principles of this nation. [**Demonstrate and explain the influence of ideas**]

3-4 Describe the history of events, such as the signing of the Mayflower Compact and the Declaration of Independence, and the writing of the Constitution, the Bill of Rights, and the Emancipation Proclamation. [**Demonstrate and explain the influence of ideas and** beliefs]

4E **The student understands national symbols through which American values and principles are expressed.**

Therefore, the student is able to:

K-4 Describe the history of American symbols such as the eagle, the Liberty Bell, George Washington as the "father of our country," and the national flag. [**Demonstrate and explain the influence of ideas**]

K-4 Explain why important buildings, statues, and monuments are associated with state and national history, such as the White House, Lincoln Memorial, Statue of Liberty, Ellis Island, Angel Island, Mt. Rushmore, and veterans memorials. [**Obtain historical data**]

3-4   Analyze the Pledge of Allegiance and patriotic songs, poems, and sayings that were written long ago to demonstrate understanding of their significance. [Reconstruct the literal meaning of a historical passage]

3-4   Analyze songs, symbols, and slogans that demonstrate freedom of expression and the role of protest in a democracy. [Consider multiple perspectives]

STANDARD 5	The causes and nature of various movements of large groups of people into and within the United States, now, and long ago.

5   **The student understands the movements of large groups of people into his or her own and other states in the United States now and long ago.**

Therefore, the student is able to:

3-4   Draw upon data in historical maps, historical narratives, diaries, and other fiction or nonfiction accounts in order to chart various movements (westward, northward, and eastward) in the United States. [Obtain historical data]

K-4   Gather data in order to describe the forced relocation of Native Americans and how their lives, rights, and territories were affected by European colonization and the expansion of the United States, including examples such as Spanish colonization in the Southwest, Tecumseh's resistance to Indian removal, Cherokee Trail of Tears, Black Hawk's War, and the movement of the Nez Perce. [Obtain historical data]

K-4   Draw upon data from charts, historical maps, nonfiction and fiction accounts, and interviews in order to describe "through their eyes" the experience of immigrant groups. Include information such as where they came from and why they left, travel experiences, ports of entry and immigration screening, and the opportunities and obstacles they encountered when they arrived in America. [Appreciate historical perspectives]

3-4   Identify reasons why groups such as freed African Americans, Mexican and Puerto Rican migrant workers, and Dust Bowl farm families migrated to various parts of the country. [Consider multiple perspectives]

3-4   Analyze the experiences of those who moved from farm to city during the periods when cities grew rapidly in the United States. [Read historical narratives imaginatively]

STANDARD 6

Regional folklore and cultural contributions that helped to form our national heritage.

6A **The student understands folklore and other cultural contributions from various regions of the United States and how they help to form a national heritage.**

Therefore, the student is able to:

K-4 Describe regional folk heroes, stories, or songs that have contributed to the development of the cultural history of the U.S. [**Read historical narratives imaginatively**]

K-4 Draw upon a variety of stories, legends, songs, ballads, games, and tall tales in order to describe the environment, lifestyles, beliefs, and struggles of people in various regions of the country. [**Read historical narratives imaginatively**]

3-4 Examine art, crafts, music, and language of people from a variety of regions long ago and describe their influence on the nation. [**Draw upon visual and other historical data**]

TOPIC 4

The History of Peoples of Many Cultures Around the World

| STANDARD 7 | Selected attributes and historical developments of various societies in Africa, the Americas, Asia, and Europe. |

7A **The student understands the cultures and historical developments of selected societies in such places as Africa, the Americas, Asia, and Europe.**

Therefore, the student is able to:

3-4 Investigate the ways historians learn about the past if there are no written records. [**Compare records from the past**]

3-4 Describe the effects geography has had on societies, including their development of urban centers, food, clothing, industry, agriculture, shelter, trade, and other aspects of culture. [**Draw upon historical maps**]

K-4 Compare and contrast various aspects of family life, structures, and roles in different cultures and in many eras with students' own family lives. [**Compare and contrast**]

K-4 Illustrate or retell the main ideas in folktales, legends, myths, and stories of heroism that disclose the history and traditions of various cultures around the world. [**Reconstruct the literal meaning of a historical passage**]

3-4 Describe life in urban areas and communities of various cultures of the world at various times in their history. [**Obtain historical data**]

3-4 Describe significant historical achievements of various cultures of the world. [**Obtain historical data**]

K-4 Analyze the dance, music, and arts of various cultures around the world to draw conclusions about the history, daily life, and beliefs of the people in history. [**Draw upon visual data**]

K-4 Explain the customs related to important holidays and ceremonies in various countries in the past. [**Assess the importance of ideas and beliefs in history**]

7B **The student understands great world movements of people now and long ago.**

Therefore, the student is able to:

3-4 Trace on maps and explain the migrations of large groups, such as the movement of Native American ancestors across the Bering Strait land bridge, the Bantu migrations in Africa, the movement of Europeans and Africans to the Western Hemisphere, and the exodus of Vietnamese boat people, Haitians, and Cubans in recent decades. [**Obtain historical data**]

K-4 Draw upon historical narratives to identify early explorers and world travelers, such as Marco Polo, Zheng He, Eric the Red, and Christopher Columbus, and to describe the knowledge gained from their journeys. [**Read historical narratives imaginatively**]

K-4 Draw upon historical narratives in order to identify European explorers of the 15th and 16th centuries, and explain their reasons for exploring, the information gained from their journeys, and what happened as a result of their travels. [**Obtain historical data and read historical narratives imaginatively**]

3-4 Gather data in order to explain the effects of the diffusion of food crops and animals between the Western and Eastern hemispheres after the voyages of Columbus. [**Obtain historical data**]

STANDARD 8	Major discoveries in science and technology, their social and economic effects, and the scientists and inventors responsible for them.

8A **The student understands the development of technological innovations, the major scientists and inventors associated with them, and their social and economic effects.**

Therefore, the student is able to:

K-4 Compare and contrast the behaviors of hunters and gatherers with those of people who cultivated plants and raised domesticated animals for food. [**Compare and contrast differing sets of ideas**]

K-4 Draw upon visual data to illustrate development of the wheel and its early uses in ancient societies. [**Demonstrate and explain the influence of ideas**]

3-4 Describe the development and the influence of basic tools on work and behavior. [**Demonstrate and explain the influence of ideas**]

3-4 Identify and describe various technological developments to control fire, water, wind, and soil, and to utilize natural resources such as trees, coal, oil, and gas in order to satisfy the basic human needs for food, water, clothing, and shelter. [**Obtain historical data**]

3-4 Identify and describe technological inventions and developments that evolved during the 19th century and the influence of these changes on the lives of workers. [**Demonstrate and explain the influence of ideas**]

K-4   Identify and describe the significant achievements of important scientists and inventors. [**Assess the importance of the individual in history**]

8B   The student understands changes in transportation and their effects.

Therefore, the student is able to:

3-4   Create a timeline showing the varieties in forms of transportation and their developments over time. [**Create time lines**]

K-4   Draw upon photographs, illustrations, models, and nonfictional resource materials to demonstrate the developments in marine vessels constructed by people from ancient times until today. [**Reconstruct patterns of historical succession and duration**]

3-4   Investigate the development of extensive road systems, such as the Roman roads of the early Roman Empire; the trade routes by camel caravan linking East Asia, Southwest Asia, and Africa during the ancient and early Middle Ages; the network of roads and highways of the Incas in Peru; the National Road in the U.S.; and the interstate highway system in order to explain the travel and communication difficulties encountered by people over vast expanses of territory, and the social and economic effects of these developments. [**Obtain historical data**]

3-4   Trace the developments in rail transportation beginning in the 19th century and the effects of national systems of railroad transport on the lives of people. [**Reconstruct patterns of historical succession and duration**]

3-4   Investigate the design and development of aircraft and rocketry and the people involved. [**Reconstruct patterns of historical succession and duration**]

3-4   Identify and describe the people who have made significant contributions in the field of transportation. [**Assess the importance of the individual in history**]

8C   The student understands changes in communication and their effects.

Therefore, the student is able to:

K-4   Compare and contrast ways people communicate with each other now and long ago, and list in chronological order technological developments that facilitated communication. [**Establish temporal order**]

3-4   Illustrate the origins and changes in methods of writing over time and describe how the changes made communication between people more effective. [**Obtain historical data**]

3-4   Explain the significance of the printing press, the computer, and electronic developments in communication, and describe their impact on the spread of ideas. [**Obtain historical data**]

K-4   Compare and contrast various systems of long-distance communication, including runners, the "talking drums" of Africa, smoke signals of Native Americans, the pony express, the telegraph, telephones, and satellite systems of worldwide communication today, and analyze their effects. [**Compare and contrast**]

3-4   Identify and describe the people who have made significant contributions in the field of communication. [**Assess the importance of the individual**]

National Standards for United States and World History
Grades 5-12

PART TWO

CHAPTER 1

Developing Standards in United States History and World History

Significance of History for the Educated Citizen

Setting standards for history in the schools requires a clear vision of the place and importance of history in the general education of all students. The widespread and growing support for more and better history in the schools, beginning in the early grades of elementary education, is one of the more encouraging signs of the decade. The reasons are many, but none are more important to a democratic society than this: *knowledge of history is the precondition of political intelligence.* Without history, a society shares no common memory of where it has been, what its core values are, or what decisions of the past account for present circumstances. Without history, we cannot undertake any sensible inquiry into the political, social, or moral issues in society. And without historical knowledge and inquiry, we cannot achieve the informed, discriminating citizenship essential to effective participation in the democratic processes of governance and the fulfillment for all our citizens of the nation's democratic ideals.

Thomas Jefferson long ago prescribed history for all who would take part in self-government because it would enable them to prepare for things yet to come. The philosopher Etienne Gilson noted the special significance of the perspectives history affords. "History," he remarked, "is the only laboratory we have in which to test the consequences of thought." History opens to students the great record of human experience, revealing the vast range of accommodations individuals and societies have made to the problems confronting them, and disclosing the consequences that have followed the various choices that have been made. By studying the choices and decisions of the past, students can confront today's problems and choices with a deeper awareness of the alternatives before them and the likely consequences of each.

Current problems, of course, do not duplicate those of the past. Essential to extrapolating knowledgeably from history to the issues of today requires yet a further skill, again dependent upon one's understanding of the past: differentiating between (1) relevant historical antecedents that properly inform analyses of current issues and (2) those antecedents that are clearly irrelevant. Students must be sufficiently grounded in historical understanding in order to bring sound historical analysis to the service of informed decision making.

What is required is mastery of what Nietzsche once termed "critical history" and what Gordon Craig has explained as the "ability, after painful inquiry and sober judgment, to determine what part of history [is] relevant to one's current problems and what [is] not," whether one is assessing a situation, forming an opinion, or taking an active position on the issue. In exploring these matters, students will soon discover that history is filled with the high costs of decisions reached on the basis of false analogies from the past as well as the high costs of actions taken with little or no understanding of the important lessons the past imparts.

These learnings directly contribute to the education of the *public citizen*, but they uniquely contribute to nurturing the *private individual* as well. Historical memory is the key to self-identity, to seeing one's place in the stream of time, and one's connectedness with all of humankind. We are part of an ancient chain, and the long hand of the past is upon us—for good and for ill—just as our hands will rest on our descendants for years to come. Denied knowledge of one's roots and of one's place in the great stream of human history, the individual is deprived of the fullest sense of self and of that sense of shared community on which one's fullest personal development as well as responsible citizenship depends. For these purposes, history and the humanities must occupy an indispensable role in the school curriculum.

Finally, history opens to students opportunities to develop a comprehensive understanding of the world, and of the many cultures and ways of life different from their own. From a balanced and inclusive world history students may gain an appreciation both of the world's many peoples and of their shared humanity and common problems. Students may also acquire the habit of seeing matters through others' eyes and come to realize that they can better understand themselves as they study others, as well as the other way around. Historical understanding based on such comparative studies in world history does not require approval or forgiveness for the tragedies either of one's own society or of others; nor does it negate the importance of critically examining alternative value systems and their effects in supporting or denying the basic human rights and aspirations of all their peoples. Especially important, an understanding of the history of the world's many cultures can contribute to fostering the kind of mutual patience, respect, and civic courage required in our increasingly pluralistic society and our increasingly interdependent world.

If students are to see ahead more clearly, and be ready to act with judgment and with respect for the shared humanity of all who will be touched by the decisions they as citizens make, support, or simply acquiesce in, then schools must attend to this critical field of the curriculum.

Definition of Standards

Standards in history make explicit the goals that all students should have opportunity to acquire, if the purposes just considered are to be achieved. In history, standards are of two types:

1. *Historical thinking skills* that enable students to evaluate evidence, develop comparative and causal analyses, interpret the historical record, and construct sound historical arguments and perspectives on which informed decisions in contemporary life can be based.

2. *Historical understandings* that define what students should *know* about the history of their nation and of the world. These understandings are drawn from the record of human aspirations, strivings, accomplishments, and failures in at least five spheres of

human activity: the social, political, scientific/technological, economic, and cultural (philosophical/religious/aesthetic). They also provide students the historical perspectives required to analyze contemporary issues and problems confronting citizens today.

Historical thinking and understanding do not, of course, develop independently of one another. Higher levels of historical thinking depend upon and are linked to the attainment of higher levels of historical understanding. For these reasons, the standards presented in Chapters 3 and 4 of this volume provide an integration of historical thinking and understanding.

Criteria for the Development of Standards

The development of national standards in United States and World History presents a special challenge in deciding what, of the great storehouse of human history, is the most significant for all students to acquire. Perhaps less contentious but no less important is deciding what historical perspectives and what skills in historical reasoning, values analysis, and policy thinking are essential for all students to achieve.

The following criteria, developed and refined over the course of a broad-based national review and consensus process, were adopted by the National Council for History Standards in order to guide the development of history standards for grades kindergarten through 12.

1. Standards should be intellectually demanding, reflect the best historical scholarship, and promote active questioning and learning rather than passive absorption of facts, dates, and names.

2. Such standards should be equally expected of all students and all students should be provided equal access to the curricular opportunities necessary to achieving those standards.

3. Standards should reflect the ability of children from the earliest elementary school years to learn the meanings of history and the methods of historians.

4. Standards should be founded in chronology, an organizing approach that fosters appreciation of pattern and causation in history.

5. Standards should strike a balance between emphasizing broad themes in United States and World History and probing specific historical events, ideas, movements, persons, and documents.

6. All historical study involves selection and ordering of information in light of general ideas and values. Standards for history should reflect the principles of sound historical reasoning—careful evaluation of evidence, construction of causal relationships, balanced interpretation, and comparative analysis. The ability to detect and evaluate distortion and propaganda by omission, suppression, or invention of facts is essential.

7. Standards should include awareness of, appreciation for, and the ability to utilize a variety of sources of evidence from which historical knowledge is achieved, including written documents, oral tradition, quantitative data, popular culture, literature, artifacts, art and music, historical sites, photographs, and films.

8. Standards for United States History should reflect both the nation's diversity exemplified by race, ethnicity, social and economic status, gender, region, politics, and

religion, and the nation's commonalities. The contributions and struggles of specific groups and individuals should be included.

9. Standards in United States History should contribute to citizenship education through developing understanding of our common civic identity and shared civic values within the polity, through analyzing major policy issues in the nation's history, and through developing mutual respect among its many people.

10. History standards should emphasize the nature of civil society and its relationship to government and citizenship. Standards in United States History should address the historical origins of the nation's democratic political system and the continuing development of its ideals and institutions, its controversies, and the struggle to narrow the gap between its ideals and practices. Standards in World History should include different patterns of political institutions, ranging from varieties of democracy to varieties of authoritarianism, and ideas and aspirations developed by civilizations in all parts of the world.

11. Standards in United States and World History should be separately developed but interrelated in content and similar in format. Standards in United States History should reflect the global context in which the nation unfolded and World History should treat United States History as one of its integral parts.

12. Standards should include appropriate coverage of recent events in United States and World History, including social and political developments and international relations of the post World War II era.

13. Standards in United States and World History should utilize regional and local history by exploring specific events and movements through case studies and historical research. Local and regional history should enhance the broader patterns of United States and World History.

14. Standards in United States and World History should integrate fundamental facets of human culture such as religion, science and technology, politics and government, economics, interactions with the environment, intellectual and social life, literature, and the arts.

15. Standards in World History should treat the history and values of diverse civilizations, including those of the West, and should especially address the interactions among them.

Developing Standards in United States History

Periodization for U.S. History

Students should understand that the periods into which the written histories of the United States or the world are divided are simply constructions made by historians trying to impose some order on what is inherently an untidy past that can be read and conceptualized in a variety of ways. In a nation of such diversity as the United States, no periodizing scheme will work for all groups. American Indian history has benchmarks and eras that sometimes but not always overlap with those of European settlers in the colonial period. For that matter, Iroquois history would have to be periodized differently from Sioux or Zuni history. African American history would have its own watersheds, such as the shift from white indentured servitude to black slave labor in the South, the abolition of the slave trade, the beginning of emigrationism, and so forth. So also with women's history and with Mexican American history.

Nonetheless, we believe that teachers will appreciate a periodization that attempts to blend political and social history. For this purpose, political events in United States history such as the American Revolution, the Constitution, the Civil War, Progressivism, the New Deal, and the Cold War—all of which have fairly definite beginning and end points—continue to provide breakpoints in the United States history curriculum. The industrial revolution, the labor movement, environmentalism, shifts in childrearing and family size, and so forth have no such precise beginning and end points and cut across eras defined by revolution, civil war, depression, and the like. In fact, none of the college texts in United States History that have tried in recent years to infuse social history into political and institutional history have been able to get around the general determinacy of wars and political reform movements and the indeterminacy of demographic, cultural, and social transformations.

We have tried to overcome, in part, the difficulties inherent in periodizing history by overlapping eras to demonstrate that there really is no such thing as an era's beginning or ending, and that all such schemes are simply the historian's way of trying to give *some* structure to the course of history. The ten eras selected for periodizing United States history are presented below:

Era 1: Three Worlds Meet (Beginnings to 1620)

Era 2: Colonization and Settlement (1585-1763)

Era 3: Revolution and the New Nation (1754-1820s)

Era 4: Expansion and Reform (1801-1861)

Era 5: Civil War and Reconstruction (1850-1877)

Era 6: The Development of the Industrial United States (1870-1900)

Era 7: The Emergence of Modern America (1890-1930)

Era 8: The Great Depression and World War II (1929-1945)

Era 9: Postwar United States (1945-early 1970s)

Era 10: Contemporary United States (1968-present)

Approaching World History

These standards rest on the premise that our schools must teach a comprehensive history in which all students may share. That means a history that encompasses humanity. In writing the standards a primary task was to identify those developments in the past that involved and affected relatively large numbers of people and that had broad significance for later generations. Some of these developments pertain to particular civilizations or regions. Others involve patterns of human interconnection that extended across cultural and political boundaries. Within this framework students are encouraged to explore in depth particular cases of historical change that may have had only regional or local importance but that exemplify the drama and human substance of the past.

These standards represent a forceful commitment to world-scale history. No attempt has been made, however, to address the histories of all identifiable peoples or cultural traditions. The aim rather is to encourage students to ask large and searching questions about the human past, to compare patterns of continuity and change in different parts of the world, and to examine the histories and achievements of particular peoples or civilizations with an eye to wider social, cultural, or economic contexts.

Periodization for World History

As in United States History, arranging the study of the past into distinct periods of time is one way of imposing a degree of order and coherence on the incessant, fragmented flow of events. Historians have devised a variety of periodization designs for World History to make it intelligible. Students should understand that every one of these designs is a creative construction reflecting the historian's particular aims, preferences, and cultural or social values.

A periodization of world history that encompasses the grand sweep of the human past can make sense only at a relatively high level of generalization. Historians have also worked out periodizations for particular civilizations, regions, and nations, and these have their own validity, their own benchmarks and turning points. The history of India, for example, would necessarily be periodized differently than would the history of China or Europe, since the major shifts in Indian history relate to the Gupta age, the Mughal empire, the post-independence era, and so on.

We believe that as teachers work toward a more integrated study of world history in their classrooms they will appreciate having a periodization design that encourages study of those broad developments that have involved large segments of the world's population and that have had lasting significance. The standards are divided into nine eras of world history. The title of each era attempts to capture the very general character of that age. Note that the time periods of some of the eras overlap in order to incorporate both the closure of certain developments and the start of others. The beginning and ending dates should be viewed as approximations representing broad shifts in the human scene.

Era 1: The Beginnings of Human Society

Era 2: Early Civilizations and the Emergence of Pastoral Peoples, 4000-1000 BCE

Era 3: Classical Traditions, Major Religions, and Giant Empires, 1000 BCE-300 CE

Era 4: Expanding Zones of Exchange and Encounter, 300-1000 CE

Era 5: Intensified Hemispheric Interactions, 1000-1500 CE

Era 6: Emergence of the First Global Age, 1450-1770

Era 7: An Age of Revolutions, 1750-1914

Era 8: A Half-Century of Crisis and Achievement, 1900-1945

Era 9: The 20th Century Since 1945: Promises and Paradoxes

Historical Understanding

History is a broadly integrative field, recounting and analyzing human aspirations and strivings in various spheres of human activity: **social, political, scientific/technological, economic, and cultural.** Studying history—inquiring into families, communities, states, nations, and various peoples of the world—at once engages students in the lives, aspirations, struggles, accomplishments, and failures of real people, in all these aspects of their lives.

Through social history, students come to deeper understandings of society: of what it means to be human, of different and changing views of family structures, of men's and women's roles, of childhood and of children's roles, of various groups and classes in society, and of relationships among all these individuals and groups. This sphere considers how economic, religious, cultural, and political changes have affected social life, and it incorporates developments shaping the destiny of millions: the history of slavery; of class conflict; of mass migration and immigration; the human consequences of plague, war, and famine; and the longer life expectancy and rising living standards following upon medical, technological, and economic advances.

Through political history, students comprehend the political sphere of activity, as it has developed in their local community, their state, their nation, and in various societies of the world. Efforts to construct governments and institutions; the drive to seize and hold power over others; the struggle to achieve and preserve basic human rights, justice, equality, law, and order in societies; and the evolution of regional and world mechanisms to promote international law are all part of the central human drama to be explored and analyzed in the study of history.

Through history of science and technology, students learn how the scientific quest to understand nature, the world we live in, and humanity itself is as old as recorded history. So, too, is the quest to improve ways of doing everything from producing food, to caring for the ill, to transporting goods, to advancing economic security and the well-being of the group. Understandings of the scientific/technological developments that have propelled change, and how these changes have altered all other spheres of human activity are central to the study of history.

Through economic history, students appreciate the economic forces that have been crucial in determining the quality of people's lives, in structuring societies, and in influencing the course of events. Exchange relationships within and between cultures have had major impacts on society and politics, producing changing patterns of regional, hemispheric, and global economic dominance and permitting the emergence in the 20th century of a truly international economy, with far-reaching consequences for all other spheres of activity.

Through cultural history, students learn how ideas, beliefs, and values have profoundly influenced human actions throughout history. Religion, philosophy, art, and popular culture have all been central to the aspirations and achievements of all societies, and have been a mainspring of historical change from earliest times. Students' explorations of this sphere of human activity, through literature, sacred writings and oral traditions, political treatises, drama, art, architecture, music, and dance deepen their understandings of the human experience.

Analyzing these five spheres of human activity requires considering them in the contexts both of *historical time* and *geographic place.* The historical record is inextricably linked to the geographic setting in which it developed. Population movements and settlements, scientific and economic activities, geopolitical agendas, and the distribution and spread of political, philosophical, religious, and aesthetic ideas are all related in some measure to geographic factors. The opportunities, limitations, and constraints with which any people have addressed the issues and challenges of their time have, to a significant degree, been influenced by the environment in which they lived or to which they have had access, and by the traces on the landscape, malignant or benign, irrevocably left by those who came before.

Because these five spheres of human activity are also interwoven in the real lives of individuals and societies, essential understandings in United States and World History often cut across these categories. Thus, to comprehend the causes of the American Revolution, students must address the *philosophical ideas* of the Enlightenment, the competing *economic interests* of British mercantilism and colonial self-interest, the *political antecedents* defining the "rights of Englishmen" under English common law, the English Bill of Rights, and the Glorious Revolution, and the varying aspirations of different social groups in the colonies, defined by gender, race, economic status, and region.

Similarly, understanding the consequences of the American victory demonstrates how change in any one of these spheres of activity often has impact on some or all of the others. The many consequences of the colonists' military victory included their development of new and lasting *political institutions*, the *social and economic effects* of the American victory on the various groups who entered the war with differing aspirations and who allied themselves with different sides during the conflict, and the long-term *philosophical consequences* of the American Revolution, inspiring what has been called the "Age of Democratic Revolution." Together, these consequences demonstrate the complexity of historical events and the broadly integrative nature of history itself. They also affirm, once again, the unique power of history to deepen students' understanding of the past, and of how we are still affected by it.

Likewise, in world history, in order to comprehend the forces leading to the Iberian Conquest of Mesoamerica in the 15th and 16th centuries, students must address the *economics* of the interregional trading system that linked peoples of Africa, Asia, and Europe on the eve of the European overseas voyages; the *political and religious* changes initiated with the rise of centralized monarchies of Spain and Portugal; and the major *technological* innovations that the Portuguese and Spanish made in shipbuilding, navigation, and naval warfare and the influence of northern Europe, Muslim, and Chinese maritime technology on these changes.

Similarly, understanding the consequences of the Iberian Conquest of Mesoamerica demonstrates how change in any one of these spheres of human activity often had impact on some or all of the others. The many consequences of the Iberian military victories included, for example, the founding of Spanish and Portuguese *colonial empires* in the Americas; the *worldwide exchange* of flora, fauna, and pathogens following the Columbian encounter; the *social changes* wrought by the subjugation and enslavement of the indigenous peoples of the Americas; the devastating *demographic effects* caused by the introduction of new disease microorganisms into the Americas; the *forced relocation and enslavement* of some 10 million Africans in the European colonies; the changes in *religious beliefs and practices* that followed the introduction of Christianity into the Americas; and the *economic and social effects* of the infusion into the European economies of the vast gold and silver resources of the Americas. These many effects demonstrate the complexity of historical events and the broadly integrative nature of history itself. They also affirm, once again, the unique power of history to deepen students' understanding of the past, and of how we are still affected by it.

Historical Thinking

Beyond defining what students should *know*—that is, the understandings in United States and World History that all students should acquire—it is essential to consider what students should be able to *do* to demonstrate their understandings and to apply their knowledge in productive ways.

The study of history involves much more than the passive absorption of facts, dates, names, and places. **History is in its essence a process of reasoning based on evidence from the past. This reasoning must be grounded in the careful gathering, weighing and sifting of factual information such as names, dates, places, ideas, and events. However, the process does not stop here.** Real historical understanding requires students to think through cause-and-effect relationships, to reach sound historical interpretations, and to conduct historical inquiries and research leading to the knowledge on which informed decisions in contemporary life can be based. These thinking skills are the processes of active learning.

Properly taught, history develops capacities for analysis and judgment. It reveals the ambiguity of choice, and it promotes wariness about quick, facile solutions which have so often brought human suffering in their wake. History fosters understanding of paradox and a readiness to distinguish between that which is beyond and that which is within human control, between the inevitable and the contingent. It trains students to detect bias, to weigh evidence, and to evaluate arguments, thus preparing them to make sensible, independent judgments, to sniff out spurious appeals to history by partisan pleaders, to distinguish between anecdote and analysis.

To acquire these capabilities, students must develop competence in the following five types of historical thinking:

▶ **Chronological thinking,** developing a clear sense of historical time—past, present, and future—in order to identify the temporal sequence in which events occurred, measure calendar time, interpret and create time lines, and explain patterns of historical succession and duration, continuity and change.

▶ **Historical comprehension,** including the ability to read historical narratives with understanding; to identify the basic elements of the narrative structure (the characters, situation, sequence of events, their causes, and their outcomes); and, to appreciate historical perspectives—that is, the ability to describe the past through the eyes and experiences of those who were there, as revealed through their literature, art, artifacts, and the like, and to avoid "present-mindedness," judging the past solely in terms of the norms and values of today.

▶ **Historical analysis and interpretation,** including the ability to compare and contrast different experiences, beliefs, motives, traditions, hopes, and fears of people from various groups and backgrounds, and at various times in the past and present; to analyze how these differing motives, interests, beliefs, hopes and fears influenced people's behaviors; to consider multiple perspectives in the records of human experience and multiple causes in analyses of historical events; to challenge arguments of historical inevitability; and to compare and evaluate competing historical explanations of the past.

‣ **Historical research,** including the ability to formulate historical questions from encounters with historical documents, artifacts, photos, visits to historical sites, and eyewitness accounts; to determine the historical time and context in which the - artifact, document, or other record was created; to judge its credibility and authority; and to construct a sound historical narrative or argument concerning it.

‣ **Historical issues-analysis and decision-making,** including the ability to identify problems that people confronted in the past; to analyze the various interests and points of view of people caught up in these situations; to evaluate alternative proposals for dealing with the problem(s); to analyze whether the decisions reached or the actions taken were sound ones and why; and, to bring historical perspectives to bear on informed decision-making in the present.

Integrating Standards in Historical Understanding and Thinking

Chapter 2 presents the standards in historical thinking, largely independent of historical content in order to specify the quality of thinking desired for each. None of these skills in historical thinking, however, can be developed or even expressed in a vacuum. Every one of them requires historical content in order to function—a relationship made explicit in Chapters 3 and 4, in which the Standards integrating historical understanding and historical thinking are presented for all eras of United States and World History for grades 5 through 12.

The diagram on page 52 illustrates the approach taken to integrate historical thinking and historical understandings in the Standards. The example is drawn from the *U.S. History Standards, Era 3, Revolution and the New Nation (1754-1820s)*. As illustrated, the five skills in historical thinking (the left side of the diagram) and the three historical understandings students should acquire concerning the American Revolution (the right side of the diagram) are integrated in the central area of overlap in the diagram in order to define (immediately below) Standard 1A: The student understands the causes of the American Revolution.

Page 53 provides a further illustration of this same standard, presented this time in the format in which the standards are stated (Chapters 3 and 4). The selection is again drawn from *Era 3, Revolution and the New Nation*. As illustrated, the standard first presents a statement defining what students should understand: "The causes of the American Revolution, the ideas and interests involved in forging the revolutionary movement, and the reasons for the American victory."

Directly below the standard is standard component 1A, a statement which zooms in on part of the full standard. This statement is followed by five elaborated standards which specify what students should be able to do to demonstrate their understanding of the causes of the American Revolution. Each elaborated standard illustrates the integration of historical thinking and understanding by marrying a particular thinking skill (e.g., comparing arguments) to a specific historical understanding (e.g., traditional rights of English people). One thinking skill appears highlighted in brackets following each statement. The particular thinking skill was selected to serve as an example of the integration of historical thinking and historical understanding, and it is by no means the only one that can be employed. In fact, the standards encourage teachers to approach content through a wide variety of thinking skills.

Finally, each elaborated standard is coded to indicate in which grades the standard can appropriately be developed.

5-12   indicates the standard is appropriate for grades 5-6, as well as for all higher levels, from grades 7-8 through grades 9-12.

7-12   indicates the standard is appropriate for grades 7-8 through grades 9-12.

9-12   indicates the standard is best reserved for students in their high school years, grades 9-12.

However, the order in which the elaborated standards are presented is driven by the logical unfolding of the particular topic rather than by grade level.

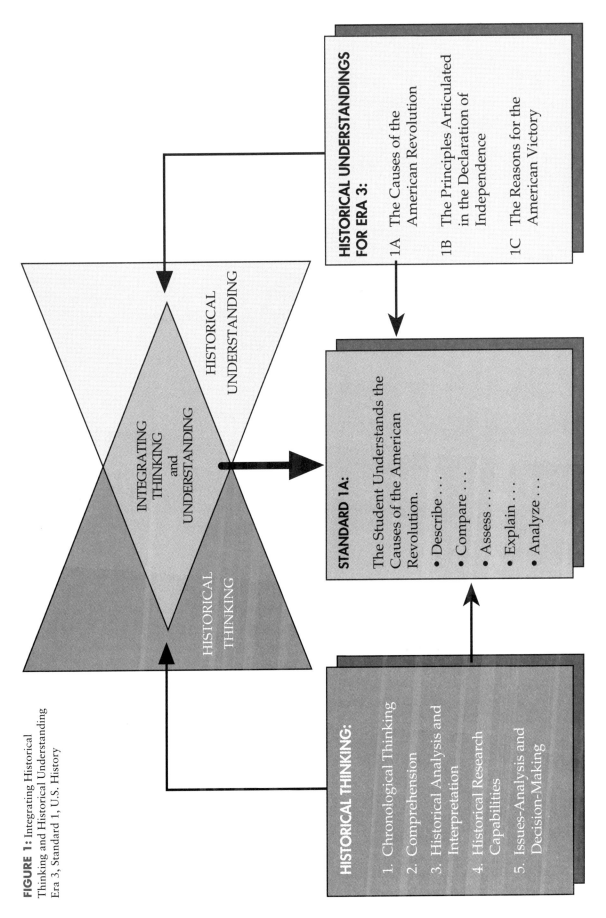

FIGURE 1: Integrating Historical Thinking and Historical Understanding Era 3, Standard 1, U.S. History

FIGURE 2: Elements of a History Standard

STANDARD:

Statement of the historical understanding that students should acquire

STANDARD COMPONENT:

Statement identifying the first understanding of Standard 1 (1A)

ELABORATED STANDARD:

Standard 1A elaborations with recommendation of grade-level appropriateness

THINKING SKILL:

One of several appropriate thinking skills

ERA 3: REVOLUTION AND THE NEW NATION (1754-1820S)

STANDARD 1   The causes of the American Revolution, the ideas and interests involved in forging the revolutionary movement, and the reasons for the American victory.

1A   **The student understands the causes of the American Revolution.**

Therefore, the student is able to:

5-12   Explain the consequences of the Seven Years War and the overhaul of English imperial policy following the Treaty of Paris in 1763. [**Marshal evidence of antecedent circumstances**]

5-12   Compare the arguments advanced by defenders and opponents of the new imperial policy on the traditional rights of English people and the legitimacy of asking the colonies to pay a share of the costs of empire. [**Consider multiple perspectives**]

5-12   Reconstruct the chronology of the critical events leading to the outbreak of armed conflict between the American colonies and England. [**Establish temporal order**]

7-12   Analyze political, ideological, religious, and economic origins of the revolution. [**Analyze multiple causation**]

9-12   Reconstruct the arguments among patriots and loyalists about independence and draw conclusions about how the decision to declare independence was reached. [**Consider multiple perspectives**]

85

53

Questions Concerning These Standards

Q: Do these Standards require that each era be taught at all three levels, grades 5-6, 7-8, and 9-12?

A: No. The local school curriculum will determine when an era is to be taught, whether at grades 5-6, 7-8, and/or 9-12. Once that curriculum decision is made, teachers can enter these standards to determine which ones are appropriate for their students, and how the standards they select are related to others within a well-articulated curriculum in history, grades 5-12.

Q: Are high school teachers expected to teach all standards identified as appropriate for grades 9-12?

A: No. These standards assume that schools will devote three years of study to United States History and three years of study to World History sometime between grades 5 and 12. Therefore, an era will probably be studied in some depth during at least one earlier school year (e.g., grade 8). In that case, the more numerous standards deemed appropriate for grades 9-12 will, in part, have already been addressed in an earlier grade, and the emphasis can be turned in the high school U.S. or World History course to those standards judged not to be appropriate for the earlier grades. Again, these are matters of well-designed, articulated curriculum planning, within the jurisdiction of local schools.

Q: Does the thinking skill identified in a particular elaborated standard limit teachers to drawing upon that one skill?

A: No. Decidedly not. Each elaborated standard highlights one important thinking skill. However, it is understood that good teaching will incorporate several, or even many, thinking skills to develop these understandings. In fact, as students' historical knowledge deepens, they will draw on a widening range of skills.

Q: Do these standards limit the instructional approaches teachers might adopt to develop these outcomes with students?

A: No. These standards are intended to open possibilities, not to limit teachers' options for engaging students in lively activities within what has been called the "thinking curriculum." To take one example from U.S. history, "Compare the arguments advanced by defenders and opponents of the new imperial policy on the traditional rights of English people," can be developed through any of a number of teaching approaches. For example, students might:

▶ Create a chart listing the competing arguments in two parallel columns.

▶ Assume the roles of defenders and opponents of England's imperial policy and debate the issue whether England was right in developing its policy.

▶ Write "Letters to the Editor" for a July 1775 issue of their classroom newspaper, the *Boston Liberator*, in which the editorial page is devoted to assessing opposing views on England's imperial policy in the context of the mounting crisis.

▶ Create a historical argument in the form of an essay, speech before the English Parliament, or an editorial in which they confront the opposing views on England's imperial policy and justify the position they judge warranted by the data.

An example from world history further illustrates a variety of instructional approaches that can be used for the 4th elaborated standard for Era 3, Standard 2A: "Describe the changing political institutions of Athens in the 6th and 5th centuries BCE, and analyze the influence of political thought on public life," can be developed through any number of teaching approaches. For example, teachers might select one episode from the time of the Persian Wars when Athens faced invasion (480 BCE) and the Assembly voted upon a bill proposed by the Athenian general Themistocles for the defense of Athens. In this case, students might:

▶ Recount or create a flow chart of the procedure for passing a bill in 5th-century BCE Athens.

▶ Prepare a speech such as Themistocles might have delivered before the Athenian Assembly setting forth the plans for the evacuation and defense of Athens, and conduct a mock session of the Assembly to debate the proposal.

▶ Consider the roles of people from different classes in Athenian society such as women, children, the elders, landowning males under the age of 50, slaves, and those who had been ostracized or disenfranchised. Analyze who was allowed to participate in the democratic process under Athenian law at this time, and how each group would be affected by the Assembly's decision on the proposed evacuation.

Q: **Won't the elaborated standards each require a separate lesson or sequence of lessons, and doesn't the total teaching load therefore far exceed the total number of teaching days available, even over three years of instruction?**

A: No. Good teaching, it should be emphasized, will often develop two or more of these elaborated standards in a single lesson or sequence of lessons. These standards are intended to signify desired *outcomes* of instruction and not to prescribe a particular teaching plan. Teachers will creatively design their own instructional plans, integrating related understandings in a variety of ways to accomplish these ends.

For example, in the teaching approaches just considered—creating a flow chart, conducting a mock meeting of the Athenian Assembly, and analyzing potential political roles of people from different classes of Athenian society—the first and second activities contribute directly to achieving the first of the five elaborated standards and the third activity contributes directly to achieving three of them: the first (describing the changing political institutions of Athens and the influence of political thought on public life); the fourth (explaining class divisions of Greek society and the social and political roles of major classes); and the fifth (analyzing the place of women in Athenian society). Teachers seeking to make the most of their instructional time will therefore probably select the third activity over the least productive activity of creating a flow chart, and thereby hit the proverbial two—or three!—birds with a single stone.

Q: Why are famous figures from U.S. and world history such as Robert E. Lee or Wilbur and Orville Wright seldom mentioned by name in the standards?

A: The standards are neither a curriculum nor a textbook where these names, and hundreds of others, will undoubtedly be mentioned and elaborated upon. Rather, the standards, which are curricular guidelines, direct teachers' attention to broad historical developments. For example, students should understand "how political, military and diplomatic leadership affected the outcome of the Civil War." In acquiring this understanding, students will find names such as Robert E. Lee, George McClelland, Ulysses S. Grant and many others, in textbooks and other sources.

Three Policy Issues

Ensuring Equity for All Students

The purposes of the national standards developed in this document are threefold: (1) to establish high expectations for what all students should know and be able to do; (2) to clarify what constitutes successful achievement; and (3) *most significantly, to promote equity in the learning opportunities and resources to be provided all students in the nation's schools.*

Standards in and of themselves cannot ensure remediation of the pervasive inequalities in the educational opportunities currently available to students. The roots of these problems are deep and widely manifested in gross inequities in school financing, in resource allocations, and in practices of discriminatory "lower tracks" and "dumbed down" curricula that continue to deny large sectors of the nation's children equal educational opportunity.

What the national commitment to high achievement standards for all students can do is to serve as an engine of change: (1) defining for all students the goals essential to success in a rapidly changing global economy and in a society undergoing wrenching social, technological, and economic change; and (2) establishing the moral obligation to provide equity in the educational resources required to help all students attain these goals.

If students are to achieve the understandings and thinking skills specified in the United States and World History Standards, they must have equal access to well-prepared history teachers and to engaging, balanced, accurate, and challenging curricular materials. For these reasons the success of these standards requires the provision of high quality professional development in United States and World History and in pedagogy for teachers who are not prepared to teach the content or thinking skills presented in this document. Equally important, all students must be provided with the best available textbooks and other curricular materials in history.

As Robert Hutchins said many years ago: "The best education for the best should be the best education for all." Every child is entitled to and must have equal access to excellence in the goals their teachers strive to help them achieve and in the instructional resources and opportunities required to reach those ends. Nothing less is acceptable in a democratic society; no commitment is more essential to meeting the challenges— economic, social, and ethical—confronting this nation in the years ahead.

Providing Adequate Instructional Time for History

In developing these standards, the National Council for History Standards kept in mind the purposes of the National Education Goals adopted by the nation's fifty governors in 1989. Developing the internationally competitive levels of student achievement called for in this reform movement clearly cannot be accomplished by limiting the study of the nation's history to one year (or less) over the eight years of middle and high school education. Excellence in history requires the instructional time to pursue an era in some depth and to engage students' active learning through the higher processes of historical thinking.

For these reasons it is important that the schools devote no less than three years of instruction to United States History and three years of instruction to World History over the eight years of students' middle and high school education, grades five through twelve. Currently, seventeen states provide three years of United States history, though under a variety of curriculum plans. Fourteen states provide two or more years of world history and six of these states provide three years, again, under a variety of curriculum plans. In formulating national standards for excellence, the Council argued, we should not be setting our sights lower than those of the numerous states that have already committed three years of instruction to this field.

Accommodating Variability in State and Local Curriculum Plans

Schools today vary widely as to when and how they offer their courses in history, and therefore the National Council sought a flexible approach to history standards which would accommodate local variability rather than impose a single national curriculum on the nation's schools. As illustrated in Figure 2 on page 53, we have tried to indicate appropriate grade levels for study of each elaborated standard. Deciding **when** these eras should be studied, whether in grades 5-6, 7-8, or 9-12, is a *curriculum* decision, and should remain under local or state control.

Thus, under Florida's state course of study, United States history is developed in relation to world history over two successive high school years—grades 10 (to World War I) and 11 (the modern world)—in addition to two successive years of study of state and national history in grade 4 (beginnings to 1880) and grade 5 (the years since 1880). Teachers of grades 4 and 10 following this plan will draw on the U.S. history standards developed for the earlier eras in U.S. history while teachers of grades 5 and 11 will draw on the standards developed for the later eras. In all cases teachers will focus on the standards designated for their particular grade levels, whether grades 5-6 or 9-12. None will use the standards developed for grades 7 or 8—two years in Florida's curriculum devoted to studies other than history.

In California, by contrast, where the state framework suggests concentrating upon the study of the early eras of U.S. history in grade 5, the 19th century in grade 8, and the 20th century in grade 11, teachers following this plan will turn to the standards in a different way. Teachers of grade 5 will turn to the standards developed for U.S. history through the Civil War; teachers of grade 8 will *selectively* draw upon these same standards in their initial review but will concentrate upon the standards developed for the 19th-century history of the United States. Teachers of grade 11 will again selectively draw upon the standards for the earlier eras in their initial reviews, but will concentrate upon the standards developed for the 20th-century history of the nation. In all cases, teachers will focus within any of these eras upon the standards developed for their particular grade level.

Likewise, under Florida's state course of study, **world history** is developed in relation to United States history over three successive high school years—grade 9 (birth of civilizations through the 18th-century democratic revolutions); grade 10 (through World War I); and grade 11 (from 1848 until today). In addition, Florida begins a three-year sequence in history with grade 3 in which students are engaged in humanities-enriched studies of significant developments of the ancient world, the middle ages, and the Renaissance. Teachers of grade 9 following this course of study will draw upon the world history standards developed for Eras 1 through 6; teachers of grade 10 will draw upon the world history standards developed for Era 7; and teachers of grade 11 will draw upon the world history standards developed for Eras 7 and 8.

California's state framework recommends concentrating upon the study of the early Eras 1-3 in world history in grade 6, Eras 4-6 in grade 7, and Eras 7-9 in grade 10; therefore, teachers following this plan will turn to the standards in a different way. Teachers of grade 6 will turn to the standards developed for the ancient world. Teachers of grade 7 will *selectively* draw upon the standards developed for eras beginning with the fall of the Roman and Han empires and continuing through 18th-century world history. Teachers of grade 10 will again *selectively* draw upon the standards for the earlier eras in their initial reviews, but will concentrate upon the standards developed for the 19th and 20th centuries of world history. Again, in utilizing these voluntary standards, teachers may choose to focus within any of these eras upon the standards developed for their particular grade level, whether for grades 5-6, 7-8, or 9-12.

2

Standards in Historical Thinking

The study of history, as noted earlier, rests on knowledge of facts, dates, names, places, events, and ideas. In addition, true historical understanding requires students to engage in historical thinking: to raise questions and to marshal solid evidence in support of their answers; to go beyond the facts presented in their textbooks and examine the historical record for themselves; to consult documents, journals, diaries, artifacts, historic sites, works of art, quantitative data, and other evidence from the past, and to do so imaginatively—taking into account the historical context in which these records were created and comparing the multiple points of view of those on the scene at the time.

Real historical understanding requires that students have opportunity to create historical narratives and arguments of their own. Such narratives and arguments may take many forms—essays, debates, and editorials, for instance. They can be initiated in a variety of ways. None, however, more powerfully initiates historical thinking than those issues, past and present, that challenge students to enter knowledgeably into the historical record and to bring sound historical perspectives to bear in the analysis of a problem.

Historical understanding also requires that students thoughtfully read the historical narratives created by others. Well-written historical narratives are interpretative, revealing and explaining connections, change, and consequences. They are also analytical, combining lively storytelling and biography with conceptual analysis drawn from all relevant disciplines. Such narratives promote essential skills in historical thinking.

Reading such narratives requires that students analyze the assumptions—stated and unstated—from which the narrative was constructed and assess the strength of the evidence presented. It requires that students consider the significance of what the author included as well as chose to omit—the absence, for example, of the voices and experiences of other men and women who were also an important part of the history of their time. Also, it requires that students examine the interpretative nature of history, comparing, for example, alternative historical narratives written by historians who have given different weight to the political, economic, social, and/or technological causes of events and who have developed competing interpretations of the significance of those events.

Students engaged in activities of the kinds just considered will draw upon skills in the following five interconnected dimensions of historical thinking:

1. Chronological Thinking
2. Historical Comprehension
3. Historical Analysis and Interpretation
4. Historical Research Capabilities
5. Historical Issues-Analysis and Decision-making

These skills, while presented in five separate categories, are nonetheless **interactive and mutually supportive.** In conducting historical research or creating a historical argument of their own, for example, students must be able to draw upon skills in all five categories. Beyond the skills of conducting their research, students must, for example, be able to comprehend historical documents and records, analyze their relevance, develop interpretations of the document(s) they select, and demonstrate a sound grasp of the historical chronology and context in which the issue, problem, or events they are addressing developed.

In short, these five sets of skills, developed in the following pages as the five Standards in Historical Thinking, are statements of the outcomes that students need to achieve. They are not mutually exclusive when put into practice, nor do they prescribe a particular teaching sequence to be followed. Teachers will draw upon all these Thinking Standards, as appropriate, to develop their teaching plans and to guide students through challenging programs of study in history.

Finally, it is important to point out that these five sets of Standards in Historical Thinking are defined in the following pages largely independent of historical content in order to specify the quality of thinking desired for each. It is essential to understand, however, that these skills do not develop, nor can they be practiced, in a vacuum. Every one of these skills requires specific historical content in order to function—a relationship that is made explicit in Chapters 3 and 4, which presents the standards integrating historical understandings and thinking for history for grades 5-12.

Overview of Standards in Historical Thinking

Standard 1. Chronological Thinking

A. Distinguish between past, present, and future time.

B. Identify in historical narratives the temporal structure of a historical narrative or story.

C. Establish temporal order in constructing historical narratives of their own.

D. Measure and calculate calendar time.

E. Interpret data presented in time lines.

F. Reconstruct patterns of historical succession and duration.

G. Compare alternative models for periodization.

Standard 2. Historical Comprehension

A. Reconstruct the literal meaning of a historical passage.

B. Identify the central question(s) the historical narrative addresses.

C. Read historical narratives imaginatively.

D. Evidence historical perspectives.

E. Draw upon data in historical maps.

F. Utilize visual and mathematical data presented in charts, tables, pie and bar graphs, flow charts, Venn diagrams, and other graphic organizers.

G. Draw upon visual, literary, and musical sources.

Standard 3. Historical Analysis and Interpretation

A. Identify the author or source of the historical document or narrative.

B. Compare and contrast differing sets of ideas, values, personalities, behaviors, and institutions.

C. Differentiate between historical facts and historical interpretations.

D. Consider multiple perspectives.

E. Analyze cause-and-effect relationships and multiple causation, including the importance of the individual, the influence of ideas, and the role of chance.

F. Challenge arguments of historical inevitability.

G. Compare competing historical narratives.

H. Hold interpretations of history as tentative.

I. Evaluate major debates among historians.

J. Hypothesize the influence of the past.

Standard 4. Historical Research Capabilities

A. Formulate historical questions.

B. Obtain historical data.

C. Interrogate historical data.

D. Identify the gaps in the available records, marshal contextual knowledge and perspectives of the time and place, and construct a sound historical interpretation.

Standard 5. Historical Issues-Analysis and Decision-Making

A. Identify issues and problems in the past.

B. Marshal evidence of antecedent circumstances and contemporary factors contributing to problems and alternative courses of action.

C. Identify relevant historical antecedents.

D. Evaluate alternative courses of action.

E. Formulate a position or course of action on an issue.

F. Evaluate the implementation of a decision.

STANDARD 1

Chronological Thinking

Chronological thinking is at the heart of historical reasoning. Without a strong sense of chronology—of when events occurred and in what temporal order—it is impossible for students to examine relationships among those events or to explain historical causality. Chronology provides the mental scaffolding for organizing historical thought.

In developing students' chronological thinking, instructional time should be given to the use of well-constructed historical narratives: literary narratives including biographies and historical literature, and well-written narrative histories that have the quality of "stories well told." Well-crafted narratives such as these have the power to grip and hold students' attention. Thus engaged, the reader is able to focus on what the narrator discloses: the temporal structure of events unfolding over time, the actions and intentions of those who were there, the temporal connections between antecedents and their consequences.

In the middle and high school years, students should be able to use their mathematical skills to measure time by years, decades, centuries, and millennia; to calculate time from the fixed points of the calendar system (BC or BCE and AD or CE); and to interpret the data presented in time lines.

Students should be able to analyze *patterns of historical duration,* demonstrated, for example, by the more than two hundred years the United States Constitution and the government it created has endured.

Students should also be able to analyze *patterns of historical succession* illustrated, for example, in the development, over time, of ever larger systems of interaction, beginning with trade among settlements of the Neolithic world; continuing through the growth of the great land empires of Rome, Han China, the Islamic world, and the Mongols; expanding in the early modern era when Europeans crossed the Atlantic and Pacific, and established the first worldwide networks of trade and communication; and culminating with the global systems of trade and communication of the modern world.

STANDARD 1   The student thinks chronologically:

Therefore, the student is able to:

A. **Distinguish between past, present, and future time.**

B. **Identify the temporal structure of a historical narrative or story:** its beginning, middle, and end (the latter defined as the outcome of a particular beginning).

C. **Establish temporal order in constructing historical narratives of their own:** working forward from some beginning through its development, to some end or outcome; working *backward* from some issue, problem, or event to explain its origins and its development over time.

D. **Measure and calculate calendar time** by days, weeks, months, years, decades, centuries, and millennia, from fixed points of the calendar system: BC (before Christ) and AD (*Anno Domini*, "in the year of our Lord") in the Gregorian calendar and the contemporary secular designation for these same dates, BCE (before the Common Era) and CE (in the Common Era); and compare with the fixed points of other calendar systems such as the Roman (753 BC, the founding of the city of Rome) and the Muslim (622 AD, the hegira).

E. **Interpret data presented in time lines and create time lines** by designating appropriate equidistant intervals of time and recording events according to the temporal order in which they occurred.

F. **Reconstruct patterns of historical succession and duration** in which historical developments have unfolded, and apply them to **explain historical continuity and change.**

G. **Compare alternative models for periodization** by identifying the organizing principles on which each is based.

STANDARD 2

Historical Comprehension

One of the defining features of historical narratives is their believable recounting of human events. Beyond that, historical narratives also have the power to disclose the intentions of the people involved, the difficulties they encountered, and the complex world in which such historical figures actually lived. To read historical stories, biographies, autobiographies, and narratives with comprehension, students must develop the ability to read imaginatively, to take into account what the narrative reveals of the humanity of the individuals and groups involved—their motives and intentions, their values and ideas, their hopes, doubts, fears, strengths, and weaknesses. Comprehending historical narratives requires, also, that students develop historical perspectives, the ability to describe the past on its own terms, through the eyes and experiences of those who were there. By studying the literature, diaries, letters, debates, arts, and artifacts of past peoples, students should learn to avoid "present-mindedness" by not judging the past solely in terms of the norms and values of today but taking into account the historical context in which the events unfolded.

Acquiring these skills begins in the early years of childhood, through the use of superbly written biographies that capture children's imagination and provide them an important foundation for continuing historical study. As students move into middle grades and high school years, historical literature should continue to occupy an important place in the curriculum, capturing historical events with dramatic immediacy, engaging students' interests, and fostering deeper understanding of the times and cultural milieu in which events occurred.

Beyond these important outcomes, students should also develop the skills needed to comprehend historical narratives that *explain* as well as recount the course of events and that *analyze* relationships among the various forces which were present at the time and influenced the ways events unfolded. These skills include: 1) identifying the central question the historical narrative seeks to answer; 2) defining the purpose, perspective, or point of view from which the narrative has been constructed; 3) reading the historical explanation or analysis with meaning; 4) recognizing the rhetorical cues that signal how the author has organized the text.

Comprehending historical narratives will also be facilitated if students are able to draw upon the data presented in historical maps; visual, mathematical, and quantitative data presented in a variety of graphic organizers; and a variety of visual sources such as historical photographs, political cartoons, paintings, and architecture in order to clarify, illustrate, or elaborate upon the information presented in the text.

STANDARD 2	The student comprehends a variety of historical sources:

Therefore, the student is able to:

A. **Identify the author or source of the historical document or narrative and assess its credibility.**

B. **Reconstruct the literal meaning of a historical passage** by identifying who was involved, what happened, where it happened, what events led to these developments, and what consequences or outcomes followed.

C. **Identify the central question(s)** the historical narrative addresses and the purpose, perspective, or point of view from which it has been constructed.

D. **Differentiate between historical facts and historical interpretations** but acknowledge that the two are related; that the facts the historian reports are selected and reflect therefore the historian's judgement of what is most significant about the past.

E. **Read historical narratives imaginatively,** taking into account what the narrative reveals of the humanity of the individuals and groups involved—their probable values, outlook, motives, hopes, fears, strengths, and weaknesses.

F. **Appreciate historical perspectives**—(a) describing the past on its own terms, through the eyes and experiences of those who were there, as revealed through their literature, diaries, letters, debates, arts, artifacts, and the like; (b) considering the historical context in which the event unfolded—the values, outlook, options, and contingencies of that time and place; and (c) avoiding "present-mindedness," judging the past solely in terms of present-day norms and values.

G. **Draw upon data in historical maps** in order to obtain or clarify information on the geographic setting in which the historical event occurred, its relative and absolute location, the distances and directions involved, the natural and man-made features of the place, and critical relationships in the spatial distributions of those features and historical event occurring there.

H. **Utilize visual, mathematical, and quantitative data** presented in charts, tables, pie and bar graphs, flow charts, Venn diagrams, and other graphic organizers to clarify, illustrate, or elaborate upon information presented in the historical narrative.

I.   **Draw upon visual, literary, and musical sources** including: (a) photographs, paintings, cartoons, and architectural drawings; (b) novels, poetry, and plays; and, (c) folk, popular and classical music, to clarify, illustrate, or elaborate upon information presented in the historical narrative.

STANDARD 3

Historical Analysis and Interpretation

One of the most common problems in helping students to become thoughtful readers of historical narrative is the compulsion students feel to find the one right answer, the one essential fact, the one authoritative interpretation. "Am I on the right track?" "Is this what you want?" they ask. Or, worse yet, they rush to closure, reporting back as self-evident truths the facts or conclusions presented in the document or text.

These problems are deeply rooted in the conventional ways in which textbooks have presented history: a succession of facts marching straight to a settled outcome. To overcome these problems requires the use of more than a single source: of history books other than textbooks and of a rich variety of historical documents and artifacts that present alternative voices, accounts, and interpretations or perspectives on the past.

Students need to realize that historians may differ on the facts they incorporate in the development of their narratives and disagree as well on how those facts are to be interpreted. Thus, "history" is usually taken to mean what happened in the past; but written history is a dialogue among historians, not only about what happened but about why and how events unfolded. The study of history is not only remembering answers. It requires following and evaluating arguments and arriving at usable, even if tentative, conclusions based on the available evidence

To engage in *historical analysis and interpretation* students must draw upon their skills of *historical comprehension*. In fact, there is no sharp line separating the two categories. Certain of the skills involved in comprehension overlap the skills involved in analysis and are essential to it. For example, identifying the author or source of a historical document or narrative and assessing its credibility (comprehension) is prerequisite to comparing competing historical narratives (analysis). Analysis builds upon the skills of comprehension; it obliges the student to assess the evidence on which the historian has drawn and determine the soundness of interpretations created from that evidence. It goes without saying that in acquiring these analytical skills students must develop the ability to differentiate between expressions of opinion, no matter how passionately delivered, and informed hypotheses grounded in historical evidence.

Well-written historical narrative has the power to promote students' analysis of historical causality—of how change occurs in society, of how human intentions matter, and how ends are influenced by the means of carrying them out, in what has been called the tangle of process and outcomes. Few challenges can be more fascinating to students than unraveling the often dramatic complications of cause. And nothing is more dangerous than a simple, monocausal explanation of past experiences and present problems.

Finally, well-written historical narratives can also alert students to the traps of *lineality and inevitability*. Students must understand the relevance of the past to their own times, but they need also to avoid the trap of lineality, of drawing straight lines between past and present, as though earlier movements were being propelled teleologically toward some rendezvous with destiny in the late 20th century.

A related trap is that of thinking that events have unfolded inevitably—that the way things are is the way they had to be, and thus that individuals lack free will and the capacity for making choices. Unless students can conceive that history could have turned out differently, they may unconsciously accept the notion that the future is also inevitable or predetermined, and that human agency and individual action count for nothing. No attitude is more likely to feed civic apathy, cynicism, and resignation—precisely what we hope the study of history will fend off. Whether in dealing with the main narrative or with a topic in depth, we must always try, in one historian's words, to "restore to the past the options it once had."

STANDARD 3	**The student engages in historical analysis and interpretation:**

Therefore, the student is able to:

A. **Compare and contrast differing sets of ideas,** values, personalities, behaviors, and institutions by identifying likenesses and differences.

B. **Consider multiple perspectives** of various peoples in the past by demonstrating their differing motives, beliefs, interests, hopes, and fears.

C. **Analyze cause-and-effect relationships** bearing in mind **multiple causation** including (a) **the importance of the individual** in history; (b) **the influence of ideas,** human interests, and beliefs; and (c) the role of chance, the accidental and the irrational.

D. **Draw comparisons across eras and regions in order to define enduring issues** as well as large-scale or long-term developments that transcend regional and temporal boundaries.

E. **Distinguish between unsupported expressions of opinion and informed hypotheses grounded in historical evidence.**

F. **Compare competing historical narratives.**

G. **Challenge arguments of historical inevitability** by formulating examples of historical contingency, of how different choices could have led to different consequences.

H. **Hold interpretations of history as tentative,** subject to changes as new information is uncovered, new voices heard, and new interpretations broached.

I. **Evaluate major debates among historians** concerning alternative interpretations of the past.

J. **Hypothesize the influence of the past,** including both the limitations and the opportunities made possible by past decisions.

STANDARD 4

Historical Research Capabilities

Perhaps no aspect of historical thinking is as exciting to students or as productive of their growth in historical thinking as "doing history." Such inquiries can arise at critical turning points in the historical narrative presented in the text. They might be generated by encounters with historical documents, eyewitness accounts, letters, diaries, artifacts, photos, a visit to a historic site, a record of oral history, or other evidence of the past. Worthy inquiries are especially likely to develop if the documents students encounter are rich with the voices of people caught up in the event and sufficiently diverse to bring alive to students the interests, beliefs, and concerns of people with differing backgrounds and opposing viewpoints on the event.

Historical inquiry proceeds with the formulation of a problem or set of questions worth pursuing. In the most direct approach, students might be encouraged to analyze a document, record, or site itself. Who produced it, when, how, and why? What is the evidence of its authenticity, authority, and credibility? What does it tell them of the point of view, background, and interests of its author or creator? What else must they discover in order to construct a useful story, explanation, or narrative of the event of which this document or artifact is a part? What interpretation can they derive from their data, and what argument can they support in the historical narrative they create from the data?

In this process students' contextual knowledge of the historical period in which the document or artifact was created becomes critically important. Only a few records of the event will be available to students. Filling in the gaps, evaluating the records they have available, and imaginatively constructing a sound historical argument or narrative requires a larger context of meaning.

For these purposes, students' ongoing narrative study of history provides important support, revealing the larger context. But just as the ongoing narrative study, supported by but not limited to the textbook, provides a meaningful context in which students' inquiries can develop, it is these inquiries themselves that imbue the era with deeper meaning. Hence the importance of providing students documents or other records beyond materials included in the textbook, that will allow students to challenge textbook interpretations, to raise new questions about the event, to investigate the perspectives of those whose voices do not appear in the textbook accounts, or to plumb an issue that the textbook largely or in part bypassed.

Under these conditions, students will view their inquiries as creative contributions. They will better understand that written history is a human construction, that many judgments about the past are tentative and arguable, and that historians regard their work as critical inquiry, pursued as ongoing explorations and debates with other historians. On the other hand, careful research can resolve cloudy issues from the past and can overturn previous arguments and theses. By their active engagement in historical inquiry, students will learn for themselves why historians are continuously reinterpreting the past, and why new interpretations emerge not only from uncovering new evidence but from rethinking old evidence in the light of new ideas springing up in our own times. Students then can also see why the good historian, like the good teacher, is interested not in manipulation or indoctrination but in acting as an honest messenger from the past—not interested in possessing student's minds but in presenting them with the power to possess their own.

| STANDARD 4 | The student conducts historical research: |

Therefore, the student is able to:

A. **Formulate historical questions** from encounters with historical documents, eyewitness accounts, letters, diaries, artifacts, photos, historical sites, art, architecture, and other records from the past.

B. **Obtain historical data from a variety of sources,** including: library and museum collections, historic sites, historical photos, journals, diaries, eyewitness accounts, newspapers, and the like; documentary films, oral testimony from living witnesses, censuses, tax records, city directories, statistical compilations, and economic indicators.

C. **Interrogate historical data** by uncovering the social, political, and economic context in which it was created; testing the data source for its credibility, authority, authenticity, internal consistency and completeness; and detecting and evaluating bias, distortion, and propaganda by omission, suppression, or invention of facts.

D. **Identify the gaps in the available records and marshal contextual knowledge and perspectives of the time and place** in order to elaborate imaginatively upon the evidence, fill in the gaps deductively, and construct a sound historical interpretation.

E. **Employ quantitative analysis** in order to explore such topics as changes in family size and composition, migration patterns, wealth distribution, and changes in the economy.

F. **Support interpretations with historical evidence** in order to construct closely reasoned arguments rather than facile opinions.

| S T A N D A R D 5 |

Historical Issues-Analysis and Decision-Making

Issue-centered analysis and decision-making activities place students squarely at the center of historical dilemmas and problems faced at critical moments in the past and the near-present. Entering into such moments, confronting the issues or problems of the time, analyzing the alternatives available to those on the scene, evaluating the consequences that might have followed those options for action that were not chosen, and comparing with the consequences of those that were adopted, are activities that foster students' deep, personal involvement in these events.

If well chosen, these activities also promote capacities vital to a democratic citizenry: the capacity to identify and define public policy issues and ethical dilemmas; analyze the range of interests and values held by the many persons caught up in the situation and affected by its outcome; locate and organize the data required to assess the consequences of alternative approaches to resolving the dilemma; assess the ethical implications as well as the comparative costs and benefits of each approach; and evaluate a particular course of action in light of all of the above and, in the case of historical issues-analysis, in light also of its long-term consequences revealed in the historical record.

Because important historical issues are frequently value-laden, they also open opportunities to consider the moral convictions contributing to social actions taken. For example, what moral and political dilemmas did Lincoln face when, in his Emancipation Proclamation, he decided to free only those slaves behind the Confederate lines? The point to be made is that teachers should not use critical events to hammer home a particular "moral lesson" or ethical teaching. Not only will many students reject that approach; it fails also to take into account the processes through which students acquire the complex skills of principled thinking and moral reasoning.

When students are invited to judge morally the conduct of historical actors, they should be encouraged to analyze the values that inform the judgment. In some instances, this will be an easy task. Students judging the Holocaust or slavery as evils will probably be able to articulate the foundation for their judgment. In other cases, a student's effort to reach a moral judgment may produce a healthy student exercise in analyzing values, and may, in some instances, lead him or her to recognize the historically conditioned nature of a particular moral value he or she may be invoking.

Particularly challenging are the many social issues throughout United States history on which multiple interests and different values have come to bear. Issues of civil rights or equal education opportunity, of the right to choice vs. the right to life, and of criminal justice have all brought such conflicts to the fore. When these conflicts have not been resolved within the social and political institutions of the nation, they have regularly found their way into the judicial system, often going to the Supreme Court for resolution.

As the history course approaches the present era, such inquiries assume special relevance, confronting students with issues that resonate in today's headlines and invite their participation in lively debates, simulations, and socratic seminars—settings in which they can confront alternative policy recommendations, judge their ethical implications, challenge one another's assessments, and acquire further skills in the public presentation and defense of positions. In these analyses, teachers have the special responsibility of helping students differentiate between (1) relevant historical antecedents and (2) those that are clearly inappropriate and irrelevant. Students need to learn how to use their knowledge of history (or the past) to bring sound historical analysis to the service of informed decision making.

| STANDARD 5 | The student engages in historical issues-analysis and decision-making: |

Therefore, the student is able to:

A. **Identify issues and problems in the past** and analyze the interests, values, perspectives, and points of view of those involved in the situation.

B. **Marshal evidence of antecedent circumstances** and current factors contributing to contemporary problems and alternative courses of action.

C. **Identify relevant historical antecedents** and differentiate from those that are inappropriate and irrelevant to contemporary issues.

D. **Evaluate alternative courses of action,** keeping in mind the information available at the time, in terms of ethical considerations, the interests of those affected by the decision, and the long- and short-term consequences of each.

E. **Formulate a position or course of action on an issue** by identifying the nature of the problem, analyzing the underlying factors contributing to the problem, and choosing a plausible solution from a choice of carefully evaluated options.

F. **Evaluate the implementation of a decision** by analyzing the interests it served; estimating the position, power, and priority of each player involved; assessing the ethical dimensions of the decision; and evaluating its costs and benefits from a variety of perspectives.

Putting Historical Thinking Skills to Work

Historical thinking skills cannot be divorced from content. The skills highlighted in brackets throughout the History Standards (see Figure 2 on page 53) reflect only one of many thinking skills that should be developed for each elaborated standard. The following are among the thinking skills that can be brought to bear on particular topics. In fact, as students deepen their historical thinking and knowledge, they will learn to draw upon an increasing range of interconnected thinking skills.

The following six **examples** illustrate how multiple historical thinking skills can be utilized in studying particular history standards. The brackets following each thinking skill indicate the skills spelled out in Chapter 2.

Grades 5-6:

United States History, Era 3, Standard 1A

The student is able to:

Reconstruct the chronology of the critical events leading to the outbreak of armed conflict between the American colonies and England.

Reconstruct temporal order (1B)
Analyze cause-and-effect relationships (3C)

Appreciate historical perspectives (2F)
Challenge arguments of historical inevitability (3E)
Consider multiple perspectives (3B)

World History, Era 2, Standard 1A

The student is able to:

Analyze how the natural environment of the Tigris-Euphrates, Nile, and the Indus Valleys shaped the early development of civilization.

Compare and contrast differing sets of ideas (3A)
Draw comparisons across regions (3D)
Interrogate historical data (4C)
Obtain historical data from a variety of sources (4B)
Draw upon data in historical maps (2G)

Grades 7-8:

United States History, Era 5, Standard 2A

The student is able to:

Analyze the purpose, meaning, and significance of the Gettysburg Address.

Identify the author of historical document and assess its credibility (2A)
Reconstruct the literal meaning of a historical passage (2B)
Identify the central question (2C)
Assess the importance of the individual in history (3C)
Support interpretations with historical evidence (4F)

World History, Era 6, Standard 1C

The student is able to:

Assess the ways in which the exchange of plants and animals around the world in the late 15th and 16th centuries affected European, Asian, African, and American Indian societies and commerce.

Analyze cause-and-effect relationships (3C)
Employ quantitative analysis (4E)
Draw comparisons across eras and regions (3D)
Marshal contextual knowledge and perspectives of the time and place (4D)
Formulate historical questions (4A)

Grades 9-12:

United States History, Era 9, Standard 4A

The student is able to:

Assess the role of the legislative and executive branches in advancing the civil rights movement and the effect of shifting the focus from *de jure* to *de facto* segregation.

Evaluate the implementation of a decision (5F)
Explain historical continuity and change (1F)
Analyze cause-and-effect relationships (3C)
Challenge arguments of historical inevitability (2E)
Formulate a position or course of action on an issue (5E)

World History, Era 8, Standard 3A

The student is able to:

Describe the conflicting aims and aspirations of the conferees at Versailles, and analyze the responses of major powers to the terms of the World War I settlement.

Differentiate between historical facts and historical interpretations (2D)
Hypothesize the influence of the past (3J)
Marshal evidence of antecedent circumstances (5B)
Evaluate the implementation of a decision (5F)

CHAPTER 3

United States History Standards for Grades 5-12

Overview

Era 1: Three Worlds Meet (Beginnings to 1620)

Standard 1: Comparative characteristics of societies in the Americas, Western Europe, and Western Africa that increasingly interacted after 1450

Standard 2: How early European exploration and colonization resulted in cultural and ecological interactions among previously unconnected peoples

Era 2: Colonization and Settlement (1585-1763)

Standard 1: Why the Americas attracted Europeans, why they brought enslaved Africans to their colonies, and how Europeans struggled for control of North America and the Caribbean

Standard 2: How political, religious, and social institutions emerged in the English colonies

Standard 3: How the values and institutions of European economic life took root in the colonies, and how slavery reshaped European and African life in the Americas

Era 3: Revolution and the New Nation (1754-1820s)

Standard 1: The causes of the American Revolution, the ideas and interests involved in forging the revolutionary movement, and the reasons for the American victory

Standard 2: The impact of the American Revolution on politics, economy, and society

Standard 3: The institutions and practices of government created during the Revolution and how they were revised between 1787 and 1815 to create the foundation of the American political system based on the U.S. Constitution and the Bill of Rights

Era 4: Expansion and Reform (1801-1861)

Standard 1: United States territorial expansion between 1801 and 1861, and how it affected relations with external powers and Native Americans

Standard 2: How the industrial revolution, increasing immigration, the rapid expansion of slavery, and the westward movement changed the lives of Americans and led toward regional tensions

Standard 3: The extension, restriction, and reorganization of political democracy after 1800

Standard 4: The sources and character of cultural, religious, and social reform movements in the antebellum period

Era 5: Civil War and Reconstruction (1850-1877)

Standard 1: The causes of the Civil War

Standard 2: The course and character of the Civil War and its effects on the American people

Standard 3: How various reconstruction plans succeeded or failed

Era 6: The Development of the Industrial United States (1870-1900)

Standard 1: How the rise of corporations, heavy industry, and mechanized farming transformed the American people

Standard 2: Massive immigration after 1870 and how new social patterns, conflicts, and ideas of national unity developed amid growing cultural diversity

Standard 3: The rise of the American labor movement and how political issues reflected social and economic changes

Standard 4: Federal Indian policy and United States foreign policy after the Civil War

Era 7: The Emergence of Modern America (1890-1930)

Standard 1: How Progressives and others addressed problems of industrial capitalism, urbanization, and political corruption

Standard 2: The changing role of the United States in world affairs through World War I

Standard 3: How the United States changed from the end of World War I to the eve of the Great Depression

Era 8: The Great Depression and World War II (1929-1945)

Standard 1: The causes of the Great Depression and how it affected American society

Standard 2: How the New Deal addressed the Great Depression, transformed American federalism, and initiated the welfare state

Standard 3: The causes and course of World War II, the character of the war at home and abroad, and its reshaping of the U.S. role in world affairs

Era 9: Postwar United States (1945 to early 1970s)

Standard 1: The economic boom and social transformation of postwar United States

Standard 2: How the Cold War and conflicts in Korea and Vietnam influenced domestic and international politics

Standard 3: Domestic policies after World War II

Standard 4: The struggle for racial and gender equality and the extension of civil liberties

Era 10: Contemporary United States (1968 to the present)

Standard 1: Recent developments in foreign and domestic politics

Standard 2: Economic, social, and cultural developments in contemporary United States

ERA 1

Three Worlds Meet (Beginnings to 1620)

The study of American history properly begins with the first peopling of the Americas more than 30,000 years ago. Students will learn about the spread of ancient human societies in the Americas, North and South, and their adaptations to diverse physical and natural environments. This prepares students to address the historical convergence of European, African, and Native American people starting in the late 15th century when the Columbian voyages began. In studying the beginnings of North American history, it is important for students to understand that Indian societies, like peoples in other parts of the world, were experiencing change—political, economic, cultural—on the eve of the arrival of Europeans. The history of the Native Americans was complex, and it was continuing even as European settlers landed on South and North American shores.

European mariners were the agents of the encounters among these many peoples of the late 15th and early 16th centuries. To understand why the trans-oceanic voyages took place students must gain an appreciation of Europe's economic growth, the rise of bureaucratic states, the pace of technological innovation, intellectual and religious ferment, and the continuing crusading tradition in the late medieval period. Students' grasp of the encounters of diverse peoples in the Americas also requires attention to the history of West and Central Africa. This study will prepare students to investigate the conditions under which the Atlantic slave trade developed.

By studying the European colonization—and partial conquest—of the Americas to 1620, mostly played out in Central and South America, students will embark upon a continuing theme—the making of the many American people of the Western Hemisphere. As a people, we were composed from the beginning of diverse ethnic and linguistic strains. The nature of these manifold and uneven beginnings spawned issues and tensions that are still unresolved. How a composite American society was created out of such human diversity was a complicated process of cultural transformation that unfolded unevenly and unremittingly as the following eras will address.

By studying early European exploration, colonization, and conquest, students will learn about five long-range changes set in motion by the Columbian voyages. First, the voyages initiated a redistribution of the world's population. Several million voluntary European immigrants flocked to the Americas; at least 10-12 million involuntary enslaved Africans relocated on the west side of the Atlantic, overwhelmingly to South America and the Caribbean; and indigenous peoples experienced catastrophic losses. Second, the arrival of Europeans led to the rise of the first trans-oceanic empires in world history. Third, the Columbian voyages sparked a world-wide commercial expansion and an explosion of European capitalist enterprise. Fourth, the voyages led in time to the planting of English settlements where ideas of representative government and religious toleration would grow and, over several centuries, would inspire similar transformations in other parts of the world. Lastly, at a time when slavery and serfdom were waning in Western Europe, new plantation economies were emerging in the Americas employing forced labor on a large scale.

Overview

Standard 1: Comparative characteristics of societies in the Americas, Western Europe, and Western Africa that increasingly interacted after 1450

Standard 2: How early European exploration and colonization resulted in cultural and ecological interactions among previously unconnected peoples

STANDARD 1	**Comparative characteristics of societies in the Americas, Western Europe, and Western Africa that increasingly interacted after 1450.**

1A   The student understands the patterns of change in indigenous societies in the Americas up to the Columbian voyages.

Therefore, the student is able to:

5-12 Draw upon data provided by archaeologists and geologists to explain the origins and migration from Asia to the Americas and contrast them with Native Americans' own beliefs concerning their origins in the Americas. [**Compare and contrast different sets of ideas**]

5-12 Trace the spread of human societies and the rise of diverse cultures from hunter-gatherers to urban dwellers in the Americas. [**Reconstruct patterns of historical succession and duration**]

9-12 Explain the common elements of Native American societies such as gender roles, family organization, religion, and values and compare their diversity in languages, shelter, labor systems, political structures, and economic organization. [**Analyze multiple causation**]

7-12 Explore the rise and decline of the Mississippian mound-building society. [**Analyze multiple causation**]

1B   The student understands changes in Western European societies in the age of exploration.

Therefore, the student is able to:

5-12 Appraise aspects of European society, such as family organization, gender roles, property holding, education and literacy, linguistic diversity, and religion. [**Identify historical antecedents**]

9-12 Describe major institutions of capitalism and analyze how the emerging capitalist economy transformed agricultural production, manufacturing, and the uses of labor. [**Analyze cause-and-effect relationships**]

7-12 Explain the causes and consequences of European Crusades in Iberia and analyze connections between the Christian crusading tradition and European overseas exploration. [**Analyze multiple causation**]

7-12 Explain dissent within the Catholic Church and analyze the beliefs and ideas of leading religious reformers. [**Explain the influence of ideas**]

9-12 Analyze relationships among the rise of centralized states, the development of urban centers, the expansion of commerce, and overseas exploration. [**Identify historical antecedents**]

1C The student understands developments in Western African societies in the period of early contact with Europeans.

Therefore, the student is able to:

5-12 Describe the physical geography of West and Central Africa and analyze its impact on settlement patterns, cultural traits, and trade. [**Draw upon data in historical maps**]

9-12 Describe general features of family organization, labor division, agriculture, manufacturing, and trade in Western African societies. [**Analyze multiple causation**]

7-12 Describe the continuing growth of Islam in West Africa in the 15th and 16th centuries and analyze interactions between Islam and local religious beliefs and practices. [**Examine the influence of ideas**]

9-12 Analyze varieties of slavery in Western Africa and the economic importance of the trans-Saharan slave trade in the 15th and 16th centuries. [**Analyze multiple causation**]

9-12 Analyze the varying responses of African states to early European trading and raiding on the Atlantic African coast. [**Analyze cause-and-effect relationships**]

1D The student understands the differences and similarities among Africans, Europeans, and Native Americans who converged in the western hemisphere after 1492.

Therefore, the student is able to:

5-12 Compare political systems, including concepts of political authority, civic values, and the organization and practice of government. [**Compare and contrast different political systems**]

5-12 Compare social organizations, including population levels, urbanization, family structure, and modes of communication. [**Compare and contrast different social organizations**]

5-12 Compare economic systems, including systems of labor, trade, concepts of property, and exploitation of natural resources. [**Compare and contrast different economic institutions**]

5-12 Compare dominant ideas and values including religious belief and practice, gender roles, and attitudes toward nature. [**Compare and contrast the influence of ideas**]

| STANDARD 2 | How early European exploration and colonization resulted in cultural and ecological interactions among previously unconnected peoples. |

2A **The student understands the stages of European oceanic and overland exploration, amid international rivalries, from the 9th to 17th centuries.**

Therefore, the student is able to:

> 5-12   Trace routes taken by early explorers, from the 15th through the 17th century, around Africa, to the Americas, and across the Pacific. [**Draw upon data in historical maps**]

> 7-12   Evaluate the significance of Columbus' voyages and his interactions with indigenous peoples. [**Assess the importance of the individual in history**]

> 5-12   Compare English, French, and Dutch motives for exploration with those of the Spanish. [**Compare and contrast different sets of ideas**]

> 9-12   Appraise the role of national and religious rivalries in the age of exploration and evaluate their long-range consequences. [**Consider multiple perspectives**]

> 7-12   Evaluate the course and consequences of the "Columbian Exchange." [**Hypothesize the influence of the past**]

2B **The student understands the Spanish and Portuguese conquest of the Americas.**

Therefore, the student is able to:

> 7-12   Describe the social composition of the early settlers and compare their various motives for exploration and colonization. [**Compare and contrast differing sets of ideas**]

> 5-12   Explain and evaluate the Spanish interactions with such people as Aztecs, Incas, and Pueblos. [**Examine the influence of ideas**]

> 9-12   Describe the evolution and long-term consequences of labor systems such as encomienda and slavery in Spanish and Portuguese America. [**Appreciate historical perspectives**]

> 7-12   Analyze connections between silver mined in Peru and Mexico and the rise of global trade and the price revolution in 16th-century Europe. [**Analyze cause-and-effect relationships**]

ERA 2

Colonization and Settlement (1585-1763)

The study of the colonial era in American history is essential because the foundations for many of the most critical developments in our subsequent national history were established in those years. The long duration of the nation's colonial period—nearly two centuries—requires that teachers establish clear themes. A continental and Caribbean approach best serves a full understanding of this era because North America and the closely linked West Indies were an international theatre of colonial development.

One theme involves the intermingling of Native Americans, Europeans, and Africans. Students first need to understand what induced hundreds of thousands of free and indentured immigrants to leave their homelands in many parts of Europe. Why did they risk the hardships of resettlement overseas, and how well did they succeed?

Students must also address two of the most tragic aspects of American history: first, the violent conflicts between Europeans and indigenous peoples, the devastating spread of European diseases among Native Americans, and the gradual dispossession of Indian land; second, the traffic in the African slave trade and the development of a slave labor system in many of the colonies. While coming to grips with these tragic events, students should also recognize that Africans and Native Americans were not simply victims but were intricately involved in the creation of colonial society and a new, hybrid American culture.

A second theme is the development of political and religious institutions and values. The roots of representative government are best studied regionally, so that students can appreciate how European colonizers in New England, the mid-Atlantic, and the South differed in the ways they groped their way toward mature political institutions. In studying the role of religion—especially noteworthy are the foundations of religious freedom, denominationalism, and the many-faceted impact of the Great Awakening—a comparative geographic approach can also be fruitful. Comparison with the role of religion in Dutch, French, and Spanish colonies can be valuable as well.

A third theme is the economic development of the colonies through agriculture and commerce. A comparative approach to French, Spanish, Dutch, and English colonies, and a regional approach to the English mainland and West Indian colonies, as part of a developing Atlantic economy, will also be instructive. As in studying politics and religion, students should ponder how economic institutions developed—in ways that were typically European or were distinctively American—and how geographical variations—climate, soil conditions, and other natural resources—helped shape regional economic development.

Overview

Standard 1: Why the Americas attracted Europeans, why they brought enslaved Africans to their colonies, and how Europeans struggled for control of North America and the Caribbean

Standard 2: How political, religious, and social institutions emerged in the English colonies

Standard 3: How the values and institutions of European economic life took root in the colonies, and how slavery reshaped European and African life in the Americas

---

STANDARD 1 | Why the Americas attracted Europeans, why they brought enslaved Africans to their colonies, and how Europeans struggled for control of North America and the Caribbean.

1A   The student understands how diverse immigrants affected the formation of European colonies.

Therefore, the student is able to:

> *5-12* Analyze the religious, political, and economic motives of free immigrants from different parts of Europe who came to North America and the Caribbean. [Consider multiple causation]

> *5-12* Explain why so many European indentured servants risked the hardships of bound labor overseas. [Consider multiple perspectives]

> *5-12* Evaluate the opportunities for European immigrants, free and indentured, in North America and the Caribbean and the difficulties they encountered. [Compare competing historical narratives]

> *9-12* Compare the social composition of English, French, and Dutch settlers in the 17th and 18th centuries. [Interrogate historical data]

> *5-12* Trace the arrival of Africans in the European colonies in the 17th century and the rapid increase of slave importation in the 18th century. [Reconstruct patterns of historical succession and duration]

1B   The student understands the European struggle for control of North America.

Therefore, the student is able to:

> *7-12* Analyze relationships between Native Americans and Spanish, English, French, and Dutch settlers. [Compare and contrast different sets of ideas]

> *5-12* Compare how English settlers interacted with Native Americans in New England, mid-Atlantic, Chesapeake, and lower South colonies. [Consider multiple perspectives]

7-12 Analyze how various Native American societies changed as a result of the expanding European settlements and how they influenced European societies. [**Examine the influence of ideas and interests**]

7-12 Analyze the significance of the colonial wars before 1754 and the causes, character, and outcome of the Seven Years War. [**Analyze multiple causation**]

9-12 Analyze Native American involvement in the colonial wars and evaluate the consequences for their societies. [**Consider multiple perspectives**]

STANDARD 2	**How political, religious, and social institutions emerged in the English colonies.**

2A **The student understands the roots of representative government and how political rights were defined.**

Therefore, the student is able to:

7-12 Analyze how the rise of individualism contributed to the idea of participatory government. [**Assess the importance of the individual**]

5-12 Compare how early colonies were established and governed. [**Compare and contrast differing sets of ideas**]

7-12 Explain the concept of the "rights of Englishmen" and the impact of the English Civil War and the Glorious Revolution on the colonies. [**Hypothesize the influence of the past**]

9-12 Analyze how gender, property ownership, religion, and legal status affected political rights. [**Analyze cause-and-effect relationships**]

7-12 Explain the social, economic, and political tensions that led to violent conflicts between the colonists and their governments. [**Examine the influence of ideas**]

9-12 Explain how the conflicts between legislative and executive branches contributed to the development of representative government. [**Analyze cause-and-effect relationships**]

2B **The student understands religious diversity in the colonies and how ideas about religious freedom evolved.**

Therefore, the student is able to:

9-12 Describe religious groups in colonial America and the role of religion in their communities. [**Consider multiple perspectives**]

5-12 Explain how Puritanism shaped New England communities and how it changed during the 17th century. [**Compare and contrast differing sets of ideas**]

7-12 Trace and explain the evolution of religious freedom in the English colonies. [**Reconstruct patterns of historical succession and duration**]

9-12 Explain the impact of the Great Awakening on colonial society. [**Examine the influence of ideas**]

2C **The student understands social and cultural change in British America.**

Therefore, the student is able to:

7-12 Explain how rising individualism challenged inherited ideas of hierarchy and deference and affected the ideal of community. [**Assess the importance of the individual**]

5-12 Explain how and why family and community life differed in various regions of colonial North America. [**Consider multiple perspectives**]

9-12 Analyze women's property rights before and after marriage in the colonial period. [**Interrogate historical data**]

5-12 Explain how Enlightenment ideas, including Benjamin Franklin's experiments with electricity, influenced American society. [**Examine the influence of ideas**]

9-12 Explore the seeds of public education in the New England colonies and explain how literacy and education differed between New England and southern colonies. [**Compare and contrast differing sets of ideas**]

STANDARD 3	How the values and institutions of European economic life took root in the colonies, and how slavery reshaped European and African life in the Americas.

3A **The student understands colonial economic life and labor systems in the Americas.**

Therefore, the student is able to:

7-12 Explain mercantilism and evaluate how it influenced patterns of economic activity. [**Analyze cause-and-effect relationships**]

5-12 Identify the major economic regions in the Americas and explain how labor systems shaped them. [**Utilize visual and mathematical data**]

9-12 Explain the development of an Atlantic economy in the colonial period. [**Reconstruct patterns of historical succession and duration**]

3B **The student understands economic life and the development of labor systems in the English colonies.**

Therefore, the student is able to:

5-12 Explain how environmental and human factors accounted for differences in the economies that developed in the colonies of New England, mid-Atlantic, Chesapeake, and lower South. [**Compare and contrast different sets of ideas**]

7-12 Analyze how the early Navigation Acts affected economic life in the colonies. [**Marshal evidence of antecedent circumstances**]

9-12 Explore how the mobility and material success of many colonists encouraged the development of a consumer society and led to the imitation of English culture. [**Utilize quantitative data**]

7-12 Compare the characteristics of free labor, indentured servitude, and chattel slavery. [**Compare and contrast differing labor systems**]

9-12 Explain the shift from indentured servitude to chattel slavery in the southern colonies. [**Challenge arguments of historical inevitability**]

3C   **The student understands African life under slavery.**

Therefore, the student is able to:

5-12 Analyze the forced relocation of Africans to the English colonies in North America and the Caribbean. [**Appreciate historical perspectives**]

7-12 Explain how varieties of slavery in African societies differed from the chattel racial slavery that developed in the English colonies. [**Compare and contrast differing institutions**]

9-12 Assess the contribution of enslaved and free Africans to economic development in different regions of the American colonies. [**Interrogate historical data**]

7-12 Analyze how Africans in North America drew upon their African past and upon selected European (and sometimes Indian) customs and values to develop a distinctive African American culture. [**Identify gaps in the historical record while constructing a sound historical interpretation**]

7-12 Analyze overt and passive resistance to enslavement. [**Analyze cause-and-effect relationships**]

ERA 3

Revolution and the New Nation (1754-1820s)

The American Revolution is of signal importance in the study of American history. First, it severed the colonial relationship with England and legally created the United States. Second, the revolutionary generation formulated the political philosophy and laid the institutional foundations for the system of government under which we live. Third, the Revolution was inspired by ideas concerning natural rights and political authority that were transatlantic in reach, and its successful completion affected people and governments over a large part of the globe for many generations. Lastly, it called into question long-established social and political relationships—between master and slave, man and woman, upper class and lower class, officeholder and constituent, and even parent and child—and thus demarcated an agenda for reform that would preoccupy Americans down to the present day.

In thinking about the causes and course of the Revolution, it is important to study the fundamental principles of the Declaration of Independence; the causes for the outbreak of the war; the main stages of the Revolutionary War and the reasons for the American victory; and the role of wartime leaders, from all strata of society, both on the battlefield and on the homefront.

In assessing the outcomes of the American Revolution, students need to confront the central issue of how revolutionary the Revolution actually was. In order to reach judgments about this, they necessarily will have to see the Revolution through different sets of eyes—enslaved and free African Americans, Native Americans, white men and women of different social classes, religions, ideological dispositions, regions, and occupations. Students should also be able to see pre- and post-Revolutionary American society in relation to reigning political institutions and practices in the rest of the world.

Students can appreciate how agendas for redefining American society in the postwar era differed by exploring how the Constitution was created and how it was ratified after a dramatic ideological debate in virtually every locale in 1787-88. The Constitution of 1787 and the Bill of Rights should be broached as the culmination of the most creative era of constitutionalism in American history. In addition, students should ponder why the Constitutional Convention sidetracked the movement to abolish slavery that had taken rise in the revolutionary era. Nor should they think that ratification of the Constitution ended debate on governmental power or how to create "a more perfect union." Economic, regional, social, ideological, religious, and political tensions would spawn continuing debates over the meaning of the Constitution for generations.

In studying the post-Revolutionary generation, students can understand how the embryo of the American two-party system took shape, how political turmoil arose as Americans debated the French Revolution, and how the Supreme Court rose to a place of prominence. Politics, political leadership, and political institutions have always bulked large in the study of this era, but students will also need to understand other less noticed topics: the beginnings of a national economy, the exuberant push westward, the military campaigns against Native American nations; the emergence of free black communities; and the democratization of religion.

Overview

Standard 1: The causes of the American Revolution, the ideas and interests involved in forging the revolutionary movement, and the reasons for the American victory

Standard 2: The impact of the American Revolution on politics, economy, and society

Standard 3: The institutions and practices of government created during the Revolution and how they were revised between 1787 and 1815 to create the foundation of the American political system based on the U.S. Constitution and the Bill of Rights

STANDARD 1	The causes of the American Revolution, the ideas and interests involved in forging the revolutionary movement, and the reasons for the American victory.

1A   The student understands the causes of the American Revolution.

Therefore, the student is able to:

5-12 Explain the consequences of the Seven Years War and the overhaul of English imperial policy following the Treaty of Paris in 1763. [**Marshal evidence of antecedent circumstances**]

5-12 Compare the arguments advanced by defenders and opponents of the new imperial policy on the traditional rights of English people and the legitimacy of asking the colonies to pay a share of the costs of empire. [**Consider multiple perspectives**]

5-12 Reconstruct the chronology of the critical events leading to the outbreak of armed conflict between the American colonies and England. [**Establish temporal order**]

7-12 Analyze political, ideological, religious, and economic origins of the Revolution. [**Analyze multiple causation**]

9-12 Reconstruct the arguments among patriots and loyalists about independence and draw conclusions about how the decision to declare independence was reached. [**Consider multiple perspectives**]

1B   The student understands the principles articulated in the Declaration of Independence.

Therefore, the student is able to:

5-12 Explain the major ideas expressed in the Declaration of Independence and their intellectual origins. [**Marshal evidence of antecedent circumstances**]

7-12 Demonstrate the fundamental contradictions between the ideals expressed in the Declaration of Independence and the realities of chattel slavery. [**Consider multiple perspectives**]

9-12   Draw upon the principles in the Declaration of Independence to construct a sound historical argument regarding whether it justified American independence. [**Interrogate historical data**]

5-12   Explain how key principles in the Declaration of Independence grew in importance to become unifying ideas of American democracy. [**Evaluate the influence of ideas**]

9-12   Compare the Declaration of Independence with the French Declaration of the Rights of Man and Citizen and construct an argument evaluating their importance to the spread of constitutional democracies in the 19th and 20th centuries. [**Compare and contrast differing sets of ideas**]

1C   The student understands the factors affecting the course of the war and contributing to the American victory.

Therefore, the student is able to:

5-12   Appraise George Washington's military and political leadership in conducting the Revolutionary War. [**Assess the importance of the individual**]

5-12   Compare and explain the different roles and perspectives in the war of men and women, including white settlers, free and enslaved African Americans, and Native Americans. [**Evaluate the influence of ideas**]

9-12   Analyze the problems of financing the war and dealing with wartime inflation, hoarding, and profiteering. [**Identify issues and problems in the past**]

7-12   Explain how the Americans won the war against superior British resources. [**Analyze multiple causation**]

5-12   Analyze United States relationships with France, Holland, and Spain during the Revolution and the contributions of each European power to the American victory. [**Analyze cause-and-effect relationships**]

7-12   Analyze the terms of the Treaty of Paris and how they affected U.S. relations with Native Americans and with European powers that held territories in North America. [**Consider multiple perspectives**]

STANDARD 2   The impact of the American Revolution on politics, economy, and society.

2A   The student understands revolutionary government-making at national and state levels.

Therefore, the student is able to:

5-12   Analyze the arguments over the Articles of Confederation. [**Examine the influence of ideas**]

9-12   Compare several state constitutions and explain why they differed. [**Analyze multiple causation**]

7-12   Assess the accomplishments and failures of the Continental Congress. [**Compare and contrast differing sets of ideas**]

7-12 Assess the importance of the Northwest Ordinance. [Interrogate historical data]

2B   **The student understands the economic issues arising out of the Revolution.**

Therefore, the student is able to:

7-12 Evaluate how the states and the Continental Congress dealt with the revolutionary war debt. [Utilize quantitative data]

5-12 Analyze the factors that led to Shay's Rebellion. [Analyze multiple causation]

7-12 Explain the dispute over the western lands and evaluate how it was resolved. [Draw upon data in historical maps]

9-12 Explain how the Continental Congress and the states attempted to rebuild the economy by addressing issues of foreign and internal trade, banking, and taxation. [Formulate a position or course of action on an issue]

2C   **The student understands the Revolution's effects on different social groups.**

Therefore, the student is able to:

7-12 Compare the reasons why many white men and women and most African Americans and Native Americans remained loyal to the British. [Consider multiple perspectives]

5-12 Compare the revolutionary goals of different groups—for example, rural farmers and urban craftsmen, northern merchants and southern planters—and how the Revolution altered social, political, and economic relations among them. [Compare and contrast differing values, behaviors, and institutions]

5-12 Explain the revolutionary hopes of enslaved and free African Americans and the gradual abolition of slavery in the northern states. [Examine the influence of ideas]

7-12 Analyze the ideas put forth arguing for new women's roles and rights and explain the customs of the 18th century that limited women's aspirations and achievements. [Examine the influence of ideas]

9-12 Explain how African American leaders and African American institutions shaped free black communities in the North. [Assess the importance of the individual]

STANDARD 3	The institutions and practices of government created during the Revolution and how they were revised between 1787 and 1815 to create the foundation of the American political system based on the U.S. Constitution and the Bill of Rights.

3A **The student understands the issues involved in the creation and ratification of the United States Constitution and the new government it established.**

Therefore, the student is able to:

5-12 Analyze the factors involved in calling the Constitutional Convention. [**Analyze multiple causation**]

7-12 Analyze the alternative plans considered by the delegates and the major compromises agreed upon to secure approval of the Constitution. [**Examine the influence of ideas**]

9-12 Analyze the fundamental ideas behind the distribution of powers and the system of checks and balances established by the Constitution. [**Examine the influence of ideas**]

5-12 Analyze the features of the Constitution which have made this the most enduring and widely imitated written constitution in world history. [**Examine the influence of ideas**]

9-12 Compare the arguments of Federalists and Anti-Federalists during the ratification debates and assess their relevance in late 20th-century politics. [**Hypothesize the influence of the past**]

3B **The student understands the guarantees of the Bill of Rights and its continuing significance.**

Therefore, the student is able to:

7-12 Evaluate the arguments over the necessity of a Bill of Rights and explain Madison's role in securing its adoption by the First Congress. [**Assess the importance of the individual**]

5-12 Analyze the significance of the Bill of Rights and its specific guarantees. [**Examine the influence of ideas**]

9-12 Analyze whether the Alien and Sedition Acts of 1798 threatened First Amendment rights and the issues the Alien and Sedition Acts posed in the absence of judicial review of acts of Congress. [**Evaluate the implementation of a decision**]

9-12 Analyze issues addressed in recent court cases involving the Bill of Rights to assess their continuing significance today. [**Identify relevant historical antecedents**]

3C **The student understands the development of the Supreme Court's power and its significance from 1789 to 1820.**

Therefore, the student is able to:

7-12 Appraise how John Marshall's precedent-setting decisions interpreted the Constitution and established the Supreme Court as an independent and equal branch of the government. [**Assess the importance of the individual**]

9-12 Trace the evolution of the Supreme Court's powers during the 1790s and early 19th century and analyze its influence today. [**Explain historical continuity and change**]

3D **The student understands the development of the first American party system.**

Therefore, the student is able to:

9-12 Explain the principles and issues that prompted Thomas Jefferson to organize an opposition party. [**Analyze multiple causation**]

5-12 Compare the leaders and social and economic composition of each party. [**Compare and contrast differing sets of ideas**]

7-12 Compare the opposing views of the two parties on the main economic and foreign policy issues of the 1790s. [**Compare and contrast differing sets of ideas**]

7-12 Assess the influence of the French Revolution on American politics. [**Analyze cause-and-effect relationships**]

ERA 4

Expansion and Reform (1801-1861)

The new American republic prior to the Civil War experienced dramatic territorial expansion, immigration, economic growth, and industrialization. The increasing complexity of American society, the growth of regionalism, and the cross-currents of change that are often bewildering require the development of several major themes to enable students to sort their way through the six decades that brought the United States to the eve of the Civil War.

One theme is the vast territorial expansion between 1800 and 1861, as restless Americans pushed westward across the Appalachians, then across the Mississippi, and finally on to the Pacific Ocean. Students should study how Americans, animated by land hunger, the ideology of "Manifest Destiny," and the optimism that anything was possible with imagination, hard work, and the maximum freedom of the individual, flocked to the western frontier. While studying how the frontier experience indelibly stamped the American character, students should explore its ambivalent aspects: the removal of many Indian nations in the Southeast and old Northwest, acquisition of a large part of Mexico through the Mexican-American War, and abrasive encounters with Native Americans, Mexicans, Chinese immigrants, and others in the West.

A second theme confronts the economic development of the expanding American republic—a complex and fascinating process that on the one hand created the sinews of national identity but on the other hand fueled growing regional tensions. In the North, the first stage of industrialization brings students face to face with the role of technology in historical change and how economic development has had profound environmental effects. In studying the rise of immigrant-filled cities, the "transportation revolution" involving railroads, canals, and trans-regional roads, the creation of a national market system, and the proliferation of family farming in newly opened territories, students will appreciate how Tocqueville might have reached the conclusion that the Americans seemed at one time "animated by the most selfish cupidity; at another by the most lively patriotism." In studying the expanding South, students must understand the enormous growth of slavery as an exploitive and morally corrupt economic and social system; but they should also comprehend how millions of African Americans struggled to shape their own lives as much as possible through family, religion, and resistance to slavery.

A third theme interwoven with the two themes above, can be organized around the extension, restriction, and reorganization of political democracy after 1800. The rise of the second party system and modern interest-group politics mark the advent of modern politics in the United States. However, students will see that the evolution of political democracy was not a smooth, one-way street as free African Americans were disenfranchised in much of the North and woman's suffrage was blocked even while white male suffrage spread throughout the states and into the newly developed territories.

Connected to all of the above is the theme of reform, for the rapid transformation and expansion of the American economy brought forth one of the greatest bursts of reformism in American history. Emerson captured the vibrancy of this era in asking,

"What is man born for but to be a reformer?" Students will find that the attempts to complete unfinished agendas of the revolutionary period and to fashion new reforms necessitated by the rise of factory labor and rapid urbanization partook of the era's democratic spirit and religious faith and yet also reflected the compulsion of well-positioned Americans to restore order to a turbulent society.

Overview

Standard 1: United States territorial expansion between 1801 and 1861, and how it affected relations with external powers and Native Americans

Standard 2: How the industrial revolution, increasing immigration, the rapid expansion of slavery, and the westward movement changed the lives of Americans and led toward regional tensions

Standard 3: The extension, restriction, and reorganization of political democracy after 1800

Standard 4: The sources and character of cultural, religious, and social reform movements in the antebellum period

---

STANDARD 1 — United States territorial expansion between 1801 and 1861, and how it affected relations with external powers and Native Americans.

1A **The student understands the international background and consequences of the Louisiana Purchase, the War of 1812, and the Monroe Doctrine.**

Therefore, the student is able to:

5-12 Analyze Napoleon's reasons for selling Louisiana to the United States. [**Draw upon the data in historical maps**]

7-12 Compare the arguments advanced by Democratic Republicans and Federalists regarding the acquisition of Louisiana. [**Compare and contrast differing sets of ideas**]

9-12 Analyze how the Louisiana Purchase influenced politics, economic development, and the concept of Manifest Destiny. [**Evaluate the implementation of a decision**]

9-12 Assess how the Louisiana Purchase affected relations with Native Americans and the lives of various inhabitants of the Louisiana Territory. [**Explain historical continuity and change**]

5-12 Explain President Madison's reasons for declaring war in 1812 and analyze the sectional divisions over the war. [**Compare and contrast differing sets of ideas**]

5-12 Assess why many Native Americans supported the British in the War of 1812 and the consequences of this policy. [**Consider multiple perspectives**]

5-12 Identify the origins and provisions of the Monroe Doctrine and how it influenced hemispheric relations. [**Reconstruct patterns of historical succession and duration**]

1B **The student understands federal and state Indian policy and the strategies for survival forged by Native Americans.**

Therefore, the student is able to:

7-12 Compare the policies toward Native Americans pursued by presidential administrations through the Jacksonian era. [**Compare and contrast differing sets of ideas**]

9-12 Compare federal and state Indian policy and explain Whig opposition to the removal of Native Americans. [**Consider multiple perspectives**]

5-12 Analyze the impact of removal and resettlement on the Cherokee, Creek, Chickasaw, Choctaw, and Seminole. [**Appreciate historical perspectives**]

5-12 Investigate the impact of trans-Mississippi expansion on Native Americans. [**Analyze cause-and-effect relationships**]

7-12 Explain and evaluate the various strategies of Native Americans such as accommodation, revitalization, and resistance. [**Compare and contrast differing sets of ideas**]

1C **The student understands the ideology of Manifest Destiny, the nation's expansion to the Northwest, and the Mexican-American War.**

Therefore, the student is able to:

5-12 Explain the economic, political, racial, and religious roots of Manifest Destiny and analyze how the concept influenced the westward expansion of the nation. [**Examine the influence of ideas**]

7-12 Explain the diplomatic and political developments that led to the resolution of conflicts with Britain and Russia in the period 1815-1850. [**Formulate a position or course of action on an issue**]

9-12 Analyze United States trading interests in the Far East and explain how they influenced continental expansion to the Pacific. [**Analyze cause-and-effect relationships**]

5-12 Compare and explain the peaceful resolution of the Oregon dispute with Great Britain and the declaration of war with Mexico. [**Challenge arguments of historical inevitability**]

5-12 Explain the causes of the Texas War for Independence and the Mexican-American War and evaluate the provisions and consequences of the Treaty of Guadalupe Hidalgo. [**Analyze multiple causation**]

9-12 Analyze different perspectives on the Mexican-American War. [**Consider multiple perspectives**]

STANDARD 2	How the industrial revolution, increasing immigration, the rapid expansion of slavery, and the westward movement changed the lives of Americans and led toward regional tensions.

2A **The student understands how the factory system and the transportation and market revolutions shaped regional patterns of economic development.**

Therefore, the student is able to:

5-12 Explain how the major technological developments that revolutionized land and water transportation arose and analyze how they transformed the economy, created international markets, and affected the environment. [**Analyze cause-and-effect relationships**]

7-12 Evaluate national and state policies regarding a protective tariff, a national bank, and federally funded internal improvements. [**Examine the influence of ideas**]

9-12 Explain how economic policies related to expansion, including northern dominance of locomotive transportation, served different regional interests and contributed to growing political and sectional differences. [**Compare and contrast differing sets of ideas**]

9-12 Compare how patterns of economic growth and recession affected territorial expansion and community life in the North, South, and West. [**Analyze cause-and-effect relationships**]

5-12 Analyze how the factory system affected gender roles and changed the lives of men, women, and children. [**Analyze cause-and-effect relationships**]

7-12 Evaluate the factory system from the perspectives of owners and workers and assess its impact on the rise of the labor movement in the antebellum period. [**Consider multiple perspectives**]

2B **The student understands the first era of American urbanization.**

Therefore, the student is able to:

5-12 Identify and explain the factors that caused rapid urbanization and compare the new industrialized centers with the old commercial cities. [**Explain historical continuity and change**]

7-12 Analyze how rapid urbanization, immigration, and industrialization affected the social fabric of early 19th-century cities. [**Analyze cause-and-effect relationships**]

7-12 Explain the growth of free African American communities in the cities and account for the rise of racial hostility. [**Examine the influence of ideas**]

5-12 Compare popular and high culture in the growing cities. [**Compare and contrast differing sets of ideas**]

2C **The student understands how antebellum immigration changed American society.**

Therefore, the student is able to:

5-12 Analyze the push-pull factors which led to increased immigration, for the first time from China but especially from Ireland and Germany. [**Analyze cause-and-effect relationships**]

7-12 Assess the connection between industrialization and immigration. [**Analyze cause-and-effect relationships**]

7-12 Explain how immigration intensified ethnic and cultural conflict and complicated the forging of a national identity. [**Interrogate historical data**]

5-12 Assess the ways immigrants adapted to life in the United States and to the hostility sometimes directed at them by the nativist movement and the Know Nothing party. [**Assess the importance of the individual in history**]

2D **The student understands the rapid growth of "the peculiar institution" after 1800 and the varied experiences of African Americans under slavery.**

Therefore, the student is able to:

7-12 Analyze the impact of the Haitian Revolution and the ending of the Atlantic slave trade. [**Analyze cause-and-effect relationships**]

5-12 Explain how the cotton gin and the opening of new lands in the South and West led to the increased demand for slaves. [**Analyze cause-and-effect relationships**]

9-12 Analyze the argument that the institution of slavery retarded the emergence of capitalist institutions and values in the South. [**Evaluate major debates among historians**]

5-12 Describe the plantation system and the roles of their owners, their families, hired white workers, and enslaved African Americans. [**Consider multiple perspectives**]

5-12 Identify the various ways in which African Americans resisted the conditions of their enslavement and analyze the consequences of violent uprisings. [**Analyze cause-and-effect relationships**]

7-12 Evaluate how enslaved African Americans used religion and family to create a viable culture and ameliorate the effects of slavery. [**Obtain historical data**]

2E **The student understands the settlement of the West.**

Therefore, the student is able to:

5-12 Explore the lure of the West and the reality of life on the frontier. [**Examine the influence of ideas**]

5-12 Contrast the causes and character of the rapid settlement of California and Oregon in the late 1840s and 1850s. [**Compare and contrast different patterns of settlement**]

5-12 Examine the origins and political organization of the Mormons, explaining the motives for their trek west and evaluating their contributions to the settlement of the West. [**Appreciate historical perspectives**]

7-12 Analyze cultural interactions among diverse groups in the trans-Mississippi region. [**Consider multiple perspectives**]

9-12 Assess the degree to which political democracy was a characteristic of the West and evaluate the factors influencing political and social conditions on the frontier. [**Differentiate between historical facts and historical interpretations**]

STANDARD 3	The extension, restriction, and reorganization of political democracy after 1800.

3A **The student understands the changing character of American political life in "the age of the common man."**

Therefore, the student is able to:

7-12 Relate the increasing popular participation in state and national politics to the evolving democratic ideal that adult white males were entitled to political participation. [**Identify relevant historical antecedents**]

5-12 Explain the contradictions between the movement for universal white male suffrage and the disenfranchisement of free African Americans as well as women in New Jersey. [**Evaluate the implementation of a decision**]

5-12 Analyze the influence of the West on the heightened emphasis on equality in the political process. [**Analyze cause-and-effect relationships**]

9-12 Explain the combination of sectional, cultural, economic, and political factors that contributed to the formation of the Democratic, Whig, and "Know-Nothing" parties. [**Analyze multiple causation**]

9-12 Evaluate the importance of state and local issues, the rise of interest-group politics, and the style of campaigning in increasing voter participation. [**Compare and contrast differing sets of ideas**]

5-12 Explain why the election of Andrew Jackson was considered a victory for the "common man." [**Assess the importance of the individual in history**]

7-12 Analyze how Jackson's veto of the U.S. Bank recharter and his actions in the nullification crisis contributed to the rise of the Whig party. [**Analyze cause-and-effect relationships**]

3B **The student understands how the debates over slavery influenced politics and sectionalism.**

Therefore, the student is able to:

5-12 Explain the Missouri Compromise and evaluate its political consequences. [**Identify issues and problems in the past**]

7-12 Explain how tariff policy and issues of states' rights influenced party development and promoted sectional differences. [**Analyze cause-and-effect relationships**]

7-12   Analyze how the debates over slavery—from agitation over the "gag rule" of the late 1830s through the war with Mexico—strained national cohesiveness and fostered rising sectionalism. [**Compare and contrast differing sets of ideas**]

STANDARD 4	The sources and character of cultural, religious, and social reform movements in the antebellum period.

4A   **The student understands the abolitionist movement.**

Therefore, the student is able to:

7-12   Analyze changing ideas about race and assess the reception of proslavery and antislavery ideologies in the North and South. [**Examine the influence of ideas**]

5-12   Explain the fundamental beliefs of abolitionism and compare the antislavery positions of the "immediatists" and "gradualists" within the movement. [**Consider multiple perspectives**]

9-12   Compare the positions of African American and white abolitionists on the issue of the African American's place in society. [**Compare and contrast differing sets of ideas**]

4B   **The student understands how Americans strived to reform society and create a distinct culture.**

Therefore, the student is able to:

5-12   Explain the importance of the Second Great Awakening and the ideas of its principal leaders. [**Examine the influence of ideas**]

7-12   Assess how the Second Great Awakening impinged on antebellum issues such as public education, temperance, women's suffrage, abolition, and commercialization. [**Analyze cause-and-effect relationships**]

7-12   Define Transcendentalism, account for the rise of the first American renaissance, and analyze ideas concerning the individual, society, and nature expressed in the literary works of major Transcendentalists. [**Examine the influence of ideas**]

5-12   Examine how literary and artistic movements fostered a distinct American identity among different groups and in different regions. [**Draw upon literary and artistic sources**]

9-12   Identify the major utopian experiments and analyze the reasons for their formation. [**Consider multiple perspectives**]

4C   **The student understands changing gender roles and the ideas and activities of women reformers.**

Therefore, the student is able to

9-12   Compare the North, South, and West in terms of men's and women's occupations, legal rights, and social status. [**Interrogate historical data**]

5-12   Analyze the activities of women of different racial and social groups in the reform movements for education, abolition, temperance, and women's suffrage. [**Examine the importance of the individual**]

7-12   Analyze the goals of the 1848 Seneca Falls "Declaration of Sentiments" and evaluate its impact. [**Reconstruct the literal meaning of a historical passage**]

9-12   Compare and contrast the antebellum women's movement for equality and 20th-century feminism. [**Hypothesize the influence of the past**]

ERA 5

Civil War and Reconstruction (1850-1877)

The Civil War was perhaps the most momentous event in American history. The survival of the United States as one nation was at risk and on the outcome of the war depended the nation's ability to bring to reality the ideals of liberty, equality, justice, and human dignity.

The war put constitutional government to its severest test as a long festering debate over the power of the federal government versus state rights reached a climax. Its enormously bloody outcome preserved the Union while releasing not only four million African Americans but the entire nation from the oppressive weight of slavery.

The war can be studied in several ways: as the final, violent phase in a conflict of two regional subcultures; as the breakdown of a democratic political system; as the climax of several decades of social reform; and as a pivotal chapter in American racial history. In studying the Civil War, students have many opportunities to study heroism and cowardice, triumph and tragedy, and hardship, pain, grief, and death wrought by conflict. Another important topic is how the war necessarily obliged both northern and southern women and children to adapt to new and unsettling situations.

As important as the war itself, once the Union prevailed, was the tangled problem of Reconstruction. Through examining the 13th, 14th, and 15th amendments—fundamental revisions of the Constitution—students can see how African Americans hoped for full equality as did many white lawmakers. They can assess the various plans for Reconstruction that were contested passionately. The retreat from Radical Reconstruction—the first attempt at establishing a biracial democracy—should be of concern to all students who need to understand how shared values of the North and South sharply limited support for social and racial democratization. The enduring republican belief in the need to respect local control made direction by central government power unpopular. Northerners, like southerners, did not support schemes to redistribute wealth under Reconstruction because of the need to protect private property. Northerners, like southerners, believed in the social inferiority of blacks.

Students should learn how southern white resistance and the withdrawal of federal supervision resulted in the "redemption" of the South through the disfranchisement of African Americans, the end of their involvement in Reconstruction state legislatures, greater racial separation, the rise of white intimidation and violence, and the creation of black rural peonage.

Balancing the success and failures of Reconstruction should test the abilities of all students. Too much stress on the unfinished agenda of the period can obscure the great changes actually wrought. Moreover, it needs to be remembered how most white Americans were diverted from completing Reconstruction toward new goals brought about by social change. A new generation sought new fields of endeavor afforded by industrialization. They were not imbued by the reformist idealism of their predecessors. Indeed, they were receptive to new doctrines of racial and social inequality. The legacies of the era of war and reconstruction needs to be considered with reference to the North and West as well as the South.

Overview

Standard 1: The causes of the Civil War

Standard 2: The course and character of the Civil War and its effects on the American people

Standard 3: How various reconstruction plans succeeded or failed

---

STANDARD 1	The causes of the Civil War.

1   **The student understands how the North and South differed and how politics and ideologies led to the Civil War.**

Therefore, the student is able to:

> **7-12** Identify and explain the economic, social, and cultural differences between the North and the South. [Draw **upon quantitative data to trace historical developments**]

> **9-12** Analyze how the disruption of the second American party system frayed the durable bonds of union, leading to the ascent of the Republican party in the 1850s. [**Analyze multiple causation**]

> **7-12** Explain how events after the Compromise of 1850 and the Dred Scott decision in 1857 contributed to increasing sectional polarization. [**Analyze cause-and-effect relationships**]

> **7-12** Analyze the importance of the "free labor" ideology in the North and its appeal in preventing the further extension of slavery in the new territories. [**Examine the influence of ideas**]

> **5-12** Explain the causes of the Civil War and evaluate the importance of slavery as a principal cause of the conflict. [**Compare competing historical narratives**]

> **7-12** Chart the secession of the southern states and explain the process and reasons for secession. [**Analyze cause-and-effect relationships**]

STANDARD 2	The course and character of the Civil War and its effects on the American people.

2A   **The student understands how the resources of the Union and Confederacy affected the course of the war.**

Therefore, the student is able to:

> **7-12** Compare the human resources of the Union and the Confederacy at the beginning of the Civil War and assess the tactical advantages of each side. [**Utilize visual and mathematical data**]

    5-12 Identify the innovations in military technology and explain their impact on humans, property, and the final outcome of the war. [**Utilize visual and mathematical data**]

    5-12 Identify the turning points of the war and evaluate how political, military, and diplomatic leadership affected the outcome of the conflict. [**Assess the importance of the individual in history**]

    5-12 Evaluate provisions of the Emancipation Proclamation, Lincoln's reasons for issuing it, and its significance. [**Examine the influence of ideas**]

    9-12 Analyze the purpose, meaning, and significance of the Gettysburg Address. [**Identify the author of the historical document and assess its credibility**]

    9-12 Describe the position of the major Indian nations during the Civil War and explain the effects of the war upon these nations. [**Reconstruct patterns of historical succession and duration**]

2B   **The student understands the social experience of the war on the battlefield and homefront.**

Therefore, the student is able to:

    7-12 Compare the motives for fighting and the daily life experiences of Confederate with those of white and African American Union soldiers. [**Evidence historical perspectives**]

    9-12 Analyze the reasons for the northern draft riots. [**Analyze multiple causation**]

    9-12 Evaluate the Union's reasons for curbing wartime civil liberties. [**Consider multiple perspectives**]

    5-12 Compare women's homefront and battlefront roles in the Union and the Confederacy. [**Compare and contrast differing sets of ideas**]

    5-12 Compare the human and material costs of the war in the North and South and assess the degree to which the war reunited the nation. [**Examine historical perspectives**]

STANDARD 3   How various reconstruction plans succeeded or failed.

3A   **The student understands the political controversy over Reconstruction.**

Therefore, the student is able to:

    7-12 Contrast the Reconstruction policies advocated by Lincoln, Andrew Johnson, and sharply divided Congressional leaders, while assessing these policies as responses to changing events. [**Compare and contrast differing sets of ideas**]

    7-12 Analyze the escalating conflict between the president and Congress and explain the reasons for and consequences of Johnson's impeachment and trial. [**Consider multiple perspectives**]

5-12 Explain the provisions of the 14th and 15th amendments and the political forces supporting and opposing each. [**Consider multiple perspectives**]

7-12 Analyze how shared values of the North and South limited support for social and racial democratization, as reflected in the Compromise of 1877. [**Analyze cause-and-effect relationships**]

9-12 Analyze the role of violence and the tactics of the "redeemers" in regaining control over the southern state governments. [**Interrogating historical data**]

3B   The student understands the Reconstruction programs to transform social relations in the South.

Therefore, the student is able to:

7-12 Explain the economic and social problems facing the South and appraise their impact on different social groups. [**Examine historical perspectives**]

5-12 Evaluate the goals and accomplishments of the Freedmen's Bureau. [**Hold interpretations of history as tentative**]

9-12 Describe the ways in which African Americans laid foundations for modern black communities during Reconstruction. [**Hypothesize the influence of the past**]

7-12 Analyze how African Americans attempted to improve their economic position during Reconstruction and explain the factors involved in their quest for land ownership. [**Analyze multiple causation**]

3C   The student understands the successes and failures of Reconstruction in the South, North, and West.

Therefore, the student is able to:

9-12 Evaluate the effects of northern capital and entrepreneurship on economic development in the postwar South. [**Consider multiple perspectives**]

5-12 Assess the progress of "Black Reconstruction" and legislative reform programs promoted by reconstructed state governments. [**Marshal evidence of antecedent circumstances**]

9-12 Evaluate Reconstruction ideals as a culminating expression of the mid-19th-century impulse of social democratization and perfectionism. [**Evaluate major debates among historians**]

7-12 Assess how the political and economic position of African Americans in the northern and western states changed during Reconstruction. [**Examine historical perspectives**]

7-12 Analyze how the Civil War and Reconstruction changed men's and women's roles and status in the North, South, and West. [**Analyze cause-and-effect relationships**]

5-12 Evaluate why corruption increased in the postwar period. [**Analyze multiple causation**]

ERA 6

The Development of the Industrial United States (1870-1900)

From the era of Reconstruction to the end of the 19th century, the United States underwent an economic transformation that involved the maturing of the industrial economy, the rapid expansion of big business, the development of large-scale agriculture, and the rise of national labor unions and pronounced industrial conflict.

Students can begin to see a resemblance to possibilities and problems that our society faces today. The late 19th century marked a spectacular outburst of technological innovation, which fueled headlong economic growth and delivered material benefits to many Americans. Yet, the advances in productive and extractive enterprises that technology permitted also had ecological effects that Americans were just beginning to understand and confront. In the last third of the 19th century, the rise of the American corporation and the advent of big business brought about a concentration of the nation's productive capacities in many fewer hands. Mechanization brought farming into the realm of big business and turned the United States into the world's premier producer of food—a position it has never surrendered.

This period also witnessed unprecedented immigration and urbanization, both of which were indispensable to industrial expansion. American society, always polyglot, became even more diverse as immigrants thronged from southern and eastern Europe—and also from Asia, Mexico, and Central America. As newcomers created a new American mosaic, the old Protestant European Americans' sway over the diverse people of this nation began to loosen. Related to this continuing theme of immigration was the search for national unity amid growing cultural diversity. How a rising system of public education promoted the assimilation of newcomers is an important topic for students to study.

Students should appreciate the cross-currents and contradictions of this period. For example, what many at the time thought was progress was regarded by others as retrogressive. Paradoxes abound. First, agricultural modernization, while innovative and productive, disrupted family farms and led American farmers to organize protest movements as never before. Second, the dizzying rate of expansion was accomplished at the cost of the wars against the Plains Indians, which produced the "second great removal" of indigenous peoples from their ancient homelands and ushered in a new federal Indian policy that would last until the New Deal. Third, muscular, wealth-producing industrial development that raised the standard of living for millions of Americans also fueled the rise of national labor unionism and unprecedented clashes in industrial and mining sites between capital and labor. Fourth, after the Civil War, women reformers, while reaching for a larger public presence, suffered an era of retrenchment on economic and political issues. Lastly, the wrenching economic dislocations of this period and the social problems that erupted in rural and urban settings captured the attention of reformers and politicians, giving rise to third-party movements and the beginning of the Progressive movement.

Overview

Standard 1: How the rise of corporations, heavy industry, and mechanized farming transformed the American people

Standard 2: Massive immigration after 1870 and how new social patterns, conflicts, and ideas of national unity developed amid growing cultural diversity

Standard 3: The rise of the American labor movement and how political issues reflected social and economic changes

Standard 4: Federal Indian policy and United States foreign policy after the Civil War

---

STANDARD 1	How the rise of corporations, heavy industry, and mechanized farming transformed the American people.

1A   The student understands the connections among industrialization, the advent of the modern corporation, and material well-being.

Therefore, the student is able to:

5-12   Explain how organized industrial research produced technological breakthroughs, especially the Bessemer steel process, conversion to electrical power, and telephonic communication, and how these innovations transformed the economy, work processes, and domestic life. [**Utilize quantitative data**]

9-12   Compare various types of business organizations in production and marketing. [**Compare and contrast differing sets of ideas**]

5-12   Evaluate the careers of prominent industrial and financial leaders. [**Assess the importance of the individual in history**]

7-12   Explain how business leaders sought to limit competition and maximize profits in the late 19th century. [**Examine the influence of ideas**]

9-12   Examine how industrialization made consumer goods more available, increased the standard of living for most Americans, and redistributed wealth. [**Utilize quantitative data**]

9-12   Compare the ascent of new industries today with those of a century ago. [**Hypothesize the influence of the past**]

1B   The student understands the rapid growth of cities and how urban life changed.

Therefore, the student is able to:

5-12   Explain how geographic factors and rapid industrialization created different kinds of cities in diverse regions of the country. [**Draw upon data in historical maps**]

5-12 Trace the migration of people from farm to city and their adjustment to urban life. [**Appreciate historical perspectives**]

7-12 Analyze how urban political machines gained power and how they were viewed by immigrants and middle-class reformers. [**Consider multiple perspectives**]

9-12 Explain how urban dwellers dealt with the problems of financing, governing, and policing the cities. [**Evaluate alternative courses of actions**]

7-12 Investigate how urban leaders, such as architects and philanthropists, responded to the challenges of rapid urbanization. [**Assess the importance of the individual in history**]

1C The student understands how agriculture, mining, and ranching were transformed.

Therefore, the student is able to:

5-12 Explain how major geographical and technological influences, including hydraulic engineering and barbed wire, affected farming, mining, and ranching. [**Draw upon data in historical maps**]

5-12 Explain the conflicts that arose during the settlement of the "last frontier" among farmers, ranchers, and miners. [**Consider multiple perspectives**]

9-12 Analyze the role of the federal government—particularly in terms of land policy, water, and Indian policy—in the economic transformation of the West. [**Analyze cause-and-effect relationships**]

7-12 Explain how commercial farming differed in the Northeast, South, Great Plains, and West in terms of crop production, farm labor, financing, and transportation. [**Compare and contrast differing economic patterns**]

7-12 Explain the gender composition and ethnic diversity of farmers, miners, and ranchers and analyze how this affected the development of the West. [**Examine the influence of ideas**]

7-12 Explain the significance of farm organizations. [**Analyze multiple causation**]

1D The student understands the effects of rapid industrialization on the environment and the emergence of the first conservation movement.

Therefore, the student is able to:

5-12 Analyze the environmental costs of pollution and the depletion of natural resources during the period 1870-1900. [**Utilize visual and mathematical data**]

7-12 Explain how rapid industrialization, extractive mining techniques, and the "gridiron" pattern of urban growth affected the scenic beauty and health of city and countryside. [**Analyze multiple causation**]

7-12 Explain the origins of environmentalism and the conservation movement in the late 19th century. [**Examine the influence of ideas**]

STANDARD 2	Massive immigration after 1870 and how new social patterns, conflicts, and ideas of national unity developed amid growing cultural diversity.

2A   The student understands the sources and experiences of the new immigrants.

Therefore, the student is able to:

7-12 Distinguish between the "old" and "new" immigration in terms of its volume and the immigrants' ethnicity, religion, language, place of origin, and motives for emigrating from their homelands. [**Analyze multiple causation**]

5-12 Trace patterns of immigrant settlement in different regions of the country and how new immigrants helped produce a composite American culture that transcended group boundaries. [**Reconstruct patterns of historical succession and duration**]

5-12 Assess the challenges, opportunities, and contributions of different immigrant groups. [**Examine historical perspectives**]

7-12 Evaluate how Catholic and Jewish immigrants responded to religious discrimination. [**Obtain historical data**]

9-12 Evaluate the role of public and parochial schools in integrating immigrants into the American mainstream. [**Analyze cause-and-effect relationships**]

2B   The student understands "scientific racism", race relations, and the struggle for equal rights.

Therefore, the student is able to:

7-12 Analyze the scientific theories of race and their application to society and politics. [**Examine the influence of ideas**]

5-12 Explain the rising racial conflict in different regions, including the anti-Chinese movement in the West and the rise of lynching in the South. [**Explain historical continuity and change**]

9-12 Analyze the role of new laws and the federal judiciary in instituting racial inequality and in disfranchising various racial groups. [**Evaluate the implementation of a decision**]

9-12 Analyze the arguments and methods by which various minority groups sought to acquire equal rights and opportunities guaranteed in the nation's charter documents. [**Identify issues and problems in the past**]

2C   The student understands how new cultural movements at different social levels affected American life.

Therefore, the student is able to:

7-12 Describe how regional artists and writers portrayed American life in this period. [**Read historical narratives imaginatively**]

    5-12   Investigate new forms of popular culture and leisure activities at different levels of American society. [**Draw upon visual sources**]

    9-12   Explain Victorianism and its impact on architecture, literature, manners, and morals. [**Employ literature, architecture, diaries, and artifacts**]

    9-12   Analyze how the rise of public education and voluntary organizations promoted national unity and American values in an era of unprecedented immigration and socioeconomic change. [**Examine the influence of ideas**]

STANDARD 3	The rise of the American labor movement and how political issues reflected social and economic changes.

3A   The student understands how the "second industrial revolution" changed the nature and conditions of work.

Therefore, the student is able to:

    7-12   Explain the change from workshop to factory and how it altered the worker's world. [**Analyze cause-and-effect relationships**]

    9-12   Account for employment in different regions of the country as affected by gender, race, ethnicity, and skill. [**Formulate historical questions**]

    7-12   Analyze how working conditions changed and how the workers responded to new industrial conditions. [**Explain historical continuity and change**]

    5-12   Analyze the causes and consequences of the industrial employment of children. [**Examine historical perspectives**]

3B   The student understands the rise of national labor unions and the role of state and federal governments in labor conflicts.

Therefore, the student is able to:

    9-12   Analyze how "reform unions" and "trade unions" differed in terms of their agendas for reform and for organizing workers by race, skill, gender, and ethnicity. [**Compare and contrast differing sets of ideas**]

    7-12   Explain the ways in which management in different regions and industries responded to labor organizing workers. [**Formulate historical questions**]

    5-12   Analyze the causes and effects of escalating labor conflict. [**Analyze cause-and-effect relationships**]

    7-12   Explain the response of management and government at different levels to labor strife in different regions of the country. [**Compare competing historical narratives**]

3C   **The student understands how Americans grappled with social, economic, and political issues.**

Therefore, the student is able to:

> *7-12*   Explain how Democrats and Republicans responded to civil service reform, monetary policy, tariffs, and business regulation. [**Consider multiple perspectives**]

> *9-12*   Explain the causes and effects of the depressions of 1873-79 and 1893-97 and the ways in which government, business, labor, and farmers responded. [**Analyze cause-and-effect relationships**]

> *7-12*   Explain the political, social, and economic roots of Populism and distinguish Populism from earlier democratic reform movements. [**Examine the influence of ideas**]

> *9-12*   Analyze the Populists' Omaha Platform of 1892 as a statement of grievances and an agenda for reform. [**Interrogate historical data**]

> *5-12*   Analyze the issues and results of the 1896 election and determine to what extent it was a turning point in American politics. [**Analyze cause-and-effect relationships**]

> *7-12*   Evaluate the successes and failures of Populism. [**Examine the influence of ideas**]

STANDARD 4	Federal Indian policy and United States foreign policy after the Civil War.

4A   **The student understands various perspectives on federal Indian policy, westward expansion, and the resulting struggles.**

Therefore, the student is able to:

> *7-12*   Identify and compare the attitudes and policies toward Native Americans by government officials, the U.S. Army, missionaries, and settlers. [**Interrogate historical data**]

> *5-12*   Compare survival strategies of different Native American societies during the "second great removal." [**Appreciate historical perspectives**]

> *7-12*   Explain the provisions of the Dawes Severalty Act of 1887 and evaluate its effects on tribal identity, land ownership, and assimilation. [**Evaluate the implementation of a decision**]

> *7-12*   Evaluate the legacy of 19th-century federal Indian policy. [**Hypothesize the influence of the past**]

4B   **The student understands the roots and development of American expansionism and the causes and outcomes of the Spanish-American War.**

Therefore, the student is able to:

> *5-12*   Trace the acquisition of new territories. [**Reconstruct patterns of historical succession and duration**]

9-12 Describe how geopolitics, economic interests, racial ideology, missionary zeal, nationalism, and domestic tensions combined to create an expansionist foreign policy. [**Analyze cause-and-effect relationships**]

5-12 Evaluate the causes, objectives, character, and outcome of the Spanish-American War. [**Interrogate historical data**]

7-12 Explain the causes and consequences of the Filipino insurrection. [**Analyze cause-and-effect relationships**]

ERA 7

The Emergence of Modern America (1890-1930)

The study of how the modern United States emerged begins with the Progressive era. It deserves careful study because, among other things, it included the nation's most vibrant set of reform ideas and campaigns since the 1830s-40s. Progressives were a diverse lot with various agendas that sometimes jostled uneasily, but all reformers focused on a set of corrosive problems arising from rapid industrialization, urbanization, waves of immigration, and business and political corruption. Students can be inspired by how fervently the Progressives applied themselves to the renewal of American democracy. They can also profit from understanding the distinctively female reform culture that contributed powerfully to the movement.

Two of the problems confronted by Progressives are still central today. First, the Progressives faced the dilemma of how to maintain the material benefits flowing from the industrial revolution while bringing the powerful forces creating those benefits under democratic control and while enlarging economic opportunity. Second, Progressives faced the knotted issue of how to maintain democracy and national identity amid an increasingly diverse influx of immigrants and amid widespread political corruption and the concentration of political power. Of all the waves of reformism in American history, Progressivism is notable for its nearly all-encompassing agenda. As its name implies, it stood for progress, and that put it squarely in the American belief in the perfectible society.

Students cannot fully understand the Progressive movement without considering its limitations, particularly its antagonism to radical labor movements and indifference to the plight of African Americans and other minorities. As in so many aspects of American history, it behooves students to understand different perspectives. Progressivism brought fusion in some areas of reform, but it also created fissures. Among those was the ongoing, heated controversy about female equality, particularly in the area of economic protectionism.

All issues of American foreign policy in the 20th century have their origins in the emergence of the United States as a major world power in the Spanish-American War at the end of the 19th century and in the involvement of the United States in World War I. The American intervention in World War I cast the die for the United States as a world power for the remainder of the century. Students can learn much about the complexities of foreign policy today by studying the difficulties of maintaining neutrality in World War I while acquiring the role of an economic giant with global interests and while fervently wishing to export democracy around the world.

In the postwar period the prosperity of the 1920s and the domination of big business and Republican politics are also important to study. The 1920s displayed dramatically the American urge to build, innovate, and explore—poignantly captured in Lindbergh's solo flight across the Atlantic in 1927, which excited more enthusiasm than any single event to that time. The cultural and social realms also contain lessons from history that have resonance today. First, students should study the women's struggle for equality, which had political, economic, and cultural dimensions. Second, students should understand how radical labor movements and radical ideologies provoked widespread fear and even hysteria. Third, they need to study the recurring racial tension that led to black nationalism, the Harlem Renaissance, and the first great northward migration of African Americans on the one hand and the resurgence of the Ku Klux Klan on the other hand. Fourth, they need to understand the powerful movement to Americanize a generation of immigrants and the momentous closing of the nation's gates through severe retrenchment of open-door immigration policies. Lastly, they should examine the continuing tension among Protestants, Catholics, and Jews, most dramatically exemplified in the resurgence of Protestant fundamentalism.

Overview

Standard 1: How Progressives and others addressed problems of industrial capitalism, urbanization, and political corruption

Standard 2: The changing role of the United States in world affairs through World War I

Standard 3: How the United States changed from the end of World War I to the eve of the Great Depression

STANDARD 1	How Progressives and others addressed problems of industrial capitalism, urbanization, and political corruption.

1A   The student understands the origin of the Progressives and the coalitions they formed to deal with issues at the local and state levels.

Therefore, the student is able to:

5-12 Explain how the Progressives drew upon the American past to develop a notion of democracy responsive to the distinctive needs of an industrial society. [**Explain historical continuity and change**]

9-12 Examine the social origins of the Progressives. [**Interrogate historical data**]

7-12 Explain how intellectuals and religious leaders laid the groundwork and publicists spread the word for Progressive plans to reform American society. [**Assess the importance of the individual**]

5-12 Evaluate Progressive reforms to expand democracy at the local and state levels. [**Examine the influence of ideas**]

9-12 Assess Progressive efforts to regulate big business, curb labor militancy, and protect the rights of workers and consumers. [**Evaluate alternative courses of action**]

5-12 Evaluate Progressive attempts at social and moral reform. [**Marshal evidence of antecedent circumstances**]

7-12 Analyze Progressive programs for assimilating the influx of immigrants before World War I. [**Formulate a position or course of action on an issue**]

1B   The student understands Progressivism at the national level.

Therefore, the student is able to:

5-12   Evaluate the presidential leadership of Theodore Roosevelt, William Howard Taft, and Woodrow Wilson in terms of their effectiveness in obtaining passage of reform measures. [**Assess the importance of the individual**]

7-12   Explain why the election of 1912 was a pivotal campaign for the Progressive movement. [**Interrogate historical data**]

7-12   Compare the New Nationalism, New Freedom, and Socialist agendas for change. [**Compare and contrast differing sets of ideas**]

5-12   Describe how the 16th, 17th, 18th, and 19th amendments reflected the ideals and goals of Progressivism and the continuing attempt to adapt the founding ideals to a modernized society. [**Evaluate the implementation of a decision**]

9-12   Explain how the decisions of the Supreme Court affected Progressivism. [**Interrogate historical data**]

1C   The student understands the limitations of Progressivism and the alternatives offered by various groups.

Therefore, the student is able to:

9-12   Compare the counter-Progressive programs of various labor organizations with the social democratic programs promulgated in industrial Europe. [**Compare and contrast differing ideas**]

5-12   Examine the perspectives of various African Americans on Progressivism and their alternative programs. [**Consider multiple perspectives**]

9-12   Specify the issues raised by various women and how mainstream Progressives responded to them. [**Consider multiple perspectives**]

9-12   Evaluate the changing attitude toward Native American assimilation under Progressivism and the consequences of the change. [**Explain historical continuity and change**]

STANDARD 2	The changing role of the United States in world affairs through World War I.

2A   The student understands how the American role in the world changed in the early 20th century.

Therefore, the student is able to:

5-12   Analyze the reasons for the Open Door policy. [**Formulate a position or course of action on an issue**]

7-12   Evaluate the Roosevelt administration's foreign policies. [**Evaluate the implementation of a decision**]

7-12   Explain relations with Japan and the significance of the "Gentleman's Agreement." [**Consider multiple perspectives**]

7-12   Compare Taft's dollar diplomacy with Roosevelt's big stick diplomacy and evaluate the results. [**Compare and contrast differing sets of ideas**]

9-12   Evaluate Wilson's moral diplomacy, especially in relation to the Mexican Revolution. [**Examine the influence of ideas**]

2B   The student understands the causes of World War I and why the United States intervened.

Therefore, the student is able to:

5-12   Explain the causes of World War I in 1914 and the reasons for the declaration of United States neutrality. [**Identify issues and problems in the past**]

7-12   Assess how industrial research in aviation and chemical warfare influenced military strategy and the outcome of World War I. [**Analyze cause-and-effect relationships**]

7-12   Analyze the impact of American public opinion on the Wilson administration's evolving foreign policy from 1914 to 1917. [**Examine the influence of ideas**]

7-12   Evaluate Wilson's leadership during the period of neutrality and his reasons for intervention. [**Assess the importance of the individual**]

2C   The student understands the impact at home and abroad of the United States involvement in World War I.

Therefore, the student is able to:

7-12   Explain U.S. military and economic mobilization for war and evaluate the role of labor, including women and African Americans. [**Identify issues and problems in the past**]

9-12   Analyze the impact of public opinion and government policies on constitutional interpretation and civil liberties. [**Evaluate the implementation of a decision**]

5-12   Explain how the American Expeditionary Force contributed to the allied victory. [**Interrogate historical data**]

7-12   Evaluate the significance of the Russian Revolution, how it affected the war, and how the United States and Allied powers responded to it. [**Marshal evidence of antecedent circumstances**]

5-12   Evaluate Wilson's Fourteen Points, his negotiations at the Versailles Treaty talks, and the national debate over treaty ratification and the League of Nations. [**Evaluate the implementation of a decision**]

| STANDARD 3 | How the United States changed from the end of World War I to the eve of the Great Depression. |

3A **The student understands social tensions and their consequences in the postwar era.**

Therefore, the student is able to:

7-12 Assess state and federal government reactions to the growth of radical political movements. [**Evaluate the implementation of a decision**]

5-12 Analyze the factors that lead to immigration restriction and the closing of the "Golden Door." [**Interrogate historical data**]

7-12 Examine rising racial tensions, the resurgence of the Ku Klux Klan, and the emergence of Garveyism. [**Analyze cause-and-effect relationships**]

7-12 Examine the rise of religious fundamentalism and the clash between traditional moral values and changing ideas as exemplified in the controversy over Prohibition and the Scopes trial. [**Examine the influence of ideas**]

9-12 Analyze how the emergence of the "New Woman" challenged Victorian values. [**Examine the influence of ideas**]

3B **The student understands how a modern capitalist economy emerged in the 1920s.**

Therefore, the student is able to:

5-12 Explain how principles of scientific management and technological innovations, including assembly lines, rapid transit, household appliances, and radio, continued to transform production, work, and daily life. [**Examine the influence of ideas**]

7-12 Examine the changes in the modern corporation, including labor policies and the advent of mass advertising and sales techniques. [**Analyze cause-and-effect relationships**]

9-12 Analyze the new business downtowns, the development of suburbs, and the role of transportation in changing urban life. [**Explain historical continuity and change**]

7-12 Explain the role of new technology and scientific research in the rise of agribusiness and agricultural productivity. [**Utilize quantitative data**]

3C **The student understands how new cultural movements reflected and changed American society.**

Therefore, the student is able to:

9-12 Specify and evaluate the extension of secondary education to new segments of American society. [**Utilize quantitative data**]

5-12 Analyze how radio, movies, newspapers, and popular magazines created mass culture. [**Examine the influence of ideas**]

7-12 Explain the growth of distinctively American art and literature from the social realists to the "lost generation." [Draw upon art and literature]

5-12 Examine the contributions of artists and writers of the Harlem Renaissance and assess their popularity. [Draw upon visual, literary, and musical sources]

5-12 Assess how increased leisure time promoted the growth of professional sports, amusement parks, and national parks. [Analyze cause-and-effect relationships]

3D   **The student understands politics and international affairs in the 1920s.**

Therefore, the student is able to:

7-12 Evaluate the waning of Progressivism and the "return to normalcy." [Explain historical continuity and change]

5-12 Assess the effects of woman suffrage on politics. [Evaluate the implementation of a decision]

7-12 Describe the goals and evaluate the effects of Republican foreign policy. [Analyze cause-and-effect relationships]

ERA 8

The Great Depression and World War II (1929-1945)

Participants of this era are still alive, and their common memories of cataclysmic events—from the Crash of 1929 through World War II—are still common points of reference today. Our closeness to this era should help students see how today's problems and choices are connected to the past. Knowledge of history is the precondition of political intelligence, setting the stage for current questions about government's role and rule, foreign policy, the continuing search for core values, and the ongoing imperative to extend the founding principles to all Americans.

The Great Depression and the New Deal deserve careful attention for four reasons. First, Americans in the 1930s endured—and conquered—the greatest economic crisis in American history. Second, the Depression wrought deep changes in people's attitudes toward government's responsibilities. Third, organized labor acquired new rights. Fourth, the New Deal set in place legislation that reshaped modern American capitalism.

In its effects on the lives of Americans, the Great Depression was one of the great shaping experiences of American history, ranking with the American Revolution, the Civil War, and the second industrial revolution. More than Progressivism, the Great Depression brought about changes in the regulatory power of the federal government. It also enlarged government's role in superimposing relief measures on the capitalist system, bringing the United States into a mild form of welfare state capitalism, such as had appeared earlier in industrial European nations. This era provides students with ample opportunities to test their analytic skills as they assay Franklin Roosevelt's leadership, the many alternative formulas for ending the Great Depression, and the ways in which the New Deal affected women, racial minorities, labor, children, and other groups.

World War II also commands careful attention. Although it was not the bloodiest in American history, the war solidified the nation's role as a global power and ushered in social changes that established reform agendas that would preoccupy public discourse in the United States for the remainder of the 20th century. The role of the United States in World War II was epochal for its defense of democracy in the face of totalitarian aggression. More than ever before, Americans fought abroad, not only winning the war but bringing a new cosmopolitanism home with them. As before, the war was an engine of social and cultural change. In this war, Americans of diverse backgrounds lived and fought together, fostering American identity and building notions of a common future. Similarly, on the homefront, public education and the mass media promoted nationalism and the blending of cultural backgrounds. Yet students should learn about the denial of the civil liberties of interned Japanese Americans and the irony of racial minorities fighting for democratic principles overseas that they were still denied at home as well as in military service itself.

Students will need to assess carefully the course of the war, the collapse of the Grand Alliance, and its unsettling effects on the postwar period. Also, they should evaluate the social effects of war on the homefront, such as internal migration to war production centers, the massive influx of women into previously male job roles, and the attempts of African Americans and others to obtain desegregation of the armed forces and end discriminatory hiring.

Overview

Standard 1: The causes of the Great Depression and how it affected American society

Standard 2: How the New Deal addressed the Great Depression, transformed American federalism, and initiated the welfare state

Standard 3: The causes and course of World War II, the character of the war at home and abroad, and its reshaping of the U.S. role in world affairs

STANDARD 1	**The causes of the Great Depression and how it affected American society.**

1A   The student understands the causes of the crash of 1929 and the Great Depression.

Therefore, the student is able to:

9-12 Assess the economic policies of the Harding and Coolidge administrations and their impact on wealth distribution, investment, and taxes. [**Analyze multiple causation**]

5-12 Analyze the causes and consequences of the stock market crash of 1929. [**Compare competing historical narratives**]

5-12 Evaluate the causes of the Great Depression. [**Analyze multiple causation**]

9-12 Explain the global context of the depression and the reasons for the worldwide economic collapse. [**Evaluate major debates among historians**]

7-12 Explore the reasons for the deepening crisis of the Great Depression and evaluate the Hoover administration's responses. [**Formulate a position or course of action on an issue**]

1B   The student understands how American life changed during the 1930s.

Therefore, the student is able to:

5-12 Explain the effects of the Great Depression and the Dust Bowl on American farm owners, tenants, and sharecroppers. [**Analyze multiple causation**]

7-12 Analyze the impact of the Great Depression on industry and workers and explain the response of local and state officials in combating the resulting economic and social crises. [**Analyze multiple causation**]

7-12 Analyze the impact of the Great Depression on the American family and on ethnic and racial minorities. [**Consider multiple perspectives**]

9-12 Explain the cultural life of the Depression years in art, literature, and music and evaluate the government's role in promoting artistic expression. [**Draw upon visual, literary, and musical sources**]

STANDARD 2	How the New Deal addressed the Great Depression, transformed American federalism, and initiated the welfare state.

2A   The student understands the New Deal and the presidency of Franklin D. Roosevelt.

Therefore, the student is able to:

5-12 Contrast the background and leadership abilities of Franklin D. Roosevelt with those of Herbert Hoover. [**Assess the importance of the individual in history**]

7-12 Analyze the links between the early New Deal and Progressivism. [**Compare and contrast differing sets of ideas**]

9-12 Contrast the first and second New Deals and evaluate the success and failures of the relief, recovery, and reform measures associated with each. [**Compare and contrast differing sets of ideas**]

7-12 Analyze the factors contributing to the forging of the Roosevelt coalition in 1936 and explain its electoral significance in subsequent years. [**Examine the influence of ideas**]

9-12 Analyze the involvement of minorities and women in the New Deal and its impact upon them. [**Assess the importance of the individual in history**]

7-12 Explain renewed efforts to protect the environment during the Great Depression and evaluate their success in places such as the Dust Bowl and the Tennessee Valley. [**Analyze cause-and-effect relationships**]

2B   The student understands the impact of the New Deal on workers and the labor movement.

Therefore, the student is able to:

5-12 Explain how New Deal legislation and policies affected American workers and the labor movement. [**Analyze cause-and-effect relationships**]

7-12 Explain the re-emergence of labor militancy and the struggle between craft and industrial unions. [**Compare and contrast differing sets of ideas**]

7-12 Evaluate labor union positions on minority and women workers. [**Consider multiple perspectives**]

9-12 Explain the impact of the New Deal on nonunion workers. [**Formulate a position or course of action on an issue**]

2C **The student understands opposition to the New Deal, the alternative programs of its detractors, and the legacy of the New Deal.**

Therefore, the student is able to:

7-12 Identify the leading opponents of New Deal policies and assess their arguments. [**Compare and contrast differing sets of ideas and values**]

9-12 Explain the reasoning of the Supreme Court decisions on early New Deal legislation and evaluate the Roosevelt administration's response. [**Compare and contrast differing sets of ideas**]

5-12 Evaluate the significance and legacy of the New Deal. [**Evaluate the implementation of a decision**]

| **STANDARD 3** | The causes and course of World War II, the character of the war at home and abroad, and its reshaping of the U.S. role in world affairs. |

3A **The student understands the international background of World War II.**

Therefore, the student is able to:

7-12 Analyze the factors contributing to the rise of fascism, national socialism, and communism in the interwar period. [**Analyze multiple causation**]

7-12 Explain the breakdown of the Versailles settlement and League of Nations in the 1930s. [**Challenge arguments of historical inevitability**]

9-12 Analyze hemispheric relations in the 1930s, as exemplified by the Good Neighbor Policy. [**Draw upon data in historical maps**]

5-12 Analyze the reasons for American isolationist sentiment in the interwar period and its effects on international relations and diplomacy. [**Analyze cause-and-effect relationships**]

5-12 Evaluate American responses to German, Italian, and Japanese aggression in Europe, Africa, and Asia from 1935 to 1941. [**Formulate a position or course of action on an issue**]

7-12 Analyze the reasons for the growing tensions with Japan in East Asia culminating with the bombing of Pearl Harbor. [**Marshal evidence of antecedent circumstances**]

3B **The student understands World War II and how the Allies prevailed.**

Therefore, the student is able to:

5-12 Explain the major turning points of the war and contrast military campaigns in the European and Pacific theaters. [**Draw upon data in historical maps**]

7-12 Analyze Hitler's "final solution" and the Allies' responses to the Holocaust and war crimes. [**Interrogate historical data**]

9-12 Evaluate the wartime aims and strategies hammered out at conferences among the Allied powers. [**Hypothesize the influence of the past**]

7-12 Evaluate the decision to employ nuclear weapons against Japan and assess later controversies over the decision. [**Evaluate major debates among historians**]

5-12 Explain the financial, material, and human costs of the war and analyze its economic consequences for the Allies and the Axis powers. [**Utilize visual and quantitative data**]

7-12 Describe military experiences and explain how they fostered American identity and interactions among people of diverse backgrounds. [**Utilize literary sources including oral testimony**]

7-12 Explain the purposes and organization of the United Nations. [**Marshal evidence of antecedent circumstances**]

3C   **The student understands the effects of World War II at home.**

Therefore, the student is able to:

5-12 Explain how the United States mobilized its economic and military resources during World War II. [**Utilize visual and quantitative data**]

7-12 Explore how the war fostered cultural exchange and interaction while promoting nationalism and American identity. [**Analyze cause-and-effect relationships**]

7-12 Evaluate how minorities organized to gain access to wartime jobs and how they confronted discrimination. [**Formulate a position or course of action on an issue**]

5-12 Evaluate the internment of Japanese Americans during the war and assess the implication for civil liberties. [**Evaluate the implementation of a decision**]

7-12 Analyze the effects of World War II on gender roles and the American family. [**Compare and contrast differing sets of ideas**]

9-12 Evaluate the war's impact on science, medicine, and technology, especially in nuclear physics, weaponry, synthetic fibers, and television. [**Utilize quantitative data**]

9-12 Evaluate how Americans viewed their achievements and global responsibilities at war's end. [**Interrogate historical data**]

ERA 9

Postwar United States (1945 to early 1970s)

Although the study of the era following World War II can easily be dominated by a preoccupation with the Cold War, our understanding of present-day American society will be deficient without grappling with the remarkable changes in American society, the American economy, and American culture in the 1950s and 1960s. It should be remembered that the closeness of the period makes it one of continuing reinterpretation, reminding us that historical judgments should be seen as provisional, never cut in stone.

Students will need to understand how the postwar economic boom, mightily affected by the transforming hand of science, produced epic changes in American education, consumer culture, suburbanization, the return to domesticity for many women, the character of corporate life, and sexual and cultural mores—both of which involved startling changes in dress, speech, music, film and television, family structure, uses of leisure time, and more.

All of this can take on deeper meaning when connected to politics. Politically, the era was marked by the reinvigoration of New Deal liberalism and its gradual exhaustion in the 1970s. In the period of liberal activism, leaders sought to expand the role of the state to extend civil liberties and promote economic opportunity. The advent of the civil rights and women's movements thus became part of the third great reform impulse in American history. Conservative reaction stressed restrictions on the growth of the state, emphasized free enterprise, and promoted individual rather than group rights.

The Cold War set the framework for global politics for 45 years after the end of World War II. The Cold War so strongly influenced our domestic politics, the conduct of foreign affairs, and the role of the government in the economy after 1945 that it is obligatory for students to examine its origins and the forces behind its continuation into the late 20th century. They should understand how American and European antipathy to Leninist-Stalinism predated 1945, seeded by the gradual awareness of the messianic nature of Soviet communism during the interwar years, Stalin's collectivization of agriculture, and the great purges of the 1930s. Students should also consider the Soviet Union's goals following World War II. Its catastrophic losses in the war and fear of rapid German recovery were factors in Soviet demands for a sphere of influence on its western borders, achieved through the establishment of governments under Soviet military and political control. Students should also know how the American policy of containment was successfully conducted in Europe: the Truman Doctrine, the Marshall Plan, the Berlin airlift, NATO, and the maintenance of U.S. military forces in Europe under what was called the nuclear "balance of terror."

They should also recognize that the U.S. government's anti-Communist strategy of containment in Asia confronted very different circumstances and would involve the United States in the bloody, costly wars of Korea and Vietnam. The Vietnam War is especially noteworthy. It demonstrated the power of American public opinion in reversing foreign policy, it tested the democratic system to its limits, it left scars on American society that have not yet been erased, and it made many Americans deeply skeptical about future military or even peacekeeping interventions.

Overview

Standard 1: The economic boom and social transformation of postwar United States

Standard 2: How the Cold War and conflicts in Korea and Vietnam influenced domestic and international politics

Standard 3: Domestic policies after World War II

Standard 4: The struggle for racial and gender equality and for the extension of civil liberties

---

STANDARD 1 | **The economic boom and social transformation of postwar United States.**

1A **The student understands the extent and impact of economic changes in the postwar period.**

Therefore, the student is able to:

> *7-12* Analyze the debate over demobilization and economic reconversion and its effects on the economy. [**Marshal evidence of antecedent circumstances**]

> *5-12* Explain the reasons for the sustained growth of the postwar consumer economy. [**Analyze cause-and-effect relationships**]

> *7-12* Explain the growth of the service, white collar, and professional sectors of the economy that led to the enlargement of the middle class. [**Analyze cause-and-effect relationships**]

> *9-12* Analyze the impact of the Cold War on the economy. [**Identify issues and problems in the past**]

> *9-12* Analyze the continued gap between poverty and the rising affluence of the middle class. [**Consider multiple perspectives**]

1B **The student understands how the social changes of the postwar period affected various Americans.**

Therefore, the student is able to:

> *5-12* Evaluate the effects of the GI Bill on American society. [**Hypothesize the influence of the past on the present**]

> *9-12* Examine the rapid growth of secondary and collegiate education and the role of new governmental spending on educational programs. [**Analyze cause-and-effect relationships**]

> *9-12* Explain the expansion of suburbanization and analyze how the "crabgrass frontier" affected American society. [**Explain historical continuity and change**]

7-12 Explain the reasons for the "return to domesticity" and how it affected family life and women's careers. [**Consider multiple perspectives**]

9-12 Examine the place of religion in postwar American life. [**Examine the influence of ideas**]

5-12 Explore the influence of popular culture and analyze the role of the mass media in homogenizing American culture. [**Analyze cause-and-effect relationships**]

1C **The student understands how postwar science augmented the nation's economic strength, transformed daily life, and influenced the world economy.**

Therefore, the student is able to:

9-12 Explore how the new relationship between science and government after World War II created a new system of scientific research and development. [**Explain historical continuity and change**]

5-12 Identify various pioneers in modern scientific research and explain how their work has changed contemporary society. [**Assess the importance of the individual in history**]

5-12 Assess the significance of research and scientific breakthroughs in promoting the U.S. space program. [**Examine the influence of ideas**]

9-12 Explain the advances in medical science and assess how they improved the standard of living and changed demographic patterns. [**Interrogate historical data**]

7-12 Describe agricultural innovation and consolidation in the postwar period and assess their impact on the world economy. [**Analyze cause-and-effect relationships**]

9-12 Examine how American technology ushered in the communications revolution and assess its global influence. [**Analyze cause-and-effect relationships**]

STANDARD 2 How the Cold War and conflicts in Korea and Vietnam influenced domestic and international politics.

2A **The student understands the international origins and domestic consequences of the Cold War.**

Therefore, the student is able to:

5-12 Evaluate the "flawed peace" resulting from World War II and the effectiveness of the United Nations in reducing international tensions and conflicts. [**Analyze cause-and-effect relationships**]

7-12 Explain the origins of the Cold War and the advent of nuclear politics. [**Hold interpretations of history as tentative**]

7-12 Examine the U.S. response to the Chinese Revolution and its impact on the Cold War. [**Analyze cause-and-effect relationships**]

7-12 Analyze the causes of the Korean War and how a divided Korea remained a source of international tension. [**Formulate a position or course of action on an issue**]

7-12 Explain the rationale, implementation, and effectiveness of the U.S. containment policy. [**Evaluate the implementation of a decision**]

5-12 Explain the popular uprisings against communist governments in Eastern Europe and evaluate how they affected United States foreign policy. [**Analyze cause-and-effect relationships**]

7-12 Analyze the change from confrontation to coexistence between the Soviet Union and the United States. [**Analyze cause-and-effect relationships**]

2B **The student understands United States foreign policy in Africa, Asia, the Middle East, and Latin America.**

Therefore, the student is able to:

9-12 Analyze American policies toward independence movements in Africa, Asia, the Caribbean, and the Middle East. [**Marshal evidence of antecedent circumstances**]

7-12 Evaluate changing foreign policy toward Latin America. [**Identify issues and problems in the past**]

5-12 Assess U.S. relations with Israel and explain how Arab-Israeli crises influenced American foreign policy during the Cold War. [**Evaluate the implementation of a decision**]

2C **The student understands the foreign and domestic consequences of U.S. involvement in Vietnam.**

Therefore, the student is able to:

7-12 Assess the Vietnam policy of the Kennedy, Johnson, and Nixon administrations and the shifts of public opinion about the war. [**Analyze multiple causation**]

9-12 Explain the composition of the American forces recruited to fight the war. [**Interrogate historical data**]

5-12 Evaluate how Vietnamese and Americans experienced the war and how the war continued to affect postwar politics and culture. [**Appreciate historical perspectives**]

7-12 Explain the provisions of the Paris Peace Accord of 1973 and evaluate the role of the Nixon administration. [**Differentiate between historical facts and historical interpretations**]

9-12 Analyze the constitutional issues involved in the war and explore the legacy of the Vietnam war. [**Formulate a position or course of action on an issue**]

| STANDARD 3 | Domestic policies after World War II. |

3A   The student understands the political debates of the post-World War II era.

Therefore, the student is able to:

9-12   Evaluate Truman's continuation of New Deal policies in labor relations, housing, education, and health. [**Formulate a position or course of action on an issue**]

5-12   Evaluate Truman's civil rights policies and their effect on splintering the Democratic party. [**Assess the importance of the individual in history**]

7-12   Explain the relationship between post-war Soviet espionage and the emergence of internal security and loyalty programs under Truman and Eisenhower. [**Analyze cause-and-effect relationships**]

7-12   Analyze the rise and fall of McCarthyism, its effects on civil liberties, and its repercussions. [**Analyze cause-and-effect relationships**]

7-12   Evaluate Eisenhower's "Modern Republicanism" in relation to the economy and other domestic issues. [**Formulate a position or course of action on an issue**]

3B   The student understands the "New Frontier" and the "Great Society."

Therefore, the student is able to:

9-12   Examine the role of the media in the election of 1960. [**Utilize visual and quantitative data**]

5-12   Evaluate the domestic policies of Kennedy's "New Frontier." [**Hold interpretations of history as tentative**]

5-12   Evaluate the legislation and programs enacted during Johnson's presidency. [**Evaluate the implementation of a decision**]

7-12   Assess the effectiveness of the "Great Society" programs. [**Evaluate major debates among historians**]

7-12   Compare the so-called second environmental movement with the first at the beginning of the 20th century. [**Compare and contrast different movements**]

| STANDARD 4 | The struggle for racial and gender equality and for the extension of civil liberties. |

4A   The student understands the "Second Reconstruction" and its advancement of civil rights.

Therefore, the student is able to:

7-12   Explain the origins of the postwar civil rights movement and the role of the NAACP in the legal assault on segregation. [**Analyze multiple causation**]

5-12 Evaluate the Warren Court's reasoning in *Brown* v. *Board of Education* and its significance in advancing civil rights. [**Analyze cause-and-effect relationships**]

5-12 Explain the resistance to civil rights in the South between 1954 and 1965. [**Identify issues and problems in the past**]

7-12 Analyze the leadership and ideology of Martin Luther King, Jr. and Malcolm X in the civil rights movement and evaluate their legacies. [**Assess the importance of the individual in history**]

7-12 Assess the role of the legislative and executive branches in advancing the civil rights movement and the effect of shifting the focus from *de jure* to *de facto* segregation. [**Evaluate the implementation of a decision**]

5-12 Evaluate the agendas, strategies, and effectiveness of various African Americans, Asian Americans, Latino Americans, and Native Americans, as well as the disabled, in the quest for civil rights and equal opportunities. [**Explain historical continuity and change**]

9-12 Assess the reasons for and effectiveness of the escalation from civil disobedience to more radical protest in the civil rights movement. [**Marshal evidence of antecedent circumstances**]

4B   The student understands the women's movement for civil rights and equal opportunities.

Therefore, the student is able to:

7-12 Analyze the factors contributing to modern feminism and compare the ideas, agendas, and strategies of feminist and counter-feminist organizations. [**Marshal evidence of antecedent circumstances**]

5-12 Identify the major social, economic, and political issues affecting women and explain the conflicts these issues engendered. [**Formulate a position or course of action on an issue**]

9-12 Evaluate the conflicting perspectives over the Equal Rights Amendment, Title VII, and *Roe* v. *Wade*. [**Consider multiple perspectives**]

4C   The student understands the Warren Court's role in addressing civil liberties and equal rights

Therefore, the student is able to:

9-12 Analyze the expansion of due process rights in such cases as *Gideon* v. *Wainwright* and *Miranda* v. *Arizona* and evaluate criticism of the extension of these rights for the accused. [**Interrogate historical data**]

9-12 Explain the Supreme Court's reasoning in establishing the "one man, one vote" principle. [**Interrogate historical data**]

5-12 Evaluate the Supreme Court's interpretation of freedom of religion. [**Formulate a position or course of action on an issue**]

9-12 Assess the effectiveness of the judiciary as opposed to the legislative and executive branches of government in promoting civil liberties and equal opportunities. [**Challenge arguments of historical inevitability**]

ERA 10

Contemporary United States (1968 to the present)

Examining the history of our own time presents special difficulties. The historian ordinarily has the benefit of hindsight but never less so than in examining the last few decades. Furthermore, the closer we approach the present the less likely it is that historians will be able to transcend their own biases. Historians can never attain complete objectivity, but they tend to fall shortest of the goal when they deal with current or very recent events. For example, writers and teachers of history who voted for a particular candidate will likely view that candidate's actions in office more sympathetically than a historian who voted the other way.

There can be little doubt, however, that in global politics the role of the United States has led to seismic changes that every student, as a person approaching voting age, should understand. The detente with the People's Republic of China under Nixon's presidency represents the beginning of a new era, though the outcome is still far from determined. Perhaps more epochal is the collapse of the Soviet Union, the overthrow of communist governments in Eastern Europe, and the consequent end of the Cold War and the nuclear arms race. Students can understand little about American attempts to adjust to a post-bipolar world without comprehending these momentous events.

In politics, students ought to explore how the political balance has tilted away from liberalism since 1968. They should also study the ability of the political and constitutional system to check and balance itself against potential abuses as exemplified in the Watergate and Iran-Contra affairs. They can hone their ability to think about the American political system by exploring and evaluating debates over government's role in the economy, environmental protection, social welfare, international trade policies, and more.

No course in American history should reach a conclusion without considering some of the major social and cultural changes of the most recent decades. Among them, several may claim precedence: first, the reopening of the nation's gates to immigrants that for the first time come primarily from Asia and Central America; second, renewed reform movements that promote environmental, feminist, and civil rights agendas that lost steam in the 1970s; third, the resurgence of religious evangelicalism; fourth, the massive alteration in the character of work through technological innovation and corporate reorganization; and lastly, the continuing struggle for *e pluribus unum* amid contentious debates over national vs. group identity, group rights vs. individual rights, and the overarching goal of making social and political practice conform to the nation's founding principles.

Overview

Standard 1: Recent developments in foreign policy and domestic politics

Standard 2: Economic, social, and cultural developments in contemporary United States

STANDARD 1	Recent developments in foreign policy and domestic politics.

1A   The student understands domestic politics from Nixon to Carter.

Therefore, the student is able to:

> 5-12   Evaluate the effectiveness of the Nixon, Ford, and Carter administrations in addressing social and environmental issues. [**Assess the importance of the individual in history**]

> 9-12   Assess the efforts of the Nixon, Ford, and Carter administrations to combat recession and inflation. [**Compare and contrast differing policies**]

> 5-12   Explain the Nixon administration's involvement in Watergate and examine the role of the media in exposing the scandal. [**Formulate historical questions**]

> 9-12   Analyze the constitutional issues raised by the Watergate affair and evaluate the effects of Watergate on public opinion. [**Examine the influence of ideas**]

1B   The student understands domestic politics in contemporary society.

Therefore, the student is able to:

> 7-12   Explain the conservative reaction to liberalism and evaluate supply-side economic strategies of the Reagan and Bush administrations. [**Compare and contrast differing sets of ideas**]

> 5-12   Examine the impact of the "Reagan Revolution" on federalism and public perceptions of the role of government. [**Examine the influence of ideas**]

> 9-12   Analyze constitutional issues in the Iran-Contra affair. [**Identify issues and problems in the past**]

> 9-12   Explain why labor unionism has declined in recent decades. [**Interrogate historical data**]

> 9-12   Evaluate the impact of recurring recessions and the growing national debt on the domestic agendas of recent presidential administrations. [**Compare and contrast differing policies**]

1C   The student understands major foreign policy initiatives.

Therefore, the student is able to:

> 7-12   Assess U.S. policies toward arms limitation and explain improved relations with the Soviet Union. [**Examine the influence of ideas**]

7-12 Assess Nixon's policy of detente with the USSR and the People's Republic of China. [**Analyze multiple causation**]

9-12 Examine the U.S. role in political struggles in the Middle East, Africa, Asia, and Latin America. [**Analyze cause-and-effect relationships**]

5-12 Evaluate Reagan's efforts to reassert American military power and rebuild American prestige. [**Hypothesize the influence of the past**]

7-12 Explain the reasons for the collapse of communist governments in Eastern Europe and the USSR. [**Analyze multiple causation**]

9-12 Evaluate the reformulation of foreign policy in the post-Cold War era. [**Analyze cause-and-effect relationships**]

STANDARD 2	**Economic, social, and cultural developments in contemporary United States.**

2A   The student understands economic patterns since 1968.

Therefore, the student is able to:

9-12 Explain the sluggishness in the overall rate of economic growth and the relative stagnation of wages since 1973. [**Utilize quantitative data**]

7-12 Analyze the economic and social effects of the sharp increase in the labor force participation of women and new immigrants. [**Analyze cause-and-effect relationships**]

9-12 Explain the increase in income disparities and evaluate its social and political consequences. [**Analyze cause-and-effect relationships**]

7-12 Examine the consequences of the shift of the labor force from manufacturing to service industries. [**Evaluate debates among historians**]

5-12 Evaluate how scientific advances and technological changes such as robotics and the computer revolution affect the economy and the nature of work. [**Explain historical continuity and change**]

9-12 Assess the effects of international trade, transnational business organization, and overseas competition on the economy. [**Utilize quantitative data**]

2B   The student understands the new immigration and demographic shifts.

Therefore, the student is able to:

5-12 Analyze the new immigration policies after 1965 and the push-pull factors that prompted a new wave of immigrants. [**Analyze cause-and-effect relationships**]

9-12 Identify the major issues that affected immigrants and explain the conflicts these issues engendered. [**Identify issues and problems in the past**]

7-12 Explore the continuing population flow from cities to suburbs, the internal migrations from the "Rustbelt" to the "Sunbelt," and the social and political effects of these changes. [**Analyze cause-and-effect relationships**]

9-12 Explain changes in the size and composition of the traditional American family and their ramifications. [**Explain historical continuity and change**]

7-12 Explain the shifting age structure of the population with the aging of the "baby boomers," and grasp the implications of the "greying of America." [**Utilize quantitative data**]

2C   **The student understands changing religious diversity and its impact on American institutions and values.**

Therefore, the student is able to:

5-12 Analyze how the new immigrants have affected religious diversity. [**Explain historical continuity and change**]

9-12 Analyze the position of major religious groups on political and social issues. [**Analyze cause-and-effect relationships**]

7-12 Explain the growth of the Christian evangelical movement. [**Consider multiple perspectives**]

7-12 Analyze how religious organizations use modern telecommunications to promote their faiths. [**Interrogate historical data**]

2D   **The student understands contemporary American culture.**

Therefore, the student is able to:

7-12 Evaluate the desegregation of education and assess its role in the creation of private white academies. [**Analyze multiple causation**]

9-12 Analyze how social change and renewed ethnic diversity has affected artistic expression and popular culture. [**Analyze cause-and-effect relationships**]

7-12 Explain the influence of media on contemporary American culture. [**Explain historical continuity and change**]

5-12 Explore the international influence of American culture. [**Draw upon visual and musical sources**]

5-12 Explain the reasons for the increased popularity of professional sports and examine the influence of spectator sports on popular culture. [**Reconstruct patterns of historical succession and duration**]

2E   **The student understands how a democratic polity debates social issues and mediates between individual or group rights and the common good.**

Therefore, the student is able to:

9-12 Evaluate to what degree affirmative action policies have achieved their goals and assess the current debate over affirmative action. [**Consider multiple perspectives**]

5-12 Explore the range of women's organizations, the changing goals of the women's movement, and the issues currently dividing women. [**Explain historical continuity and change**]

9-12   Explain the evolution of government support for the assertion of rights by the disabled. [**Reconstruct patterns of historical succession and duration**]

7-12   Evaluate the continuing grievances of racial and ethnic minorities and their recurrent reference to the nation's charter documents. [**Explain historical continuity and change**]

9-12   Examine the emergence of the Gay Liberation Movement and evaluate the invocation of democratic ideals concerning the civil rights of gay Americans. [**Consider multiple perspectives**]

9-12   Evaluate the continuing struggle for *e pluribus unum* amid debates over national vs. group identity, group rights vs. individual rights, multiculturalism, and bilingual education. [**Consider multiple perspectives**]

4

World History Standards for Grades 5-12

Approaches to World History

These guidelines call for a minimum of three years of World History instruction between grades 5 and 12. They also advocate courses that are genuinely global in scope. The Standards set forth in this chapter are intended as a guide and resource for schools in developing or improving World History courses. **They are not meant to serve as a prescribed syllabus or day-to-day course outline.** Teachers may wish to explore a number of different conceptual and organizational approaches to curriculum design. How much time should be devoted to particular periods, regions, or historical issues? What subject matter should be emphasized and what topics excluded? What is the proper balance between generalization and detail? Different teachers and schools will arrive at different answers to these questions. The Standards presented here are compatible with and will support a variety of curricular frameworks. Among possible approaches, four are perhaps most widely used:

Comparative civilizations. This approach invites students to investigate the histories of major civilizations one after another. A single civilization may be studied over a relatively long period of time, and ideas and institutions of different civilizations may be compared. This framework emphasizes continuities within cultural traditions rather than historical connections between civilizations or wider global developments.

Civilizations in global context. This conceptualization strikes a balance between the study of particular civilizations and attention to developments resulting from interactions among societies. This approach may also emphasize contacts between urban civilizations and non-urban peoples such as pastoral nomads. Students are likely to investigate the major civilized traditions in less detail than in the comparative civilizations model but will devote relatively more time to studying the varieties of historical experience world-wide.

Interregional history. Teachers have been experimenting with this model in recent years. Here students focus their study on broad patterns of change that may transcend the boundaries of nations or civilizations. Students investigate in comparative perspective events occurring in different parts of the world *at the same time*, as well as developments that involve peoples of different languages and cultural traditions in shared experience. This approach includes study of particular societies and civilizations but gives special attention to larger fields of human interaction, such as the Indian Ocean basin, the "Pacific rim," or even the world as a whole. In comparison with the other two models, this one puts less emphasis on long-term development of ideas and institutions within civilizations and more on large-scale forces of social, cultural, and economic change.

Thematic history. Here students identify and explore particular historical issues or problems over determined periods of time. For example, one unit of study might be concerned with urbanization in different societies from ancient to modern times, a second with slavery through the ages, and a third with nationalism in modern times. This approach allows students to explore a single issue in great depth, often one that has contemporary relevance. Teachers may want to consider, however, the hazards of separating or isolating particular phenomena from the wider historical context of the times. A useful compromise may be to choose a range of themes for emphasis but then weave them into chronological study based on one of the other three models.

A Note on Terminology

These standards employ certain terms that may be unfamiliar to some readers. **Southwest Asia** is used to designate the area commonly referred to as the Middle East, that is, the region extending from the eastern coast of the Mediterranean Sea to Afghanistan, including Turkey and the Arabian Peninsula. Middle East is used only in certain standards pertaining to the 20th century. The term **Afro-Eurasia** appears occasionally to express the geographical context of historical developments that embrace both Africa and Eurasia. The secular designations **BCE** (before the Common Era) and **CE** (in the Common Era) are used throughout the Standards in place of BC and AD. This change in no way alters the conventional Gregorian calendar.

Overview

Era 1: The Beginnings of Human Society

Standard 1: The biological and cultural processes that gave rise to the earliest human communities

Standard 2: The processes that led to the emergence of agricultural societies around the world

Era 2: Early Civilizations and the Emergence of Pastoral Peoples, 4000-1000 BCE

Standard 1: The major characteristics of civilization and how civilizations emerged in Mesopotamia, Egypt, and the Indus valley

Standard 2: How agrarian societies spread and new states emerged in the third and second millennia BCE

Standard 3: The political, social, and cultural consequences of population movements and militarization in Eurasia in the second millennium BCE

Standard 4: Major trends in Eurasia and Africa from 4000-1000 BCE

Era 3: Classical Traditions, Major Religions, and Giant Empires, 1000 BCE-300 CE

Standard 1: Innovation and change from 1000-600 BCE: horses, ships, iron, and monotheistic faith

Standard 2: The emergence of Aegean civilization and how interrelations developed among peoples of the eastern Mediterranean and Southwest Asia, 600-200 BCE

Standard 3: How major religions and large-scale empires arose in the Mediterranean basin, China, and India, 500 BCE-300 CE

Standard 4: The development of early agrarian civilizations in Mesoamerica

Standard 5: Major global trends from 1000 BCE-300 CE

Era 4: Expanding Zones of Exchange and Encounter, 300-1000 CE

Standard 1: Imperial crises and their aftermath, 300-700 CE

Standard 2: Causes and consequences of the rise of Islamic civilization in the 7th-10th centuries

Standard 3: Major developments in East Asia and Southeast Asia in the era of the Tang dynasty, 600-900 CE

Standard 4: The search for political, social, and cultural redefinition in Europe, 500-1000 CE

Standard 5: The development of agricultural societies and new states in tropical Africa and Oceania

Standard 6: The rise of centers of civilization in Mesoamerica and Andean South America in the first millennium CE

Standard 7: Major global trends from 300-1000 CE

Era 5: Intensified Hemispheric Interactions, 1000-1500 CE

Standard 1: The maturing of an interregional system of communication, trade, and cultural exchange in an era of Chinese economic power and Islamic expansion

Standard 2: The redefining of European society and culture, 1000-1300 CE

Standard 3: The rise of the Mongol empire and its consequences for Eurasian peoples, 1200-1350

Standard 4: The growth of states, towns, and trade in Sub-Saharan Africa between the 11th and 15th centuries

Standard 5: Patterns of crisis and recovery in Afro-Eurasia, 1300-1450

Standard 6: The expansion of states and civilizations in the Americas, 1000-1500

Standard 7: Major global trends from 1000-1500 CE

Era 6: The Emergence of the First Global Age, 1450-1770

Standard 1: How the transoceanic interlinking of all major regions of the world from 1450-1600 led to global transformations

Standard 2: How European society experienced political, economic, and cultural transformations in an age of global intercommunication, 1450-1750

Standard 3: How large territorial empires dominated much of Eurasia between the 16th and 18th centuries

Standard 4: Economic, political, and cultural interrelations among peoples of Africa, Europe, and the Americas, 1500-1750

Standard 5: Transformations in Asian societies in the era of European expansion

Standard 6: Major global trends from 1450-1770

Era 7: An Age of Revolutions, 1750-1914

Standard 1: The causes and consequences of political revolutions in the late 18th and early 19th centuries

Standard 2: The causes and consequences of the agricultural and industrial revolutions, 1700-1850

Standard 3: The transformation of Eurasian societies in an era of global trade and rising European power, 1750-1870

Standard 4: Patterns of nationalism, state-building, and social reform in Europe and the Americas, 1830-1914

Standard 5: Patterns of global change in the era of Western military and economic domination, 1800-1914

Standard 6: Major global trends from 1750-1914

Era 8: A Half-Century of Crisis and Achievement, 1900-1945

Standard 1: Reform, revolution, and social change in the world economy of the early century

Standard 2: The causes and global consequences of World War I

Standard 3: The search for peace and stability in the 1920s and 1930s

Standard 4: The causes and global consequences of World War II

Standard 5: Major global trends from 1900 to the end of World War II

Era 9: The 20th Century Since 1945: Promises and Paradoxes

Standard 1: How post-World War II reconstruction occurred, new international power relations took shape, and colonial empires broke up

Standard 2: The search for community, stability, and peace in an interdependent world

Standard 3: Major global trends since World War II

World History Across the Eras

Standard 1: Long-term changes and recurring patterns in world history

ERA 1

The Beginnings of Human Society

Giving Shape to World History

So far as we know, humanity's story began in Africa. For millions of years it was mainly a story of biological change. Then some hundreds of thousands of years ago our early ancestors began to form and manipulate useful tools. Eventually they mastered speech. Unlike most other species, early humans gained the capacity to learn from one another and transmit knowledge from one generation to the next. The first great experiments in creating culture were underway. Among early hunter-gatherers cultural change occurred at an imperceptible speed. But as human populations rose and new ideas and techniques appeared, the pace of change accelerated. Moreover, human history became global at a very early date. In the long period from human beginnings to the rise of the earliest civilization two world-circling developments stand in relief:

The Peopling of the Earth: The first great global event was the peopling of the earth and the astonishing story of how communities of hunters, foragers, or fishers adapted creatively and continually to a variety of contrasting, changing environments in Africa, Eurasia, Australia, and the Americas.

The Agricultural Revolution: Over a period of several thousand years and as a result of countless small decisions, humans learned how to grow crops, domesticate plants, and raise animals. The earliest agricultural settlements probably arose in Southwest Asia, but the agricultural revolution spread round the world. Human population began to soar relative to earlier times. Communities came into regular contact with one another over longer distances, cultural patterns became far more complex, and opportunities for innovation multiplied.

Why Study This Era?

▶ To understand how the human species fully emerged out of biological evolution and cultural development is to understand in some measure what it means to be human.

▶ The common past that all students share begins with the peopling of our planet and the spread of settled societies around the world.

▶ The cultural forms, social institutions, and practical techniques that emerged in the Neolithic age laid the foundations for the emergence of all early civilizations.

▶ Study of human beginnings throws into relief fundamental problems of history that pertain to all eras: the possibilities and limitations of human control over their environment; why human groups accept, modify, or reject innovations; the variety of social and cultural paths that different societies may take; and the acceleration of social change through time.

Overview

Standard 1: The biological and cultural processes that gave rise to the earliest human communities

Standard 2: The processes that led to the emergence of agricultural societies around the world

---

STANDARD 1 | The biological and cultural processes that gave rise to the earliest human communities.

1A **The student understands early hominid development in Africa.**

Therefore, the student is able to:

> *5-12* Infer from archaeological evidence the characteristics of early African hunter-gatherer communities, including tool kits, shelter, diet, and use of fire. [**Interrogate historical data**]

> *7-12* Describe types of evidence and methods of investigation that anthropologists, archaeologists, and other scholars have used to reconstruct early human evolution and cultural development. [**Interrogate historical data**]

> *7-12* Trace the approximate chronology, sequence, and territorial range of early hominid evolution in Africa from the *Australopithecines* to *Homo erectus*. [**Establish temporal order in constructing historical narratives**]

1B **The student understands how human communities populated the major regions of the world and adapted to a variety of environments.**

Therefore, the student is able to:

> *7-12* Analyze current and past theories regarding the emergence of *Homo sapiens sapiens* and the processes by which human ancestors migrated from Africa to the other major world regions. [**Evaluate major debates among historians**]

> *5-12* Compare the way of life of hunter-gatherer communities in Africa, the Americas, and western Eurasia and explain how such communities in different parts of the world responded creatively to local environments. [**Compare and contrast differing behaviors and institutions**]

> *7-12* Assess theories regarding the development of human language and its relationship to the development of culture. [**Evaluate major debates among historians**]

> *5-12* Infer from archaeological evidence the characteristics of Cro-Magnon hunter-gatherer communities of western Eurasia including tool kits, shelter, clothing, ritual life, aesthetic values, relations between men and women, and trade among communities. [**Analyze cause-and-effect relationships and multiple causation**]

> *7-12* Analyze possible links between environmental conditions associated with the last Ice Age and changes in the economy, culture, and organization of human communities. [**Analyze cause-and-effect relationships and multiple causation**]

| STANDARD 2 | The processes that led to the emergence of agricultural societies around the world. |

2A **The student understands how and why humans established settled communities and experimented with agriculture.**

Therefore, the student is able to:

5-12   Infer from archaeological evidence the technology, social organization, and cultural life of settled farming communities in Southwest Asia. [**Draw upon visual sources**]

9-12   Describe types of evidence and methods of investigation by which scholars have reconstructed the early history of domestication and agricultural settlement. [**Appreciate historical perspectives**]

9-12   Describe leading theories to explain how and why human groups domesticated wild grains as well as cattle, sheep, goats, and pigs after the last Ice Age. [**Evaluate major debates among historians**]

7-12   Identify areas in Southwest Asia and the Nile valley where early farming communities probably appeared and analyze the environmental and technological factors that made possible experiments with farming in these regions. [**Incorporate multiple causation**]

2B **The student understands how agricultural societies developed around the world.**

Therefore, the student is able to:

5-12   Analyze differences between hunter-gatherer and agrarian communities in economy, social organization, and quality of living. [**Compare and contrast differing behaviors and institutions**]

5-12   Describe social, cultural, and economic characteristics of large agricultural settlements such as Çatal Hüyuk or Jericho. [**Obtain historical data**]

7-12   Analyze how peoples of West Africa, Europe, Southeast Asia, East Asia, and the Americas domesticated food plants and developed agricultural communities in response to local needs and conditions. [**Compare and contrast behaviors and institutions**]

7-12   Analyze archaeological evidence from agricultural village sites in Southwest Asia, North Africa, China, or Europe indicating the emergence of social class divisions, occupational specializations, and differences in the daily tasks that men and women performed. [**Hold interpretations of history as tentative**]

7-12   Assess archaeological evidence for long-distance trade in Southwest Asia. [**Draw upon visual sources**]

9-12   Assess archaeological evidence for the emergence of complex belief systems, including widespread worship of female deities. [**Interrogate historical data**]

ERA 2

Early Civilizations and the Emergence of Pastoral Peoples, 4000-1000 BCE

Giving Shape to World History

When farmers began to grow crops on the irrigated floodplain of Mesopotamia in Southwest Asia, they had no consciousness that they were embarking on a radically new experiment in human organization. The nearly rainless but abundantly watered valley of the lower Tigris and Euphrates rivers was an environment capable of supporting far larger concentrations of population and much greater cultural complexity than could the hill country where agriculture first emerged. Shortly after 4000 BCE, a rich culture and economy based on walled cities was appearing along the banks of the two rivers. The rise of civilization in Mesopotamia marked the beginning of 3,000 years of far-reaching transformations that affected peoples across wide areas of Eurasia and Africa.

The four standards in this era present a general chronological progression of developments in world history from 4000 to 1000 BCE. Two major patterns of change may be discerned that unite the developments of this period.

Early Civilizations and the Spread of Agricultural Societies: Societies exhibiting the major characteristics of civilization spread widely during these millennia. Four great floodplain civilizations appeared, first in Mesopotamia, shortly after in the Nile valley, and from about 2500 BCE in the Indus valley. These three civilizations mutually influenced one another and came to constitute a single region of intercommunication and trade. The fourth civilization arose in the Yellow River valley of northwestern China in the second millennium BCE. As agriculture continued to spread, urban centers also emerged on rain-watered lands, notably in Syria and on the island of Crete. Finally, expanding agriculture and long-distance trade were the foundations of increasingly complex societies in the Aegean Sea basin and western Europe. During this same era, it must be remembered, much of the world's population lived in small farming communities and hunted or foraged. These peoples were no less challenged than city-dwellers to adapt continually and creatively to changing environmental and social conditions.

Pastoral Peoples and Population Movements: In this era pastoralism—the practice of herding animals as a society's primary source of food—made it possible for larger communities than ever before to inhabit the semi-arid steppes and deserts of Eurasia and Africa. Consequently, pastoral peoples began play an important role in world history. In the second millennium BCE migrations of pastoral folk emanating from the steppes of Central Asia contributed to a quickening pace of change across the entire region from Europe and the Mediterranean basin to India. Some societies became more highly militarized, new kingdoms appeared, and languages of the Indo-European family became much more widely spoken.

Why Study This Era?

◗ This is the period when civilizations appeared, shaping all subsequent eras of history. Students must consider the nature of civilization as both a particular way of organizing society and a historical phenomenon subject to transformation and collapse.

◗ In this era many of the world's most fundamental inventions, discoveries, institutions, and techniques appeared. All subsequent civilizations would be built on these achievements.

◗ Early civilizations were not self-contained but developed their distinctive characteristics partly as a result of interactions with other peoples. In this era students will learn about the deep roots of encounter and exchange among societies.

◗ The era introduces students to one of the most enduring themes in history, the dynamic interplay, for good or ill, between the agrarian civilizations and pastoral peoples of the great grasslands.

Overview

Standard 1: The major characteristics of civilization and how civilizations emerged in Mesopotamia, Egypt, and the Indus valley

Standard 2: How agrarian societies spread and new states emerged in the third and second millennia BCE

Standard 3: The political, social, and cultural consequences of population movements and militarization in Eurasia in the second millennium BCE

Standard 4: Major trends in Eurasia and Africa from 4000 to 1000 BCE

STANDARD 1	The major characteristics of civilization and how civilizations emerged in Mesopotamia, Egypt and the Indus valley.

1A   The student understands how Mesopotamia, Egypt, and the Indus valley became centers of dense population, urbanization, and cultural innovation in the fourth and third millennia BCE.

Therefore, the student is able to:

5-12   Analyze how the natural environments of the Tigris-Euphrates, Nile, and Indus valleys shaped the early development of civilization. [**Compare and contrast differing sets of ideas**]

5-12   Compare the character of urban development in Mesopotamia, Egypt, and the Indus valley, including the emergence of social hierarchies and occupational specializations, as well as differences in the tasks that urban women and men performed. [**Compare and contrast differing values and institutions**]

5-12 Compare the forms of writing that developed in the three civilizations and how written records shaped political, legal, religious, and cultural life. [**Compare and contrast differing sets of ideas, values, and institutions**]

7-12 Compare the development of religious and ethical belief systems in the three civilizations and how they legitimized the political and social order. [**Compare and contrast differing sets of ideas**]

9-12 Analyze the character of government and military institutions in Egypt and Mesopotamia and ways in which central authorities commanded the labor services and tax payments of peasant farmers. [**Consider multiple perspectives**]

9-12 Describe architectural, artistic, literary, technological, and scientific achievements of these civilizations and relate these achievements to economic and social life. [**Analyze cause-and-effect relationships**]

1B   The student understands how commercial and cultural interactions contributed to change in the Tigris-Euphrates, Indus, and Nile regions.

Therefore, the student is able to:

5-12 Analyze the importance of trade in Mesopotamian civilization of the fourth and third millennia and describe the networks of commercial exchange that connected various regions of Southwest Asia. [**Interrogate historical data**]

5-12 Assess the importance of commercial, cultural, and political connections between Egypt and peoples of Nubia along the upper Nile. [**Identify issues and problems in the past**]

7-12 Trace the network of trade routes connecting Egypt, Mesopotamia, and the Indus valley in the third millennium and assess the economic and cultural significance of those commercial connections. [**Analyze cause-and-effect relationships**]

STANDARD 2   How agrarian societies spread and new states emerged in the third and second millennia BCE.

2A   The student understands how civilization emerged in northern China in the second millennium BCE.

Therefore, the student is able to:

5-12 Explain the fundamentals of bronze-making technology and assess the uses and significance of bronze tools, weapons, and luxury goods in the third and second millennia BCE. [**Analyze cause-and-effect relationships**]

5-12 Compare the climate and geography of the Huang He (Yellow River) valley with the natural environments of Mesopotamia, Egypt, and the Indus valley. [**Clarify information on the geographic setting**]

9-12 Describe royal government under the Shang Dynasty and the development of social hierarchy, religious institutions, and writing. [**Appreciate historical perspectives**]

    5-12   Infer from archaeological or written evidence the character of early Chinese urban societies and compare these centers with cities of Mesopotamia or the Indus valley. [**Formulate historical questions**]

    9-12   Assess the part that Chinese peasants played in sustaining the wealth and power of the Shang political centers. [**Consider multiple perspectives**]

2B   **The student understands how new centers of agrarian society arose in the third and second millennia BCE.**

Therefore, the student is able to:

    5-12   Describe the relationship between the development of plow technology and the emergence of new agrarian societies in Southwest Asia, the Mediterranean basin, and temperate Europe. [**Analyze cause-and-effect relationships**]

    7-12   Analyze how an urban civilization emerged on Crete and evaluate its cultural achievements. [**Marshal evidence of antecedent circumstances**]

    9-12   Explain the development of commercial communities in such Mediterranean cities as Byblos and Ugarit and analyze the cultural significance of expanding commercial exchange among peoples of Southwest Asia, Egypt, and the Aegean Sea. [**Reconstruct patterns of historical succession and duration**]

    5-12   Infer from the evidence of megalithic stone building at Stonehenge and other centers the emergence of complex agrarian societies in temperate Europe. [**Draw upon visual sources**]

    9-12   Analyze evidence for the growth of agricultural societies in tropical West Africa and Southeast Asia in the second millennium BCE. [**Interrogate historical data**]

STANDARD 3	The political, social, and cultural consequences of population movements and militarization in Eurasia in the second millennium BCE.

3A   **The student understands how population movements from western and Central Asia affected peoples of India, Southwest Asia, and the Mediterranean region.**

Therefore, the student is able to:

    5-12   Define pastoralism as a specialized way of life and explain how the climate and geography of Central Asia were linked to the rise of pastoral societies on the steppes. [**Analyze multiple causation**]

    7-12   Identify the probable geographic homeland of speakers of early Indo-European languages and trace the spread of Indo-European languages from north of the Black and Caspian seas to other parts of Eurasia. [**Reconstruct patterns of historical succession and duration**]

    5-12   Explain the concept of kinship as the basis of social organization among pastoral peoples and compare the structure of kinship-based societies with that of agrarian states. [**Compare and contrast differing behaviors and institutions**]

9-12 Describe major characteristics of economy, social relations, and political authority among pastoral peoples and analyze why women tended to experience greater social equality with men in pastoral communities than in agrarian societies of Eurasia. [Identify issues and problems in the past]

3B **The student understands the social and cultural effects that militarization and the emergence of new kingdoms had on peoples of Southwest Asia and Egypt in the second millennium BCE.**

Therefore, the student is able to:

5-12 Analyze ways in which chariot transport and warfare affected Southwest Asian societies. [Analyze cause-and-effect relationships]

7-12 Analyze the origins of the Hittite people and their empire in Anatolia and assess Hittite political and cultural achievements. [Marshal evidence of antecedent circumstances]

7-12 Describe the spread of Egyptian power into Nubia and Southwest Asia under the New Kingdom and assess the factors that made Egyptian expansion possible. [Analyze multiple causation]

9-12 Explain the religious ideas of Akhenaton (Amenhotep IV) and assess the viewpoint that Atonism was an early form of monotheism. [Interrogate historical data]

3C **The student understands how urban society expanded in the Aegean region in the era of Mycenaean dominance.**

Therefore, the student is able to:

5-12 Describe the political and social organization of the Mycenaean Greeks as revealed in the archaeological and written record. [Interrogate historical data]

7-12 Assess the cultural influences of Egypt, Minoan Crete, and Southwest Asian civilizations on the Mycenaeans. [Analyze cause-and-effect relationships]

9-12 Analyze the impact of Mycenaean expansion and city-building on commerce and political life in the eastern Mediterranean. [Analyze cause-and-effect relationships]

3D **The student understands the development of new cultural patterns in northern India in the second millennium BCE.**

Therefore, the student is able to:

7-12 Infer from geographical and archaeological information why Indo-Aryan-speaking groups moved from Central Asia into India beginning in the second millennium. [Draw upon visual sources]

5-12 Analyze possible causes of the decline and collapse of Indus valley civilization. [Hypothesize the influence of the past]

9-12 Assess the early political, social, and cultural impact of Indo-Aryan movements on peoples of North India. [Analyze cause-and-effect relationships]

| STANDARD 4 | Major trends in Eurasia and Africa from 4000 to 1000 BCE. |

4 **The student understands major trends in Eurasia and Africa from 4000 to 1000 BCE.**

Therefore, the student is able to:

7-12 Explain the various criteria that have been used to define "civilization" and the fundamental differences between civilizations and other forms of social organization, notably hunter-gatherer bands, Neolithic agricultural societies, and pastoral nomadic societies. [**Consider multiple perspectives**]

5-12 Identify areas of Eurasia and Africa where cities and dense farming populations appeared between 4000 and 1000 BCE and analyze connections between the spread of agriculture and the acceleration of world population growth. [**Analyze cause-and-effect relationships**]

7-12 Compare conditions under which civilizations developed in Southwest Asia, the Nile valley, India, China, and the Eastern Mediterranean and analyze ways in which the emergence of civilizations represented a decisive transformation in human history. [**Draw comparisons across eras and regions**]

7-12 Explain why geographic, environmental, and economic conditions favored hunter-gatherer, pastoral, and small-scale agricultural ways of life rather than urban civilization in many parts of the world. [**Utilize mathematical and quantitative data**]

7-12 Describe fundamental inventions, discoveries, techniques, and institutions that appeared during this period and assess the significance of bronze technology for economic, cultural, and political life. [**Interrogate historical data**]

9-12 Analyze connections between the cultural achievements of early civilizations and the development of state authority, aristocratic power, taxation systems, and institutions of coerced labor, including slavery. [**Analyze cause-and-effect relationships**]

5-12 Describe how new ideas, products, techniques, and institutions spread from one region to another and analyze conditions under which peoples assimilated or rejected new things or adapted them to prevailing cultural traditions. [**Analyze the importance of ideas**]

7-12 Define "patriarchal society" and analyze ways in which the legal and customary position of aristocratic, urban, or peasant women may have changed in early civilizations. [**Employ quantitative analyses**]

9-12 Analyze the role of pastoral peoples in the history of Eurasia and Africa up to 1000 BCE and explain why relations between herding and agrarian societies tended to involve both conflict and mutual dependence. [**Draw comparisons across eras and regions**]

ERA 3

Classical Traditions, Major Religions, and Giant Empires, 1000 BCE-300 CE

Giving Shape to World History

By 1000 BCE urban civilizations of the Eastern Hemisphere were no longer confined to a few irrigated river plains. World population was growing, interregional trade networks were expanding, and towns and cities were appearing where only farming villages or nomad camps had existed before. Iron-making technology had increasing impact on economy and society. Contacts among diverse societies of Eurasia and Africa were intensifying, and these had profound consequences in the period from 1000 BCE to 300 CE. The pace of change was quickening in the Americas as well. If we stand back far enough to take in the global scene, three large-scale patterns of change stand out. These developments can be woven through the study of particular regions and societies as presented in Standards 1-5 below.

Classical Civilizations Defined: The civilizations of the irrigated river valleys were spreading to adjacent regions, and new centers of urban life and political power were appearing in rain-watered lands. Several civilizations were attaining their classical definitions, that is, they were developing institutions, systems of thought, and cultural styles that would influence neighboring peoples and endure for centuries.

Major Religions Emerge: Judaism, Christianity, Buddhism, Brahmanism/Hinduism, Confucianism, and Daoism all appeared in this period as systems of belief capable of stabilizing and enriching human relations across large areas of the world and providing avenues of cultural interchange between one region and another. Each of these religions united peoples of diverse political and ethnic identities. Religions also, often enough, divided groups into hostile camps and gave legitimacy to war or social repression.

Giant Empires Appear: Multi-ethnic empires became bigger than ever before and royal bureaucracies more effective at organizing and taxing ordinary people in the interests of the state. Empire building in this era also created much larger spheres of economic and cultural interaction. Near the end of the period the Roman and Han empires together embraced a huge portion of the hemisphere, and caravans and ships were relaying goods from one extremity of Eurasia to the other.

Why Study This Era?

▶ The classical civilizations of this age established institutions and defined values and styles that endured for many centuries and that continue to influence our lives today.

▶ Six of the world's major faiths and ethical systems emerged in this period and set forth their fundamental teachings.

▶ Africa and Eurasia together moved in the direction of forming a single world of human interchange in this era as a result of trade, migrations, empire-building, missionary activity, and the diffusion of skills and ideas. These interactions had profound consequences for all the major civilizations and all subsequent periods of world history.

▶ This was a formative era for many fundamental institutions and ideas in world history, such as universalist religion, monotheism, the bureaucratic empire, the city-state, and the relation of technology to social change. Students' explorations in the social sciences, literature, and contemporary affairs will be enriched by understanding such basic concepts as these.

▶ This era presents rich opportunities for students to compare empires, religions, social systems, art styles, and other aspects of the past, thus sharpening their understanding and appreciation of the varieties of human experience.

Overview

Standard 1: Innovation and change from 1000-600 BCE: horses, ships, iron, and monotheistic faith

Standard 2: The emergence of Aegean civilization and how interrelations developed among peoples of the eastern Mediterranean and Southwest Asia, 600-200 BCE

Standard 3: How major religions and large-scale empires arose in the Mediterranean basin, China, and India, 500 BCE-300 CE

Standard 4: The development of early agrarian civilizations in Mesoamerica

Standard 5: Major global trends from 1000 BCE-300 CE

STANDARD 1	**Innovation and change from 1000-600 BCE: horses, ships, iron, and monotheistic faith.**

1A **The student understands state-building, trade, and migrations that led to increasingly complex interrelations among peoples of the Mediterranean basin and Southwest Asia.**

Therefore, the student is able to:

7-12 Explain the fundamentals of iron-making technology and analyze the early significance of iron tools and weapons in Southwest Asia and the Mediterranean region. [**Analyze cause-and-effect relationships**]

7-12 Describe the extent of the Assyrian and New Babylonian empires and assess the sources of their power and wealth. [**Obtain historical data**]

5-12 Explain the patterns of Phoenician trade, political organization, and culture in the Mediterranean basin. [**Reconstruct patterns of historical succession and duration**]

5-12 Describe the emergence of Greek city-states in the Aegean region and the political, social, and legal character of the polis. [**Marshal evidence of antecedent circumstances**]

7-12 Analyze the factors that led Greeks to found colonies in the Mediterranean and Black Sea regions. [**Analyze multiple causation**]

9-12 Analyze the social and cultural effects of the spread of alphabetic writing in Southwest Asia and the Mediterranean basin. [**Analyze cause-and-effect relationships**]

1B   The student understands the emergence of Judaism and the historical significance of the Hebrew kingdoms.

Therefore, the student is able to:

5-12 Explain the fundamental teachings and practices of Judaism and compare Jewish monotheism with polytheistic religions of Southwest Asia. [**Compare and contrast differing sets of ideas**]

7-12 Explain the development of the Jewish kingdoms and analyze how the Jews maintained religious and cultural traditions despite the destruction of these kingdoms. [**Reconstruct patterns of historical succession and duration**]

9-12 Assess the significance of the Babylonian captivity for the survival of Judaism. [**Appreciate historical perspectives**]

9-12 Analyze the significance of the Jewish diaspora for the transmission of Judaism in the Mediterranean region and Southwest Asia. [**Analyze cause-and-effect relationships**]

1C   The student understands how states developed in the upper Nile valley and Red Sea region and how iron technology contributed to the expansion of agricultural societies in Sub-Saharan Africa.

Therefore, the student is able to:

9-12 Assess the importance of political, commercial, and cultural relations between Egypt and Nubia/Kush. [**Analyze multiple causation**]

5-12 Analyze the effects of Nile valley trade and the decline of the New Kingdom as factors in the power of Kush in the first millennium BCE. [**Analyze cause-and-effect relationships**]

7-12 Evaluate the linguistic, architectural, and artistic achievements of Kush in the Meroitic period. [**Interrogate historical data**]

7-12 Analyze how Kushite and Assyrian invasions affected Egyptian society. [**Evidence multiple perspectives**]

7-12 Explain connections between maritime trade and the power of the kingdom of Aksum in Northeast Africa. [**Analyze cause-and-effect relationships**]

9-12 Describe the emergence of states south of the Sahara desert and appraise theories of how iron-working technology spread in West and East Africa. [**Evaluate major debates among historians**]

1D   **The student understands how pastoral nomadic peoples of Central Asia began to play an important role in world history.**

Therefore, the student is able to:

5-12   Explain the relationship between the mastery of horse riding on the steppes and the development of pastoral nomadism and cavalry warfare. [**Analyze cause-and-effect relationships**]

9-12   Analyze how the warrior states of the Scythians and the Xiongnu arose among pastoral nomadic peoples of Central Asia. [**Analyze multiple causation**]

7-12   Infer from archaeological or other evidence basic characteristics of Scythian or Xiongnu society and culture. [**Formulate historical questions**]

5-12   Analyze why relations between pastoral nomadic peoples of Central Asia and major agrarian states of Eurasia involved both conflict and economic interdependence. [**Analyze cause-and-effect relationships**]

STANDARD 2	The emergence of Aegean civilization and how interrelations developed among peoples of the eastern Mediterranean and Southwest Asia, 600-200 BCE.

2A   **The student understands the achievements and limitations of the democratic institutions that developed in Athens and other Aegean city-states.**

Therefore, the student is able to:

5-12   Compare Athenian democracy with the military aristocracy of Sparta. [**Compare and contrast differing sets of ideas, values, and institutions**]

5-12   Explain hierarchical relationships within Greek society and analyze the civic, economic, and social tasks that men and women of different classes performed. [**Appreciate historical perspectives**]

7-12   Describe the changing political institutions of Athens in the 6th and 5th centuries BCE and analyze the influence of political thought on public life. [**Reconstruct patterns of historical succession and duration**]

9-12   Assess the importance of Greek ideas about democracy and citizenship for the development of Western political thought and institutions. [**Hypothesize the influence of the past**]

2B   **The student understands the major cultural achievements of Greek civilization.**

Therefore, the student is able to:

5-12   Identify the major characteristics of Hellenic architecture and sculpture and assess the ways in which architecture, sculpture, and painting expressed or influenced social values and attitudes. [**Draw upon visual sources**]

7-12   Identify major Greek myths and dramas and assess how they reflected social values and attitudes. [**Formulate historical questions**]

9-12   Explain the leading ideas of Socrates, Plato, Aristotle, Herodotus, and other philosophers and historians. [**Appreciate historical perspective**]

2C   **The student understands the development of the Persian (Achaemenid) empire and the consequences of its conflicts with the Greeks.**

Therefore, the student is able to:

7-12   Explain the founding, expansion, and political organization of the Persian empire. [**Reconstruct patterns of historical succession and duration**]

5-12   Analyze the major events of the wars between Persia and the Greek city-states and the reasons why the Persians failed to conquer the Aegean region. [**Analyze multiple causation**]

9-12   Describe the basic teachings of Zoroastrianism. [**Interrogate historical data**]

2D   **The student understands Alexander of Macedon's conquests and the interregional character of Hellenistic society and culture.**

Therefore, the student is able to:

7-12   Analyze the rise of Macedonia under Philip II and explain the campaigns and scope and success of Alexander's imperial conquests. [**Reconstruct patterns of historical succession and duration**]

5-12   Assess Alexander's achievements as a military and political leader and analyze why the empire broke up into successor kingdoms. [**Analyze cause-and-effect relationships**]

7-12   Evaluate major achievements of Hellenistic art, philosophy, science, and political thought. [**Appreciate historical perspectives**]

9-12   Assess the character of Greek impact on Southwest Asia and Egypt in the 4th and 3rd centuries and the influence of Greek, Egyptian, Persian, and Indian cultural traditions on one another. [**Analyze cause-and-effect relationships**]

9-12   Analyze the significance of the interaction of Greek and Jewish traditions for the emergence of both Rabbinic Judaism and early Christianity. [**Reconstruct patterns of historical succession and duration**]

| **STANDARD 3** | How major religions and large-scale empires arose in the Mediterranean basin, China, and India, 500 BCE–300 CE. |

3A   **The student understands the causes and consequences of the unification of the Mediterranean basin under Roman rule.**

Therefore, the student is able to:

> *5-12*   Assess the contributions of the Etruscans and the western Greek colonies to the development of Roman society and culture. [**Analyze multiple causation**]

> *5-12*   Describe the political and social institutions of the Roman Republic and analyze why Rome was transformed from republic to empire. [**Analyze cause-and-effect relationships**]

> *9-12*   Describe the major phases in the expansion of the empire through the 1st century CE. [**Reconstruct patterns of historical succession and duration**]

> *9-12*   Assess ways in which imperial rule over a vast area transformed Roman society, economy, and culture. [**Analyze cause-and-effect relationships**]

> *7-12*   Analyze how Roman unity contributed to the growth of trade among the lands of the Mediterranean basin and assess the importance of Roman commercial connections by land or sea with Sub-Saharan Africa, India, and East Asia. [**Interrogate historical data**]

> *7-12*   Evaluate the major legal, artistic, architectural, technological, and literary achievements of the Romans and the influence of Hellenistic cultural traditions on Roman Europe. [**Appreciate historical perspectives**]

3B   **The student understands the emergence of Christianity in the context of the Roman Empire.**

Therefore, the student is able to:

> *5-12*   Describe the lives of Jesus and Paul and explain the fundamental teachings of Christianity. [**Appreciate historical perspectives**]

> *5-12*   Analyze how Christianity spread widely in the Roman Empire. [**Analyze multiple causation**]

> *9-12*   Trace the extent and consequences of Christian expansion in Asia, Africa, and Europe to the 4th century. [**Reconstruct patterns of historical succession and duration**]

3C   **The student understands how China became unified under the early imperial dynasties.**

Therefore, the student is able to:

> *7-12*   Assess the significance of the Zhou dynasty for the development of imperial rule and the concept of the Mandate of Heaven. [**Analyze cause-and-effect relationships**]

5-12 Assess the policies and achievements of the Qin emperor Shi Huangdi in establishing a unified imperial realm. [**Evaluate the implementation of a decision**]

9-12 Analyze the political and ideological contributions of the Han to the development of the imperial bureaucratic state and the expansion of the empire. [**Analyze cause-and-effect relationships**]

7-12 Evaluate the literary, artistic, and technological achievements of the Han dynasty. [**Appreciate historical perspectives**]

7-12 Analyze the importance of iron technology and family division of labor on the expansion of agriculture and the southeastward migration of Chinese farmers. [**Analyze multiple causation**]

5-12 Analyze the commercial and cultural significance of the trans-Eurasian "silk roads" in the period of the Han and Roman empires. [**Interrogate historical data**]

5-12 Describe the life of Confucius and explain comparatively the fundamental teachings of Confucianism and Daoism. [**Compare and contrast differing sets of ideas**]

3D   The student understands religious and cultural developments in India in the era of the Gangetic states and the Mauryan Empire.

Therefore, the student is able to:

7-12 Explain the major beliefs and practices of Brahmanism in India and how they evolved into early Hinduism. [**Appreciate historical perspectives**]

5-12 Describe the life and teachings of the Buddha and explain ways in which those teachings were a response to the Brahmanic system. [**Analyze cause-and-effect relationships**]

9-12 Explain the growth of the Mauryan Empire in the context of rivalries among Indian states. [**Consider multiple perspectives**]

5-12 Evaluate the achievements of the emperor Ashoka and assess his contribution to the expansion of Buddhism in India. [**Evaluate the implementation of a decision**]

9-12 Analyze how Brahmanism responded to the social, political, and theological challenges posed by Buddhism and other reform movements. [**Analyze cause-and-effect relationships**]

7-12 Analyze how Buddhism spread in India, Ceylon, and Central Asia. [**Analyze multiple causation**]

STANDARD 4	The development of early agrarian civilizations in Mesoamerica.

4   The student understands the achievements of Olmec civilization.

Therefore, the student is able to:

5-12 Analyze the relationship between maize cultivation and the development of complex societies in Mesoamerica. [**Analyze cause-and-effect relationships**]

7-12   Interpret archaeological evidence for the development of Olmec civilization in the second and first millennia BCE. [**Formulate historical questions**]

5-12   Evaluate major Olmec contributions to Mesoamerican civilization, including the calendar, glyphic writing, sculpture, and monumental building. [**Appreciate historical perspectives**]

9-12   Assess Olmec cultural influence on the emergence of civilization in the Oaxaca valley and other regions. [**Analyze multiple causation**]

STANDARD 5	Major global trends from 1000 BCE–300 CE.

5   **The student understands major global trends from 1000 BCE to 300 CE.**

Therefore, the student is able to:

7-12   Define the concept of "classical civilizations" and assess the enduring importance of ideas, institutions, and art forms that emerged in the classical periods. [**Analyze the importance of ideas**]

7-12   Analyze the significance of military power, state bureaucracy, legal codes, belief systems, written languages, and communications and trade networks in the development of large regional empires. [**Interrogate historical data**]

5-12   Compare institutions of slavery or other forms of coerced labor in the Han empire, the Maurya empire, the Greek city-states, and the Roman empire. [**Draw comparisons across eras and regions**]

5-12   Analyze how new religious or ethical systems contributed to cultural integration of large regions of Afro-Eurasia. [**Analyze cause-and-effect relationships**]

7-12   Explain the significance of Greek or Hellenistic ideas and cultural styles in the history of the Mediterranean basin, Europe, Southwest Asia, and India. [**Analyze the importance of ideas**]

7-12   Analyze ways in which trade networks, merchant communities, state power, tributary systems of production, and other factors contributed to the economic integration of large regions of Afro-Eurasia. [**Employ quantitative analysis**]

9-12   Explain the fundamentals of iron metallurgy and assess the economic, cultural, and political significance of iron technology in Eurasia and Africa. [**Employ quantitative analysis**]

9-12   Identify patterns of social and cultural continuity in various societies and analyze ways in which peoples maintained traditions and resisted external challenges in the context of increasing interregional contacts. [**Draw comparisons across eras and regions**]

ERA 4

Expanding Zones of Exchange and Encounter, 300-1000 CE

Giving Shape to World History

Beginning about 300 CE almost the entire region of Eurasia and northern Africa experienced severe disturbances. By the 7th century, however, peoples of Eurasia and Africa entered a new period of more intensive interchange and cultural creativity. Underlying these developments was the growing sophistication of systems for moving people and goods here and there throughout the hemisphere—China's canals, trans-Saharan camel caravans, high-masted ships plying the Indian Ocean. These networks tied diverse peoples together across great distances. In Eurasia and Africa a single region of intercommunication was taking shape that ran from the Mediterranean to the China seas. A widening zone of interchange also characterized Mesoamerica.

A sweeping view of world history reveals three broad patterns of change that are particularly conspicuous in this era.

Islamic Civilization: One of the most dramatic developments of this 700-year period was the rise of Islam as both a new world religion and a civilized tradition encompassing an immense part of the Eastern Hemisphere. Commanding the central region of Afro-Eurasia, the Islamic empire of the Abbasid dynasty became in the 8th-10th-century period the principal intermediary for the exchange of goods, ideas, and technologies across the hemisphere.

Buddhist, Christian, and Hindu Traditions: Not only Islam but other major religions also spread widely during this 700-year era. Wherever these faiths were introduced, they carried with them a variety of cultural traditions, aesthetic ideas, and ways of organizing human endeavor. Each of them also embraced peoples of all classes and diverse languages in common worship and moral commitment. Buddhism declined in India but took root in East and Southeast Asia. Christianity became the cultural foundation of a new civilization in western Europe. Hinduism flowered in India under the Gupta Empire and also exerted growing influence in the princely courts of Southeast Asia.

New Patterns of Society in East Asia, Europe, West Africa, Oceania, and Mesoamerica: The third conspicuous pattern, continuing from the previous era, was the process of population growth, urbanization, and flowering of culture in new areas. The 4th to 6th centuries witnessed serious upheavals in Eurasia in connection with the breakup of the Roman and Han empires and the aggressive movements of pastoral peoples to the east, west, and south. By the 7th century, however, China was finding new unity and rising economic prosperity under the Tang. Japan emerged as a distinctive civilization. At the other end of the hemisphere Europe laid new foundations for political and social order. In West Africa towns flourished amid the rise of Ghana and the trans-Saharan gold trade. In both lower Africa and the Pacific basin migrant pioneers laid new foundations of agricultural societies. Finally, this era saw a remarkable growth of urban life in Mesoamerica in the age of the Maya.

Why Study This Era?

◗ In these seven centuries Buddhism, Christianity, Hinduism, and Islam spread far and wide beyond their lands of origin. These religions became established in regions where today they command the faith of millions.

◗ In this era the configuration of empires and kingdoms in the world changed dramatically. Why giant empires have fallen and others risen rapidly to take their place is an enduring question for all eras.

◗ In the early centuries of this era Christian Europe was marginal to the dense centers of population, production, and urban life of Eurasia and northern Africa. Students should understand this perspective but at the same time investigate the developments that made possible the rise of a new civilization in Europe after 1000 CE.

◗ In this era no sustained contact existed between the Eastern Hemisphere and the Americas. Peoples of the Americas did not share in the exchange and borrowing that stimulated innovations of all kinds in Eurasia and Africa. Therefore, students need to explore the conditions under which weighty urban civilizations arose in Mesoamerica in the first millennium CE.

Overview

Standard 1: Imperial crises and their aftermath, 300-700 CE

Standard 2: Causes and consequences of the rise of Islamic civilization in the 7th-10th centuries

Standard 3: Major developments in East Asia and Southeast Asia in the era of the Tang dynasty, 600-900 CE

Standard 4: The search for political, social, and cultural redefinition in Europe, 500-1000 CE

Standard 5: The development of agricultural societies and new states in tropical Africa and Oceania

Standard 6: The rise of centers of civilization in Mesoamerica and Andean South America in the first millennium CE

Standard 7: Major global trends from 300-1000 CE

| STANDARD 1 | Imperial crises and their aftermath, 300-700 CE. |

1A The student understands the decline of the Roman and Han empires.

Therefore, the student is able to:

5-12 Analyze various causes that historians have proposed to account for the decline of the Han and Roman empires. [**Evaluate major debates among historians**]

5-12 Trace the migrations and military movements of major pastoral nomadic groups into both the Roman Empire and China. [**Reconstruct patterns of historical succession and duration**]

7-12 Compare the consequences of these movements in China and the western part of the Roman Empire. [**Analyze cause-and-effect relationships**]

9-12 Analyze comparatively the collapse of the western part of the classical Roman Empire and the survival of the eastern part. [**Compare and contrast differing sets of ideas**]

9-12 Describe the consolidation of the Byzantine state after the breakup of the Roman Empire and assess how Byzantium transmitted ancient traditions and created a new Christian civilization. [**Reconstruct patterns of historical succession and duration**]

1B The student understands the expansion of Christianity and Buddhism beyond the lands of their origin.

Therefore, the student is able to:

5-12 Assess how Christianity and Buddhism won converts among culturally diverse peoples across wide areas of Afro-Eurasia. [**Demonstrate and explain the influence of ideas**]

7-12 Analyze the spread of Christianity and Buddhism in the context of change and crisis in the Roman and Han empires. [**Analyze cause-and-effect relationships**]

7-12 Analyze the importance of monasticism in the growth of Christianity and Buddhism and the participation of both men and women in monastic life and missionary activity. [**Compare and contrast differing values, behaviors, and institutions**]

1C The student understands the synthesis of Hindu civilization in India in the era of the Gupta Empire.

Therefore, the student is able to:

5-12 Describe fundamental features of the Hindu belief system as they emerged in the early first millennium CE. [**Appreciate historical perspectives**]

7-12 Explain the rise of the Gupta Empire and analyze factors that contributed to the empire's stability and economic prosperity. [**Analyze multiple causation**]

7-12 Analyze how Hinduism responded to the challenges of Buddhism and prevailed as the dominant faith in India. [**Reconstruct patterns of historical succession and duration**]

7-12 Analyze the basis of social relationships in India and compare the social and legal position of women and men during the Gupta era. [**Interrogate historical data**]

5-12 Evaluate Gupta achievements in art, literature, and mathematics. [**Appreciate historical perspective**]

9-12 Analyze the Gupta decline and the importance of Hun invasions in the empire's disintegration. [**Analyze multiple causation**]

1D **The student understands the expansion of Hindu and Buddhist traditions in Southeast Asia in the first millennium CE.**

Therefore, the student is able to:

5-12 Assess the relationship between long-distance trade of Indian and Malay peoples and the introduction of Hindu and Buddhist traditions in Southeast Asia. [**Analyze cause-and-effect relationships**]

7-12 Explain the impact of Indian civilization on state-building in mainland Southeast Asia and the Indonesian archipelago. [**Analyze cause-and-effect relationships**]

7-12 Evaluate monumental religious architecture exemplifying the spread of Buddhist and Hindu belief and practice in Southeast Asia. [**Draw upon visual sources**]

9-12 Explain how aspects of Buddhism and Hinduism were combined in Southeast Asian religious life. [**Interrogate historical data**]

STANDARD 2	Causes and consequences of the rise of Islamic civilization in the 7th-10th centuries.

2A **The student understands the emergence of Islam and how it spread in Southwest Asia, North Africa, and Europe.**

Therefore, the student is able to:

9-12 Analyze the political, social, and religious problems confronting the Byzantine and Sassanid Persian empires in the 7th century and the commercial role of Arabia in the Southwest Asian economy. [**Analyze multiple causation**]

5-12 Describe the life of Muhammad, the development of the early Muslim community, and the basic teachings and practices of Islam. [**Assess the importance of the individual**]

7-12 Explain how Muslim forces overthrew the Byzantines in Syria and Egypt and the Sassanids in Persia and Iraq. [**Interrogate historical data**]

5-12 Analyze how Islam spread in Southwest Asia and the Mediterranean region. [**Analyze the influence of ideas**]

9-12 Analyze how the Arab Caliphate became transformed into a Southwest Asian and Mediterranean empire under the Umayyad dynasty and explain how the Muslim community became divided into Sunnis and Shi'ites. [**Reconstruct patterns of historical succession and duration**]

7-12 Analyze Arab Muslim success in founding an empire stretching from western Europe to India and China and describe the diverse religious, cultural, and geographic factors that influenced the ability of the Muslim government to rule. [**Analyze cause-and-effect relationships**]

2B **The student understands the significance of the Abbasid Caliphate as a center of cultural innovation and hub of interregional trade in the 8th-10th centuries.**

Therefore, the student is able to:

9-12 Compare Abbasid government and military institutions with those of Sassanid Persia and Byzantium. [**Compare and contrast differing values and institutions**]

7-12 Describe sources of Abbasid wealth, including taxation, and analyze the economic and political importance of domestic, military, and gang slavery. [**Employ quantitative data**]

7-12 Analyze why the Abbasid state became a center of Afro-Eurasian commercial and cultural exchange. [**Analyze cause-and-effect relationships**]

5-12 Analyze the sources and development of Islamic law and the influence of law and religious practice on such areas as family life, moral behavior, marriage, inheritance, and slavery. [**Examine the influence of ideas**]

7-12 Describe the emergence of a center of Islamic civilization in Iberia and evaluate its economic and cultural achievements. [**Appreciate historical perspectives**]

9-12 Describe the cultural and social contributions of various ethnic and religious communities, particularly the Christian and Jewish, in the Abbasid lands and Iberia. [**Appreciate historical perspectives**]

7-12 Evaluate Abbasid contributions to mathematics, science, medicine, literature, and the preservation of Greek learning. [**Interrogate historical data**]

5-12 Assess how Islam won converts among culturally diverse peoples across wide areas of Afro-Eurasia. [**Analyze cause-and-effect relationships**]

2C **The student understands the consolidation of the Byzantine state in the context of expanding Islamic civilization.**

Therefore, the student is able to:

5-12 Explain how the Byzantine state withstood Arab Muslim attacks between the 7th and 10th centuries. [**Analyze cause-and-effect relationships**]

9-12 Compare Byzantium's imperial political system with that of the Abbasid state. [**Compare and contrast differing values and institutions**]

7-12 Evaluate the Byzantine role in preserving and transmitting ancient Greek learning. [**Reconstruct patterns of historical succession and duration**]

9-12 Analyze the expansion of Greek Orthodox Christianity into the Balkans and Kievan Russia between the 9th and 11th centuries. [**Analyze multiple causation**]

| **STANDARD 3** | Major developments in East Asia and Southeast Asia in the era of the Tang dynasty, 600-900 CE. |

3A The student understands China's sustained political and cultural expansion in the Tang period.

Therefore, the student is able to:

7-12 Explain how relations between China and pastoral peoples of Inner Asia in the Tang period reflect long-term patterns of interaction along China's grassland frontier. [**Explain historical continuity and change**]

9-12 Describe political centralization and economic reforms that marked China's reunification under the Sui and Tang dynasties. [**Analyze cause-and-effect relationships**]

5-12 Describe Tang imperial conquests in Southeast and Central Asia. [**Reconstruct patterns of historical succession and duration**]

5-12 Describe the cosmopolitan diversity of peoples and religions in Chinese cities of the early- and mid-Tang period. [**Appreciate historical perspectives**]

7-12 Assess explanations for the spread and power of Buddhism in Tang China, Korea, and Japan. [**Analyze cause-and-effect relationships**]

7-12 Evaluate creative achievements in painting and poetry in relation to the values of Tang society. [**Appreciate historical perspectives**]

3B The student understands developments in Japan, Korea, and Southeast Asia in an era of Chinese ascendancy.

Therefore, the student is able to:

7-12 Explain how Korea assimilated Chinese ideas and institutions yet preserved its political independence. [**Compare and contrast different sets of ideas**]

5-12 Describe the indigenous development of Japanese society up to the 7th century. [**Interrogate historical data**]

7-12 Assess the patterns of borrowing and adaptation of Chinese culture in Japanese society from the 7th to the 11th century. [**Analyze the influence of ideas**]

5-12 Describe the establishment of the imperial state in Japan and assess the role of the emperor in government. [**Reconstruct patterns of historical succession and duration**]

5-12 Assess the political, social, and cultural contributions of aristocratic women of the Japanese imperial court. [**Appreciate historical perspectives**]

5-12 Describe the indigenous development of Japanese society up to the 7th century CE. [**Reconstruct patterns of historical succession and duration**]

7-12   Explain China's colonization of Vietnam and analyze the effects of Chinese rule on Vietnamese society, including resistance to Chinese domination. [**Evaluate alternative courses of action**]

5-12   Explain the commercial importance of the Straits of Melaka and the significance of the empire of Srivijaya for maritime trade between China and the Indian Ocean. [**Draw upon data in historical maps**]

STANDARD 4	The search for political, social, and cultural redefinition in Europe, 500-1000 CE.

4A   **The student understands the foundations of a new civilization in Western Christendom in the 500 years following the breakup of the western Roman Empire.**

Therefore, the student is able to:

5-12   Assess the importance of monasteries, convents, the Latin Church, and missionaries from Britain and Ireland in the Christianizing of western and central Europe. [**Analyze cause-and-effect relationships**]

5-12   Explain the development of the Merovingian and Carolingian states and assess their success at maintaining public order and local defense in western Europe. [**Reconstruct patterns of historical succession and duration**]

7-12   Analyze how the preservation of Greco-Roman and early Christian learning in monasteries and convents and in Charlemagne's royal court contributed to the emergence of European civilization. [**Reconstruct patterns of historical succession and duration**]

7-12   Analyze the growth of papal power and the changing political relations between the popes and the secular rulers of Europe. [**Identify issues and problems of the past**]

9-12   Compare the successes of the Latin and Greek churches in introducing Christianity and Christian culture to eastern Europe. [**Compare and contrast differing sets of ideas**]

4B   **The student understands the coalescence of political and social order in Europe.**

Therefore, the student is able to:

5-12   Assess the impact of Norse (Viking) and Magyar migrations and invasions, as well as internal conflicts, on the emergence of independent lords and the knightly class. [**Analyze cause-and-effect relationships**]

7-12   Assess changes in the legal, social, and economic status of peasants in the 9th and 10th centuries. [**Interrogate historical data**]

7-12   Analyze the importance of monasteries and convents as centers of political power, economic productivity, and communal life. [**Examine the influence of ideas**]

9-12 Explain how royal officials such as counts and dukes transformed delegated powers into hereditary, autonomous power over land and people in the 9th and 10th centuries. [Reconstruct patterns of historical succession and duration]

STANDARD 5	The development of agricultural societies and new states in tropical Africa and Oceania.

5A **The student understands state-building in Northeast and West Africa and the southward migrations of Bantu-speaking peoples.**

Therefore, the student is able to:

7-12 Explain how the contrasting natural environments of West Africa defined agricultural production, and analyze the importance of the Niger River in promoting agriculture, commerce, and state-building. [**Analyze cause-and-effect relationships**]

7-12 Explain how Ghana became West Africa's first large-scale empire. [**Interrogate historical data**]

7-12 Assess the importance of labor specialization, regional commerce, trans-Saharan camel trade, and Islam in the development of states and cities in West Africa. [**Analyze multiple causation**]

9-12 Infer from archaeological evidence the importance of Jenné-jeno or Kumbi-Saleh as early West African commercial cities. [**Interrogate historical data**]

9-12 Analyze causes and consequences of the settling of East, Central, and Southern Africa by Bantu-speaking farmers and cattle herders up to 1000 CE. [**Analyze cause-and-effect relationships**]

5B **The student understands the peopling of Oceania and the establishment of agricultural societies and states.**

Therefore, the student is able to:

9-12 Analyze various theories drawing on linguistic, biological, and cultural evidence to explain when and how humans migrated to the Pacific Islands and New Zealand. [**Evaluate major debates among historians**]

5-12 Describe the routes by which migrants settled the Pacific Islands and New Zealand and the navigational techniques they used on long-distance voyages. [**Draw upon data in historical maps**]

7-12 Describe the plants and animals that early migrants carried with them and analyze how agricultural societies were established on the Pacific Islands and New Zealand. [**Clarify information on the geographic setting**]

9-12 Analyze how complex social structures, religions, and states developed in Oceania. [**Analyze multiple causation**]

| STANDARD 6 | The rise of centers of civilization in Mesoamerica and Andean South America in the first millennium CE. |

6A   The student understands the origins, expansion, and achievements of Maya civilization.

Therefore, the student is able to:

5-12 Describe the natural environment of southern Mesoamerica and its relationship to the development of Maya urban society. [**Analyze cause-and-effect relationships**]

7-12 Analyze the Maya system of agricultural production and trade and its relationship to the rise of city-states. [**Analyze cause-and-effect relationships**]

9-12 Interpret the Maya cosmic world view as evidenced in art and architecture and evaluate Maya achievements in astronomy, mathematics, and the development of a calendar. [**Appreciate historical perspectives**]

5-12 Analyze how monumental architecture and other evidence portrays the lives of elite men and women. [**Draw upon visual sources**]

7-12 Assess interpretations of how and why Maya civilization declined. [**Evaluate major debates among historians**]

6B   The student understands the rise of the Teotihuacán, Zapotec/Mixtec, and Moche civilizations.

Therefore, the student is able to:

7-12 Analyze the character of the Zapotec state in the valley of Oaxaca as reflected in the art and architecture of Monte Albán. [**Draw upon visual sources**]

9-12 Explain the growth of the urban society centered on Teotihuacán and the importance of this city as a transmitter of Mesoamerican cultural traditions to later societies. [**Examine the influence of ideas**]

5-12 Analyze how the diverse natural environment of the Andes region shaped systems of agriculture and animal herding. [**Analyze cause-and-effect relationships**]

7-12 Describe how archaeological discoveries have led to greater understanding of the character of Moche society. [**Hold interpretations of history as tentative**]

| STANDARD 7 | Major global trends from 300-1000 CE. |

7   The student understands major global trends from 300 to 1000 CE.

Therefore, the student is able to:

7-12 Analyze factors contributing to the weakening of empires or civilized traditions in world history up to 1000 CE and compare causes of the decline or collapse of various empires. [**Draw comparisons across eras and regions**]

7-12   Trace the migratory and military movements of pastoral nomadic peoples from Central Asia and the Arabian Peninsula between the 4th and 11th centuries and analyze the consequences of these movements for empires and agrarian civilizations of Eurasia and Africa. [Interrogate historical data]

5-12   Trace major changes in the religious map of Eurasia and Africa between 300 and 1000 and account for the success of Christianity, Buddhism, Hinduism, and Islam in making converts among peoples of differing ethnic and cultural traditions. [Analyze the influence of ideas]

5-12   Describe maritime and overland trade routes linking regions of Afro-Eurasia and analyze the importance of international trade for African and Eurasian societies. [Draw evidence from historical maps]

7-12   Explain the importance of Muslims and Muslim civilization in mediating long-distance commercial, cultural, intellectual, and food crop exchange across Eurasia and parts of Africa. [Analyze the influence of ideas]

7-12   Trace migrations of farming peoples to new regions of Europe, Sub-Saharan Africa, China, Oceania, and Mesoamerica and analyze connections between new settlement and the development of towns, trade, and greater cultural complexity in these regions. [Analyze cause-and-effect relationships]

ERA 5

Intensified Hemispheric Interactions, 1000-1500 CE

Giving Shape to World History

In this era the various regions of Eurasia and Africa became more firmly interconnected than at any earlier time in history. The sailing ships that crossed the wide sea basins of the Eastern Hemisphere carried a greater volume and variety of goods than ever before. In fact, the chain of seas extending across the hemisphere—China seas, Indian Ocean, Persian Gulf, Red Sea, Black Sea, Mediterranean, and Baltic—came to form a single interlocking network of maritime trade. In the same centuries caravan traffic crossed the Inner Asian steppes and the Sahara Desert more frequently. As trade and travel intensified so did cultural exchanges and encounters, presenting local societies with a profusion of new opportunities and dangers. By the time of the transoceanic voyages of the Portuguese and Spanish, the Eastern Hemisphere already constituted a single zone of intercommunication possessing a unified history of its own.

A global view reveals four "big stories" that give shape to the entire era.

China and Europe—Two Centers of Growth: In two regions of the Eastern Hemisphere, China and Europe, the era witnessed remarkable growth. China experienced a burst of technological innovation, commercialization, and urbanization, emerging as the largest economy in the world. As China exported its silks and porcelains to other lands and imported quantities of spices from India and Southeast Asia, patterns of production and commerce all across the hemisphere were affected. At the opposite end of Eurasia, Western and Central Europe emerged as a new center of Christian civilization, expanding in agricultural production, population, commerce, and military might. Powerful European states presented a new challenge to Muslim dominance in the Mediterranean world. At the same time Europe was drawn more tightly into the commercial economy and cultural interchange of the hemisphere.

The Long Reach of Islam: In this era Islamic faith and civilization encompassed extensive new areas of Eurasia and Africa. The continuing spread of Islam was closely connected to the migrations of Turkic conquerors and herding folk and to the growth of Muslim commercial enterprise all across the hemisphere. By about 1400 CE Muslim societies spanned the central two-thirds of Afro-Eurasia. New Muslim states and towns were appearing in West Africa, the East African coast, Central Asia, India, and Southeast Asia. Consequently, Muslim merchants, scholars, and a host of long-distance travelers were the principal mediators in the interregional exchange of goods, ideas, and technical innovations.

The Age of Mongol Dominance: The second half of the era saw extraordinary developments in interregional history. The Mongols under Chinggis Khan created the largest land empire the world had ever seen. Operating from Poland to Korea and Siberia to

Indonesia, the Mongol warlords intruded in one way or another on the lives of almost all peoples of Eurasia. The conquests were terrifying, but the stabilizing of Mongol rule led to a century of fertile commercial and cultural interchange across the continent. Eurasian unification, however, had a disastrous consequence in the 14th century—the Black Death and its attendant social impact on Europe, the Islamic world, and probably China.

Empires of the Americas: In the Western Hemisphere empire building reached an unprecedented scale. The political styles of the Aztec and Inca states were profoundly different. Even so, both enterprises demonstrated that human labor and creative endeavor could be organized on a colossal scale despite the absence of iron technology or wheeled transport.

Why Study This Era?

▶ The civilizations that flourished in this era—Chinese, Japanese, Indian, Islamic, European, West African, Mesoamerican, and others—created a legacy of cultural and social achievements of continuing significance today. To understand how cultural traditions affect social change or international relations in the contemporary world requires study of the specific historical contexts in which those traditions took form.

▶ The modern world with all its unique complexities did not emerge suddenly in the past 500 years but had its roots in the developments of the 1000-1500 era, notably the maturing of long-distance trade and the economic and social institutions connected with it.

▶ To understand both the history of modern Europe and the United States requires a grasp of the variety of institutions, ideas, and styles that took shape in western Christendom during this era of expansion and innovation.

Overview

Standard 1: The maturing of an interregional system of communication, trade, and cultural exchange in an era of Chinese economic power and Islamic expansion

Standard 2: The redefining of European society and culture, 1000-1300 CE

Standard 3: The rise of the Mongol empire and its consequences for Eurasian peoples, 1200-1350

Standard 4: The growth of states, towns, and trade in Sub-Saharan Africa between the 11th and 15th centuries

Standard 5: Patterns of crisis and recovery in Afro-Eurasia, 1300-1450

Standard 6: The expansion of states and civilizations in the Americas, 1000-1500

Standard 7: Major global trends from 1000-1500 CE

STANDARD 1	The maturing of an interregional system of communication, trade, and cultural exchange in an era of Chinese economic power and Islamic expansion.

1A   The student understands China's extensive urbanization and commercial expansion between the 10th and 13th centuries.

Therefore, the student is able to:

7-12   Explain the major dynastic transitions in China and how Confucianism changed. [**Analyze cause-and-effect relationships**]

7-12   Analyze how improved agricultural production, population growth, urbanization, and commercialization were interconnected. [**Analyze multiple causation**]

5-12   Identify major technological and scientific innovations and analyze their effects on Chinese life. [**Examine the influence of ideas**]

5-12   Analyze the expansion of China's external trade with peoples of Southeast Asia and the lands rimming the Indian Ocean. [**Analyze cause-and-effect relationships**]

7-12   Analyze the growth of an economically powerful merchant class in China. [**Formulate historical questions**]

9-12   Assess the importance of women of gentry families in preserving and transmitting Chinese cultural values. [**Interrogate historical data**]

1B   The student understands developments in Japanese and Southeast Asian civilization.

Therefore, the student is able to:

5-12   Describe Japanese government in the Kamakura and early Ashikaga periods and assess the applicability of the concept of feudalism to Japan. [**Interrogate historical data**]

5-12   Analyze the rise of the warrior class and how changes in inheritance laws and patterns of land ownership affected peasants and both upper-class and commoner women in the context of feudal society. [**Reconstruct patterns of historical succession and duration**]

7-12   Explain the development of distinctive forms of Japanese Buddhism. [**Examine the influence of ideas**]

5-12   Evaluate the arts and aesthetic values in warrior culture. [**Appreciate historical perspectives**]

7-12   Explain the sources of wealth of the Southeast Asian states of Vietnam (Dai Viet), Champa, and Angkor (Cambodia) and analyze the role of Islam and Buddhism in the decline of classical states. [**Compare and contrast differing institutions**]

9-12 Explain the struggle for Vietnamese independence from China and the subsequent reconstruction of Vietnamese society and government. [**Marshal evidence of antecedent circumstances**]

1C The student understands how pastoral migrations and religious reform movements between the 11th and 13th centuries contributed to the rise of new states and the expansion of Islam.

Therefore, the student is able to:

7-12 Analyze how the migrations of Turkic peoples from Turkestan into Southwest Asia and India in the 11th and 12th centuries contributed to Islamic expansion and the retreat of Byzantium and Greek Christian civilization. [**Analyze cause-and-effect relationships**]

9-12 Assess the growth of North African Islamic reform movements and the success of the Almoravids and Almohads in creating empires spanning Iberia and North Africa. [**Examine the influence of ideas**]

5-12 Evaluate scientific, artistic, and literary achievements of Islamic civilization. [**Appreciate historical perspectives**]

9-12 Assess Sufism as an important dimension of Islamic faith and practice and how it enriched Muslim life and contributed to Islamic expansion. [**Examine the influence of ideas**]

1D The student understands how interregional communication and trade led to intensified cultural exchanges among diverse peoples of Eurasia and Africa.

Therefore, the student is able to:

5-12 Identify the maritime routes extending from East Asia to northern Europe and assess the importance of trade across the Indian Ocean for societies of Asia, East Africa, and Europe. [**Draw upon data in historical maps**]

5-12 Explain how camel caravan transport facilitated long-distance trade across Central Asia and the Sahara Desert. [**Interrogate historical data**]

7-12 Compare the importance of such cities as Canton (Kuang-Chou), Melaka, Calicut, Samarkand, Kilwa, Cairo, Constantinople, and Venice as centers of international trade and cosmopolitan culture. [**Clarify information on the geographical setting**]

7-12 Explain connections between trade and the spread of Islam in Central Asia, East Africa, West Africa, the coasts of India, and Southeast Asia. [**Analyze cause-and-effect relationships**]

| STANDARD 2 | The redefining of European society and culture, 1000-1300 CE. |

2A **The student understands feudalism and the growth of centralized monarchies and city-states in Europe.**

Therefore, the student is able to:

5-12 Describe feudal lordship and explain how feudal relationships provided a foundation of political order in parts of Europe. [**Interrogate historical data**]

5-12 Describe manorialism and serfdom as institutions of medieval Europe and analyze how population growth and agricultural expansion affected the legal position and working lives of peasant men and women. [**Appreciate historical perspective**]

7-12 Analyze how European monarchies expanded their power at the expense of feudal lords and assess the growth and limitations of representative institutions in these monarchies. [**Analyze cause-and-effect relationships**]

5-12 Analyze the significance of developments in medieval English legal and constitutional practice and their importance for modern democratic thought and institutions. [**Identify relevant historical antecedents**]

7-12 Explain the changing political relationship between the Catholic Church and secular states. [**Analyze cause-and-effect relationships**]

7-12 Explain the importance of inheritance laws, arranged marriages, dowries, and family alliances for dynastic and aristocratic politics. [**Formulate historical questions**]

9-12 Analyze how prosperous city-states arose in Italy and northern Europe and compare the political institutions of city-states with those of centralizing monarchies. [**Compare and contrast differing institutions**]

2B **The student understands the expansion of Christian Europe after 1000.**

Therefore, the student is able to:

7-12 Analyze connections between population growth and increased agricultural production and technological innovation. [**Analyze cause-and-effect relationships**]

9-12 Explain urban growth in the Mediterranean region and northern Europe and analyze causes for the expansion of manufacturing, interregional trade, and a money economy in Europe. [**Analyze cause-and-effect relationships**]

5-12 Analyze the success of Christian states in overthrowing Muslim powers of central and southern Iberia. [**Interrogate historical data**]

5-12 Analyze the causes and consequences of the European Crusades against Syria and Palestine. [**Analyze cause-and-effect relationships**]

7-12 Assess the consequences of German military and cultural encounters with the peoples of Poland and the Baltic region. [**Analyze cause-and-effect relationships**]

2C **The student understands the patterns of social change and cultural achievement in Europe's emerging civilizations.**

Therefore, the student is able to:

5-12 Analyze ways in which ideals of chivalry and courtly love affected feudal society. [**Analyze cause-and-effect relationships**]

5-12 Describe the life of Jewish communities and their contributions to Europe's cultural and economic development. [**Examine the influence of ideas**]

5-12 Analyze how the rise of schools and universities in Italy, France, and England contributed to literacy, learning, and scientific advancement. [**Analyze cause-and-effect relationships**]

7-12 Evaluate major works of art, architecture, and literature and analyze how they shed light on values and attitudes in Christian society. [**Draw upon visual sources**]

9-12 Assess the importance of the Islamic states of Iberia and Sicily as well as the Byzantine empire in transmitting scientific and philosophical knowledge to and influencing the literature and arts of Western and Central Europe. [**Analyze the importance of ideas**]

9-12 Assess the importance of Orthodox and Latin Christianity in the cultural and social life of Eastern Europe and Russia. [**Examine the importance of ideas**]

STANDARD 3	The rise of the Mongol empire and its consequences for Eurasian peoples, 1200-1350.

3A **The student understands the world-historical significance of the Mongol empire.**

Therefore, the student is able to:

5-12 Assess the career of Chinggis Khan as a conqueror and military innovator in the context of Mongol society. [**Assess the importance of the individual**]

7-12 Describe the Mongol conquests of 1206-1279 and assess their effects on peoples of China, Southeast Asia, Russia, and Southwest Asia. [**Analyze cause-and-effect relationships**]

9-12 Describe the founding and political character of Mongol rule in China, Central Asia, Southwest Asia, and Russia and explain why the unified empire divided into four major successor kingdoms. [**Reconstruct patterns of historical succession and duration**]

9-12 Assess the usefulness and limitations of the concept of the "Pax Mongolica" and analyze how long-distance communication and trade led to cultural and technological diffusion across Eurasia. [**Interrogate historical data**]

3B **The student understands the significance of Mongol rule in China, Korea, Russia, and Southwest Asia.**

Therefore, the student is able to:

5-12 Analyze how Mongol rule affected economy, society, and culture in China and Korea. [**Analyze cause-and-effect relationships**]

5-12 Explain how Southeast Asians and Japanese successfully resisted incorporation into the Mongol empire. [**Analyze cause-and-effect relationships**]

7-12 Explain the growth of the kingdom of the Golden Horde (Khanate of Kipchak) and its impact on the peoples of Russia, Ukraine, Poland, and Hungary. [**Interrogate historical data**]

9-12 Explain how the Golden Horde and the Khanate of Persia-Iraq became Islamicized. [**Formulate a position or course of action on an issue**]

9-12 Describe major characteristics of the Mamluk and Delhi sultanates and explain the Mongol failure to conquer Egypt and India. [**Identify issues and problems in the past**]

STANDARD 4 | The growth of states, towns, and trade in Sub-Saharan Africa between the 11th and 15th centuries.

4A **The student understands the growth of imperial states in West Africa and Ethiopia.**

Therefore, the student is able to:

5-12 Analyze the importance of agriculture, gold production, and the trans-Saharan caravan trade in the growth of the Mali and Songhay empires. [**Analyze cause-and-effect relationships**]

7-12 Explain how Islam expanded in West Africa and assess its importance in the political and cultural life of Mali and Songhay. [**Examine the influence of ideas**]

5-12 Infer from bronze sculpture or other evidence the characteristics of the West African forest states of Ile-Ife and Benin. [**Draw upon visual sources**]

7-12 Explain the expansion of the Christian Ethiopian kingdom and its search for wider connections in the Christian world. [**Interrogate historical data**]

4B **The student understands the development of towns and maritime trade in East and Southern Africa.**

Therefore, the student is able to:

5-12 Explain the rise of commercial towns on the East African coast and the significance of Swahili as a language of trade. [**Interrogate historical data**]

7-12 Assess the importance of Islam, Arab settlement, and maritime trade in the economic and cultural life of Kilwa and other East African coastal cities. [**Analyze cause-and-effect relationships**]

7-12 Analyze the importance of Great Zimbabwe as a state and commercial center with links to the Indian Ocean trade. [Interrogate historical data]

STANDARD 5	Patterns of crisis and recovery in Afro-Eurasia, 1300-1450.

5A   The student understands the consequences of Black Death and recurring plague pandemic in the 14th century.

Therefore, the student is able to:

5-12 Explain the origins and characteristics of the plague pandemic of the mid-14th century, and describe its spread across Eurasia and North Africa. [**Reconstruct patterns of historical succession and duration**]

7-12 Analyze the demographic, economic, social, and political effects of the plague pandemic in Eurasia and North Africa in the second half of the 14th century. [**Appreciate historical perspectives**]

9-12 Assess ways in which long-term climatic change contributed to Europe's economic and social crisis in the 14th century. [Interrogate historical data]

5B   The student understands transformations in Europe following the economic and demographic crises of the 14th century.

Therefore, the student is able to:

5-12 Analyze major changes in the agrarian and commercial economies of Europe in the context of drastic population decline. [**Appreciate historical perspective**]

7-12 Assess the effects of crises in the Catholic Church on its organization and prestige. [**Analyze cause-and-effect relationships**]

5-12 Analyze causes and consequences of the Hundred Years War and repeated popular uprisings in Europe in the 14th century. [**Analyze cause-and-effect relationships**]

9-12 Analyze the resurgence of centralized monarchies and economically powerful city-states in western Europe in the 15th century. [**Reconstruct patterns of historical succession and duration**]

7-12 Define humanism as it emerged in Italy in the 14th and 15th centuries and analyze how study of Greco-Roman antiquity and critical analysis of texts gave rise to new forms of literature, philosophy, and education. [**Examine the influence of ideas**]

5-12 Evaluate the aesthetic and cultural significance of major changes in the techniques of painting, sculpture, and architecture. [**Appreciate historical perspectives**]

5C **The student understands major political developments in Asia in the aftermath of the collapse of Mongol rule and the plague pandemic.**

Therefore, the student is able to:

9-12 Analyze reasons for the collapse of Mongol rule in China and the reconstituting of the empire under the Chinese Ming dynasty. [**Reconstruct patterns of historical succession and duration**]

7-12 Describe the Zheng He maritime expeditions of the early 15th century and analyze why the Ming state initiated, then terminated, these voyages. [**Evaluate the implementation of a decision**]

7-12 Assess the impact of the conquests of Timur (Tamerlane) on Central Asia, Southwest Asia, and India and evaluate Timurid contributions to arts and sciences. [**Assess the importance of the individual**]

5-12 Analyze the origins and early expansion of the Ottoman state up to the capture of Constantinople. [**Reconstruct patterns of historical succession and duration**]

STANDARD 6	The expansion of states and civilizations in the Americas, 1000-1500.

6A **The student understands the development of complex societies and states in North America and Mesoamerica.**

Therefore, the student is able to:

7-12 Explain major characteristics of Toltecs, Anasazi, Pueblo, and North American mound-building peoples. [**Compare and contrast differing values and institutions**]

5-12 Analyze how the Aztec empire arose in the 14th and 15th centuries and explain major aspects of Aztec government, society, religion, and culture. [**Interrogate historical data**]

7-12 Analyze patterns of long-distance trade centered in Mesoamerica. [**Formulate historical questions**]

6B **The student understands the development of the Inca empire in Andean South America.**

Therefore, the student is able to:

5-12 Analyze Inca expansion and methods of imperial unification. [**Appreciate historical perspectives**]

7-12 Explain Inca social, political, religious, and economic institutions. [**Interrogate historical data**]

7-12 Compare the government, economy, religion, and social organization of the Aztec and Inca empires. [**Compare and contrast differing values and institutions**]

STANDARD 7   Major global trends from 1000-1500 CE.

7   The student understands major global trends from 1000 to 1500 CE.

Therefore, the student is able to:

9-12 Account for the growth, decline, and recovery of the overall population of Afro-Eurasia and analyze ways in which large demographic swings might have affected economic, social, and cultural life in various regions. [**Utilize mathematical and quantitative data**]

7-12 Trace major migratory and military movements of pastoral peoples of Asia and Africa and analyze the consequences of these movements for agrarian states and societies of Eurasia and Africa. [**Clarify information on the geographic setting**]

7-12 Compare Europe and China in relation to causes and consequences of productive growth, commercialization, urbanization, and technological or scientific innovation. [**Analyze cause-and-effect relationships**]

5-12 Account for the continuing spread of Islam and explain the importance of Muslims and Muslim civilization in mediating long-distance commercial, cultural, and intellectual exchange. [**Examine the influence of ideas**]

5-12 Explain why new ports, manufacturing centers, merchant communities, and long-distance trade routes emerged during this period in the region of the "Southern Seas" stretching from the Arabian Sea to the coasts of China. [**Analyze cause-and-effect relationships**]

7-12 Analyze ways in which encounters, both hostile and peaceful, between Muslims and Christians in the Mediterranean region affected political, economic, and cultural life in Europe, North Africa, and Southwest Asia. [**Analyze cause-and-effect relationships**]

7-12 Identify similarities and differences in society, economy, and political organization of Europe and Japan and compare the causes of economic growth, urbanization, and cultural innovation in these two regions. [**Draw comparisons across eras and regions**]

7-12 Define "capitalism" and analyze the extent to which capitalistic institutions and productive methods were emerging in Europe and other parts of Afro-Eurasia. [**Examine the influence of ideas**]

7-12 Compare the Inca or Aztec empires with empires of Afro-Eurasia in relation to political institutions, warfare, social organization, and cultural achievements. [**Draw comparisons across eras and regions**]

ERA 6

The Emergence of the First Global Age, 1450-1770

Giving Shape to World History

The Iberian voyages of the late 15th and early 16th centuries linked not only Europe with the Americas but laid down a communications net that ultimately joined every region of the world with every other region. As the era progressed ships became safer, bigger, and faster, and the volume of world commerce soared. The web of overland roads and trails expanded as well to carry goods and people in and out of the interior regions of Eurasia, Africa, and the American continents. The demographic, social, and cultural consequences of this great global link-up were immense.

The deep transformations that occurred in the world during this era may be set in the context of three overarching patterns of change.

The Acceleration of Change: The most conspicuous characteristic of this era was the great acceleration of change in the way people lived, worked, and thought. In these 300 years human society became profoundly different from the way it had been in the entire 5,000 years since the emergence of civilizations. Five aspects of change were especially prominent. Though American Indian populations declined catastrophically in the aftermath of the first European intrusions, world numbers on the whole started their steep upward curve that continues to the present. The globalizing of communications produced intensified economic and cultural encounters and exchanges among diverse peoples of Eurasia, Africa, and the Americas. Capitalism emerged as the dominant system for organizing production, labor, and trade in the world. Innovations in technology and science multiplied and continuously built on one another. European thinkers, drawing on a worldwide fund of ideas, formulated revolutionary new views of nature and the cosmos, ideas that challenged older religious and philosophical perspectives.

Europe and the World; the World and Europe: Europeans came to exert greater power and influence in the world at large than any people of a single region had ever done before. In the Americas Europeans erected colonial regimes and frontiers of European settlement that drew upon various European traditions of law, religion, government, and culture. Europeans seized relatively little territory in Africa and Asia in this era, but their naval and commercial enterprises profoundly affected patterns of production and interregional trade. The trade in human beings between Africa and the Americas to provide a labor force for European commercial agriculture was a particularly catastrophic aspect of the expanding global economy. Closely linked to Europe's far-reaching global involvement was its own internal transformation—political, social, economic, and intellectual. In this era peoples almost everywhere at some time had to come to terms with European arms and economic clout, but as of 1750 Europe by no means dominated the world scene.

Empires of Eurasia: Indeed, the greater share of the world's peoples, cities, agrarian wealth, and land-based military power were in this era still concentrated in the region stretching from the eastern Mediterranean to China. Between the late 14th and early 16th centuries four huge empires arose to dominate the greater part of Eurasia and Northern Africa. Effectively employing artillery and other firearms to expand territorially and maintain law and order among diverse populations, the Ming, Ottoman, Mughal, and Safavid states have sometimes been called "gunpowder empires." They unified such large areas of Afro-Eurasia—politically, economically, and culturally—that they contributed much to processes of globalization.

Why Study This Era?

▶ All the forces that have made the world of the past 500 years "modern" were activated during this era. A grasp of the complexities of global interdependence today requires a knowledge of how the world economy arose and the ways in which it produced both enormous material advances and wider social and political inequalities.

▶ The founding of the British colonies in North America in the 17th century took place within a much wider context of events: the catastrophic decline of American Indian populations, the rise of the Spanish empire, the African slave trade, and the trans-Atlantic trade and migration of Europeans. The history of colonial America makes sense only in relation to this larger scene.

▶ Any useful understanding of American political institutions and cultural values depends on a critical grasp of the European heritage of this era.

▶ The great empires of Eurasia—Ottoman, Persian, Mughal, and Ming/Qing—all experienced cultural flowerings that paralleled the Renaissance in Europe. These achievements are an important part of our contemporary global heritage.

Overview

Standard 1: How the transoceanic interlinking of all major regions of the world from 1450 to 1600 led to global transformations

Standard 2: How European society experienced political, economic, and cultural transformations in an age of global intercommunication, 1450-1750

Standard 3: How large territorial empires dominated much of Eurasia between the 16th and 18th centuries

Standard 4: Economic, political, and cultural interrelations among peoples of Africa, Europe, and the Americas, 1500-1750

Standard 5: Transformations in Asian societies in the era of European expansion

Standard 6: Major global trends from 1450 to 1770

STANDARD 1	How the transoceanic interlinking of all major regions of the world from 1450-1600 led to global transformations.

1A **The student understands the origins and consequences of European overseas expansion in the 15th and 16th centuries.**

Therefore, the student is able to:

5-12 Explain major characteristics of the interregional trading system that linked peoples of Africa, Asia, and Europe on the eve of the European overseas voyages. **[Consider multiple perspectives]**

9-12 Analyze the major social, economic, political, and cultural features of European society, and in particular of Spain and Portugal, that stimulated exploration and conquest overseas. **[Identify issues and problems in the past]**

5-12 Identify major technological developments in shipbuilding, navigation, and naval warfare and trace the cultural origins of various innovations. **[Analyze cause-and-effect relationships]**

7-12 Analyze the motives, nature, and short-term significance of the major Iberian military and commercial expeditions to Sub-Saharan Africa, Asia, and the Americas. **[Identify issues and problems in the past]**

1B **The student understands the encounters between Europeans and peoples of Sub-Saharan Africa, Asia, and the Americas in the late 15th and early 16th centuries.**

Therefore, the student is able to:

5-12 Analyze Portuguese maritime expansion to Africa, India, and Southeast Asia and interactions between the Portuguese and the peoples of these regions. **[Formulate historical questions]**

7-12 Compare the success of the Ottoman, Indian, Chinese, Japanese, Vietnamese, and Siamese (Thai) powers in restricting European commercial, military, and political penetration. **[Analyze cause-and-effect relationships]**

5-12 Describe the political and military collision between the Spanish and the Aztec and Inca empires and analyze why these empires collapsed. **[Identify issues and problems in the past]**

7-12 Explain the founding and organization of Spanish and Portuguese colonial empires in the Americas and Southeast Asia and assess the role of the Catholic Church in colonial administration and policies regarding indigenous populations. **[Interrogate historical data]**

1C **The student understands the consequences of the worldwide exchange of flora, fauna, and pathogens.**

Therefore, the student is able to:

> *5-12* Assess ways in which the exchange of plants and animals around the world in the late 15th and the 16th centuries affected European, Asian, African, and American Indian societies and commerce. [**Analyze cause-and-effect relationships**]

> *7-12* Analyze why the introduction of new disease microorganisms in the Americas after 1492 had such devastating demographic and social effects on American Indian populations. [**Analyze cause-and-effect relationships**]

> *9-12* Assess the effects that knowledge of the peoples, geography, and natural environment of the Americas had on European religious and intellectual life. [**Clarify information on the geographic setting**]

STANDARD 2 | How European society experienced political, economic, and cultural transformations in an age of global intercommunication, 1450-1750.

2A **The student understands demographic, economic, and social trends in Europe.**

Therefore, the student is able to:

> *5-12* Describe characteristics of the family and peasant society in early modern Europe and explain changes in institutions of serfdom in eastern and western Europe. [**Analyze cause-and-effect relationships**]

> *7-12* Analyze the social and economic consequences of population growth and urbanization in Europe from the 15th to the 18th centuries. [**Utilize visual and mathematical data**]

> *9-12* Describe major institutions of capitalism and analyze how the emerging capitalist economy transformed agricultural production, manufacturing, and ways in which women and men worked. [**Analyze cause-and-effect relationships**]

2B **The student understands the Renaissance, Reformation, and Catholic Reformation.**

Therefore, the student is able to:

> *7-12* Analyze the social and intellectual significance of the technological innovation of printing with movable type. [**Demonstrate and explain the influence of ideas**]

> *7-12* Explain connections between the Italian Renaissance and the development of humanist ideas in Europe north of the Alps. [**Compare and contrast differing sets of ideas and values**]

> *5-12* Evaluate major achievements in literature, music, painting, sculpture, and architecture in 16th-century Europe. [**Draw upon visual data and literary sources**]

7-12 Explain discontent among Europeans with the late medieval Church and analyze the beliefs and ideas of the leading Protestant reformers. [**Marshal evidence of antecedent circumstances**]

7-12 Explain the aims and policies of the Catholic Reformation and assess the impact of religious reforms and divisions on European cultural values, family life, convent communities, and men's and women's education. [**Analyze cause-and-effect relationships**]

9-12 Analyze causes of religious wars in 16th- and 17th-century Europe and account for the rise of religious pluralism. [**Marshal evidence of antecedent circumstances**]

2C **The student understands the rising military and bureaucratic power of European states between the 16th and 18th centuries.**

Therefore, the student is able to:

7-12 Analyze the character, development, and sources of wealth of strong bureaucratic monarchies in the 16th century. [**Analyze cause-and-effect relationships**]

7-12 Explain how the Dutch Republic emerged as a powerful European state. [**Formulate historical questions**]

5-12 Explain how the English civil war and the Revolution of 1688 affected government, religion, economy, and society in that country. [**Analyze cause-and-effect relationships**]

5-12 Explain the impact of the English Revolution on political institutions and attitudes in the North American colonies and on the outbreak of the American Revolution. [**Examine the influence of ideas**]

7-12 Account for the growth of bureaucratic monarchy in Russia and analyze the significance of Peter the Great's westernizing reforms. [**Interrogate historical data**]

9-12 Trace Russian expansion in the Caucasus, Central Asia, and Siberia and explain the success of the tsars in transforming the Duchy of Moscow into a Eurasian empire. [**Draw comparisons across regions.**]

2D **The student understands how the Scientific Revolution contributed to transformations in European society.**

Therefore, the student is able to:

7-12 Explain connections between the Scientific Revolution and its antecedents such as Greek rationalism, medieval theology, Muslim science, Renaissance humanism, and new global knowledge. [**Marshal evidence of antecedent circumstances**]

5-12 Explain the cultural, religious, and scientific impact of astronomical discoveries and innovations from Copernicus to Newton. [**Examine the influence of ideas**]

7-12 Analyze the importance of discoveries in mathematics, physics, biology, and chemistry for European society. [**Employ quantitative analysis**]

7-12 Explain the development and significance of the "scientific method." [**Examine the influence of ideas**]

9-12 Explain the importance of royal societies and other international networks in disseminating scientific ideas and methods. [**Interrogate historical data**]

9-12 Account for the coexistence of the new scientific rationalism with traditional learning and practices such as astrology, magic, and witchcraft. [**Formulate historical questions**]

2E **The student understands the significance of the Enlightenment in European and world history.**

Therefore, the student is able to:

7-12 Explain connections between the Enlightenment and its antecedents such as Roman republicanism, the Renaissance, and the Scientific Revolution. [**Marshal evidence of antecedent circumstances**]

5-12 Explain principal ideas of the Enlightenment, including rationalism, secularism, progress, toleration, empiricism, natural rights, contractual government, and new theories of education. [**Examine the influence of ideas**]

7-12 Assess the impact of Enlightenment ideas on the development of modern nationalism and democratic thought and institutions. [**Hypothesize the influence of the past**]

9-12 Analyze connections between Europeans' growing knowledge of other regions of the globe and the development of new concepts of universalism, toleration, and world history. [**Analyze cause-and-effect relationships**]

7-12 Describe ways in which Enlightenment thought contributed to reform of church and state and assess the reform programs of absolutist monarchs of Central Europe and Russia. [**Analyze cause-and-effect relationships**]

9-12 Explain how academies, salons, and popular publishing contributed to the dissemination of Enlightenment ideas. [**Examine the influence of ideas**]

STANDARD 3   How large territorial empires dominated much of Eurasia between the 16th and 18th centuries.

3A **The student understands the extent and limits of Chinese regional power under the Ming dynasty.**

Therefore, the student is able to:

5-12 Analyze the power and limits of imperial absolutism under the Ming dynasty. [**Analyze cause-and-effect relationships**]

7-12 Explain China's self-concept as the "middle kingdom" and the character of its political, commercial, and cultural relations with Korea, Vietnam, and other societies of East and Southeast Asia. [**Interrogate historical data**]

9-12 Analyze the effects of commercialization on social relations among gentry elites, urban merchants, and peasants. [**Analyze cause-and-effect relationships**]

5-12 Analyze China's changing attitudes toward external political and commercial relations following the Zheng He voyages from 1405 to 1433. [**Formulate historical questions**]

7-12 Assess the effects of the introduction of American food crops and importation of American silver on demographic, economic, and social change in China. [**Analyze cause-and-effect relationships**]

9-12 Compare the role of Neo-Confucianism, Buddhism, and Taoism in Chinese government and society. [**Compare and contrast differing sets of ideas**]

3B   **The student understands how Southeast Europe and Southwest Asia became unified under the Ottoman Empire.**

Therefore, the student is able to:

5-12 Analyze how the capture of Constantinople and the destruction of the Byzantine empire contributed to the expansion of Ottoman power. [**Hypothesize the influence of the past**]

5-12 Analyze reasons for Ottoman military successes against Persia, Egypt, North African states, and Christian European kingdoms. [**Analyze cause-and-effect relationships**]

7-12 Analyze the political, institutional, and economic development of the empire in the context of its religious and ethnic diversity. [**Analyze multiple causation**]

5-12 Evaluate the empire's artistic, architectural, and literary achievements. [**Draw upon visual, literary, and musical sources**]

9-12 Analyze how Muslim, Orthodox, Catholic, and Jewish peoples interacted in southeastern Europe under Ottoman rule. [**Examine the influence of ideas, human interests, and beliefs**]

3C   **The student understands the rise of the Safavid and Mughal empires.**

Therefore, the student is able to:

5-12 Explain the unification of Persia under the Turkic Safavids and evaluate Safavid political and cultural achievements under Shah Abbas. [**Analyze cause-and-effect relationships**]

5-12 Explain the Mughal conquest of India and the success of the Turkic warrior class in uniting the diverse peoples of the Indian subcontinent. [**Formulate a position or course of action on an issue**]

7-12 Analyze the relationship between Muslims and Hindus in the empire and compare Akbar's governing methods and religious ideas with those of other Mughal emperors. [**Examine the influence of ideas, human interests, and beliefs**]

9-12 Evaluate the interplay of indigenous Indian, Persian, and European influences in Mughal artistic, architectural, literary, and scientific achievements. [**Draw upon visual and literary sources**]

5-12 Assess the importance of Indian textiles, spices, and other products in the network of Afro-Eurasian trade. [**Formulate historical questions**]

STANDARD 4	Economic, political, and cultural interrelations among peoples of Africa, Europe, and the Americas, 1500-1750.

4A **The student understands how states and peoples of European descent became dominant in the Americas between the 16th and 18th centuries.**

Therefore, the student is able to:

5-12 Define and compare four major types of European activity and control in the Americas: large territorial empires, trading-post empires, plantation colonies, and settler colonies. [**Compare and contrast differing sets of ideas**]

9-12 Describe the administrative system of the Spanish viceroyalties of Peru and Mexico and analyze the importance of silver production and Indian agriculture in the Spanish colonial economy. [**Interrogate historical data**]

5-12 Analyze how the Netherlands, England, and France became naval, commercial, and political powers in the Atlantic basin. [**Marshal evidence of antecedent circumstances**]

7-12 Assess the moral, political, and cultural role of Catholic and Protestant Christianity in the European colonies in the Americas. [**Examine the influence of ideas, human interests, and beliefs**]

7-12 Explain why historians have called the Seven Years War the first "global war" and assess its consequences for Britain, France, Spain, and the indigenous peoples of the American colonial territories. [**Analyze cause-and-effect relationships**]

4B **The student understands the origins and consequences of the trans-Atlantic African slave trade.**

Therefore, the student is able to:

7-12 Analyze the ways in which entrepreneurs and colonial governments exploited American Indian labor and why commercial agriculture came to rely overwhelmingly on African slave labor. [**Evidence historical perspectives**]

7-12 Compare ways in which slavery or other forms of social bondage were practiced in the Islamic lands, Christian Europe, and West Africa. [**Compare and contrast differing sets of ideas**]

5-12 Explain how commercial sugar production spread from the Mediterranean to the Americas and analyze why sugar, tobacco, and other crops grown in the Americas became so important in the world economy. [**Analyze cause-and-effect relationships**]

7-12 Explain the organization of long-distance trade in West and Central Africa and analyze the circumstances under which African governments, elites, merchants, and other groups participated in the sale of slaves to Europeans. [**Identify issues and problems in the past**]

5-12 Explain how European governments and firms organized and financed the trans-Atlantic slave trade; and describe the conditions under which slaves made the "middle passage" from Africa to the Americas. [**Appreciate historical perspectives**]

9-12 Analyze the emergence of social hierarchies based on race and gender in the Iberian, French, and British colonies in the Americas. [**Interrogate historical data**]

5-12 Describe conditions of slave life on plantations in the Caribbean, Brazil, and British North America and analyze ways in which slaves perpetuated aspects of African culture and resisted plantation servitude. [**Appreciate historical perspectives**]

4C **The student understands patterns of change in Africa in the era of the slave trade.**

Therefore, the student is able to:

7-12 Describe the institutions and economies of Ashanti, Dahomey, Benin, Lunda, and Kongo in the period of the Atlantic slave trade. [**Formulate historical questions**]

5-12 Analyze how the Atlantic slave trade affected population, economic life, polygynous marriage, family life, and the use of male and female slave labor in West and Central Africa. [**Analyze cause-and-effect relationships**]

9-12 Describe government, trade, cultural traditions, and urban life in the Songhay Empire in the 16th century and analyze reasons for the empire's collapse at the end of the century. [**Interrogate historical data**]

7-12 Analyze causes and consequences of encounters among Khoisan groups, Bantu-speaking peoples, and European settlers in South Africa in the 17th and 18th centuries. [**Identify the gaps in the available records**]

STANDARD 5   Transformations in Asian societies in the era of European expansion.

5A **The student understands the development of European maritime power in Asia.**

Therefore, the student is able to:

5-12 Explain how the Netherlands, England, and France became naval and commercial powers in the Indian Ocean basin in the 17th and 18th centuries. [**Evaluate the implementation of a decision**]

5-12 Assess the impact of British and French commercial and military initiatives on politics, economy, and society in India. [**Marshal evidence of antecedent circumstances**]

5-12 Analyze motives for Dutch commercial and military penetration of Indonesia and the effects of Dutch imperialism on the region's economy and society. [**Analyze cause-and-effect relationships**]

9-12 Analyze the character and significance of contacts between Christian missionaries and peoples of India, Vietnam, and the Philippines. [**Examine the influence of ideas, human interests, and beliefs**]

9-12 Assess the impact of the Seven Years War on the relative power of Britain and France in Asia. [**Analyze cause-and-effect relationships**]

5B **The student understands the transformations in India, China, and Japan in an era of expanding European commercial power.**

Therefore, the student is able to:

9-12 Analyze causes of the decline of the Mughal Empire and the rise of regional powers such as the Marathas and Sikhs. [**Analyze multiple causation**]

7-12 Explain how the Manchus overthrew the Ming dynasty, established the multi-ethnic Qing, and doubled the size of the Chinese empire. [**Identify issues and problems in the past**]

9-12 Evaluate China's cultural and economic achievements during the reigns of the Kangxi and Qianlong emperors. [**Examine the influence of ideas, human interests, and beliefs**]

7-12 Assess the extent of European commercial penetration of China and the ability of the Chinese government to control European trade. [**Analyze cause-and-effect relationships**]

5-12 Explain the character of centralized feudalism in Japan under the Tokugawa shogunate and the reasons for Japan's political stability, economic growth, and cultural dynamism. [**Analyze cause-and-effect relationships**]

5-12 Analyze Japan's relations with Europeans between the 16th and 18th centuries and the consequences of its policy of limiting contacts with foreigners. [**Reconstruct patterns of historical succession and duration**]

5C **The student understands major cultural trends in Asia between the 16th and 18th centuries.**

Therefore, the student is able to:

9-12 Assess the influence of both new currents in Confucianism and Chinese art, architecture, and literary styles on cultural life in Korea, Vietnam, and Japan. [**Draw upon visual and literary sources**]

9-12 Describe the varieties of Buddhist and Hindu teaching and practice in Asia and compare their influence on social and cultural life. [**Demonstrate and explain the influence of ideas, human interests, and beliefs**]

7-12 Analyze how and why Islam continued to expand in India, Southeast Asia and China. [**Demonstrate and explain the influence of ideas, human interests, and beliefs**]

STANDARD 6	Major global trends from 1450-1770.

6   **The student understands major global trends from 1450 to 1770.**

Therefore, the student is able to:

5-12   Describe major shifts in world demography and urbanization in this era and analyze reasons for these changes. [**Utilize visual and mathematical data**]

7-12   Analyze ways in which expanding capitalistic enterprise and commercialization affected relations among states and contributed to changing class and race relations. [**Analyze cause-and-effect relationships**]

7-12   Assess the impact of gunpowder weaponry and other innovations in military technology on empire-building and the world balance of naval power. [**Analyze cause-and-effect relationships**]

5-12   Explain major changes in world political boundaries between 1450 and 1770 and assess the extent and limitations of European political and military power in Africa, Asia, and the Americas as of the mid-18th century. [**Clarify information on the geographic setting**]

5-12   Assess how the acceleration of scientific and technological innovations in this era affected social, economic, and cultural life in various parts of the world. [**Analyze cause-and-effect relationships**]

7-12   Identify regions where Buddhism, Christianity, and Islam were growing in this era and analyze why these religious and cultural traditions gained new adherents in various parts of the world. [**Examine the influence of ideas**]

7-12   Identify patterns of social and cultural continuity in various societies and analyze ways in which peoples maintained traditions and resisted external challenges in the context of a rapidly changing world. [**Explain historical continuity and change**]

An Age of Revolutions, 1750-1914

Giving Shape to World History

The invention of the railway locomotive, the steamship, and, later, the telegraph and telephone transformed global communications in this era. The time it took and the money it cost to move goods, messages, or armies across oceans and continents were drastically cut. People moved, or were forced to move, from one part of the world to another in record numbers. In the early part of the era African slaves continued to be transported across the Atlantic in large numbers; European migrants created new frontiers of colonial settlement in both the Northern and Southern Hemispheres; and Chinese, Indian, and other Asians migrated to Southeast Asia and the Americas. International commerce mushroomed, and virtually no society anywhere in the world stayed clear of the global market. Underlying these surges in communication, migration, and trade was the growth of world population, forcing men and women almost everywhere to experiment with new ways of organizing collective life.

This was an era of bewildering change in a thousand different arenas. One way to make sense of the whole is to focus on three world-encompassing and interrelated developments: the democratic revolution, the industrial revolution, and the establishment of European dominance over most of the world.

Political Revolutions and New Ideologies: The American and French revolutions offered to the world the potent ideas of popular sovereignty, inalienable rights, and nationalism. The translating of these ideas into political movements had the effect of mobilizing unprecedented numbers of ordinary people to participate in public life and to believe in a better future for all. Liberal, constitutional, and nationalist ideals inspired independence movements in Haiti and Latin America in the early 19th century, and they continued to animate reform and revolution in Europe throughout the era. At the same time political and social counterforces acted to limit or undermine the effectiveness of democratic governments. Democracy and nationalism contributed immensely to the social power of European states and therefore to Europe's rising dominance in world affairs in the 19th century. Under growing pressures from both European military power and the changing world economy, ruling or elite groups in Asian and African states organized reform movements that embraced at least some of the ideas and programs of democratic revolution.

The Industrial Revolution: The industrial revolution applied mechanical power to the production and distribution of goods on a massive scale. It also involved mobilizing unprecedented numbers of laborers and moving them from village to city and from one country to another. Industrialization was a consequence of centuries of expanding economic activity around the world. England played a crucial role in the onset of this revolution, but the process involved complex economic and financial linkages among societies. Together, the industrial and democratic revolutions thoroughly transformed European society. Asian, African, and Latin American peoples dealt with the new demands of the world market and Europe's economic might in a variety of ways. Some groups argued for reform through technical and industrial modernization. Others called for reassertion of established policies and values that had always served them well in times of crisis. Japan and the United States both subscribed to the industrial revolution with rapid success and became important players on the world scene.

The Age of European Dominance: In 1800 Europeans controlled about 35 percent of the world's land surface. By 1914 they dominated over 84 percent. In the long span of human history European world hegemony lasted a short time, but its consequences were profound and continue to be played out today. Western expansion took three principal forms: (1) Peoples of European descent, including Russians and North Americans, created colonial settlements, or "neo-Europes," in various temperate regions of the world, displacing or assimilating indigenous peoples; (2) European states and commercial firms exerted considerable economic power in certain places, notably Latin America and China, while Japan and the United States also participated in this economic expansionism; (3) in the later 19th century European states embarked on the "new imperialism," the competitive race to establish political as well as economic control over previously uncolonized regions of Africa and Asia. Mass production of new weaponry, coupled with the revolution of transport and communication, permitted this surge of power. The active responses of the peoples of Africa, Asia, and Latin America to the crisis of European hegemony are an important part of the developments of this era: armed resistance against invaders, collaboration or alliance with colonizers, economic reform or entrepreneurship, and movements for cultural reform. As World War I approached, accelerating social change and new efforts at resistance and renewal characterized colonial societies far more than consolidation and stability.

Why Study This Era?

▶ The global forces unleashed in the second half of the 18th century continue to play themselves out at the end of the 20th century. Students will understand the "isms" that have absorbed contemporary society—industrialism, capitalism, nationalism, liberalism, socialism, communism, imperialism, colonialism and so on—by investigating them within the historical context of the 18th and 19th centuries.

▶ At the beginning of the 20th century, Western nations enjoyed a dominance in world affairs that they no longer possess. By studying this era students may address some of the fundamental questions of the modern age: How did a relatively few states achieve such hegemony over most of the world? In what ways was Western domination limited or inconsequential? Why was it not to endure?

▶ The history of the United States, in this era, was not self-contained but fully embedded in the context of global change. To understand the role of the United States on the global scene, students must be able to relate it to world history.

Overview

Standard 1: The causes and consequences of political revolutions in the late 18th and early 19th centuries

Standard 2: The causes and consequences of the agricultural and industrial revolutions, 1700-1850

Standard 3: The transformation of Eurasian societies in an era of global trade and rising European power, 1750-1870

Standard 4: Patterns of nationalism, state-building, and social reform in Europe and the Americas, 1830-1914

Standard 5: Patterns of global change in the era of Western military and economic domination, 1800-1914

Standard 6: Major global trends from 1750-1914

STANDARD 1	**The causes and consequences of political revolutions in the late 18th and early 19th centuries.**

1A **The student understands how the French Revolution contributed to transformations in Europe and the world.**

Therefore, the student is able to:

7-12 Analyze how the Seven Years War, Enlightenment thought, the American Revolution, and growing internal economic crisis affected social and political conditions in Old Regime France. [**Analyze multiple causation**]

5-12 Compare the causes, character, and consequences of the American and French revolutions. [**Compare and contrast differing movements, institutions, and ideas**]

7-12 Explain how the French Revolution developed from constitutional monarchy to democratic despotism to the Napoleonic empire. [**Reconstruct patterns of historical succession and duration**]

5-12 Analyze leading ideas of the revolution concerning social equality, democracy, human rights, constitutionalism, and nationalism and assess the importance of these ideas for democratic thought and institutions in the 20th century. [**Interrogate historical data**]

7-12 Explain how the revolution affected French society, including religious institutions, social relations, education, marriage, family life, and the legal and political position of women. [**Analyze cause-and-effect relationships**]

5-12 Describe how the wars of the revolutionary and Napoleonic period changed Europe and assess Napoleon's effects on the aims and outcomes of the revolution. [**Analyze multiple causation**]

9-12 Analyze connections between the French and Haitian revolutions and assess the impact of the Haitian movement on race relations and slavery in the Americas and the French empire. [**Analyze cause-and-effect relationships**]

1B   The student understands how Latin American countries achieved independence in the early 19th century.

Therefore, the student is able to:

5-12 Analyze the influence of the American, French, and Haitian revolutions, as well as late 18th-century South American rebellions, on the development of independence movements in Latin America. [**Analyze multiple causation**]

7-12 Explain the effects of Napoleon's invasion of Iberia and the growth of British power in the Atlantic basin on the struggles for independence. [**Evaluate the implementation of a decision**]

5-12 Analyze the political and ideological objectives of the independence movements between 1808 and 1830 and explain why these movements succeeded. [**Interrogate historical data**]

9-12 Compare the political roles of Creole elites, the Catholic Church, and mestizo, mulatto, and Indian populations in the independence movements. [**Marshal evidence of antecedent circumstances**]

| **STANDARD 2** | The causes and consequences of the agricultural and industrial revolutions, 1700-1850. |

2A   The student understands the early industrialization and the importance of developments in England.

Therefore, the student is able to:

5-12 Describe the characteristics of the "agricultural revolution" that occurred in England and Western Europe and analyze its effects on population growth, industrialization, and patterns of land-holding. [**Analyze cause-and-effect relationships**]

5-12 Identify the major characteristics of the industrial revolution and compare industrial economies with other forms of economic organization. [**Compare and contrast differing institutions**]

9-12 Analyze relationships between the expanding world market economy of the 16th through 18th centuries and the development of industrialization. [**Analyze cause-and-effect relationships**]

7-12 Analyze connections between early industrialization and Britain's commercial relations with continental Europe, the Mediterranean, India, the Caribbean, and other world regions. [**Analyze cause-and-effect relationships**]

7-12 Assess the relative importance of geographical, economic, technological, and political factors that permitted or encouraged the rise of mechanized industry in England. [**Analyze multiple causation**]

2B **The student understands how industrial economies expanded and societies experienced transformations in Europe and the Atlantic basin.**

Therefore, the student is able to:

5-12 Explain connections among population growth, industrialization, and urbanization and evaluate the quality of life in early 19th-century cities. [**Appreciate historical perspectives**]

5-12 Explain how industrialization and urbanization affected class distinctions, family life, and the daily working lives of men, women, and children. [**Analyze cause-and-effect relationships**]

7-12 Analyze connections between industrialization and movements for political and social reform in England, Western Europe, and the United States. [**Analyze cause-and-effect relationships**]

9-12 Analyze connections between industrialization and the rise of new types of labor organizations and mobilization. [**Analyze cause-and-effect relationships**]

2C **The student understands the causes and consequences of the abolition of the trans-Atlantic slave trade and slavery in the Americas.**

Therefore, the student is able to:

9-12 Assess the relative importance of Enlightenment thought, Christian piety, democratic revolutions, slave resistance, and changes in the world economy in bringing about the abolition of the slave trade and the emancipation of slaves in the Americas. [**Analyze multiple causation**]

5-12 Describe the organization of movements in Europe and the Americas to end slavery and explain how the trans-Atlantic trade was suppressed. [**Reconstruct patterns of historical succession and duration**]

7-12 Compare contract labor migration and other forms of coerced labor with slavery as methods of organizing commercial agriculture in the Americas in the later 19th century. [**Compare and contrast differing values, behaviors, and institutions**]

7-12 Assess the degree to which emancipated slaves and their descendants achieved social equality and economic advancement in various countries of the Western Hemisphere. [**Interrogate historical data**]

STANDARD 3

The transformation of Eurasian societies in an era of global trade and rising European power, 1750-1870.

3A The student understands how the Ottoman Empire attempted to meet the challenge of Western military, political, and economic power.

Therefore, the student is able to:

9-12 Assess the effects of population growth and European commercial penetration on Ottoman society and government. [**Analyze cause-and-effect relationships**]

5-12 Analyze why the empire was forced to retreat from the Balkans and the Black Sea region. [**Analyze multiple causation**]

7-12 Explain the defensive reform programs of Selim III and Mahmud II and analyze the challenges these rulers faced in resolving the empire's political and economic crises. [**Interrogate historical data**]

5-12 Explain the impact of the French invasion of Egypt in 1798 and analyze the subsequent efforts of Muhammad Ali to found a modern state and economy. [**Analyze cause-and-effect relationships**]

3B The student understands Russian absolutism, reform, and imperial expansion in the late 18th and 19th centuries.

Therefore, the student is able to:

7-12 Analyze the effects of the French Revolution, Napoleonic invasion, and world economy on Russian absolutism to 1850. [**Analyze cause-and-effect relationships**]

9-12 Analyze relations between the Russian peasantry and land-owning aristocracy and explain the persistence of serfdom in the 19th century. [**Identify issues and problems in the past**]

7-12 Assess the significance of imperial reforms and popular opposition movements in the later 19th century. [**Compare and contrast differing ideas and values**]

5-12 Explain why Russia was successful in wars of expansion against the Ottoman empire and other Muslim states. [**Analyze multiple causation**]

5-12 Analyze motives and means of Russian expansion into Siberia and North America. [**Interrogate historical data**]

3C The student understands the consequences of political and military encounters between Europeans and peoples of South and Southeast Asia.

Therefore, the student is able to:

5-12 Explain the advance of British power in India up to 1850 and appraise the efforts of Indians to resist European conquest and achieve cultural renewal. [**Consider multiple perspectives**]

7-12 Describe patterns of British trade linking India with both China and Europe and assess ways in which Indian farmers and manufacturers responded to world trade. [**Analyze cause-and-effect relationships**]

9-12 Compare the British conquest of India with the Dutch penetration of Indonesia and assess the role of indigenous elites under these colonial regimes. [**Compare and contrast differing values, behaviors, and institutions**]

3D   The student understands how China's Qing dynasty responded to economic and political crises in the late 18th and the 19th centuries.

Therefore, the student is able to:

7-12 Analyze the economic and social consequences of rapid population growth in China. [**Analyze cause-and-effect relationships**]

7-12 Analyze causes of governmental breakdown and social disintegration in China in the late 18th century. [**Analyze multiple causation**]

5-12 Analyze why China resisted political contact and trade with Europeans and how the opium trade contributed to European penetration of Chinese markets. [**Appreciate historical perspectives**]

9-12 Assess causes and consequences of the mid-19th century Taiping rebellion. [**Analyze cause-and-effect relationships**]

9-12 Explain the growth of the Chinese diaspora in Southeast Asia and the Americas and assess the role of overseas Chinese in attempts to reform the Qing. [**Formulate historical questions**]

3E   The student understands how Japan was transformed from feudal shogunate to modern nation-state in the 19th century.

Therefore, the student is able to:

5-12 Analyze the internal and external causes of the Meiji Restoration. [**Formulate historical questions**]

5-12 Analyze the goals and policies of the Meiji state and their impact on Japan's modernization. [**Obtain historical data**]

7-12 Assess the impact of Western ideas and the role of Confucianism and Shinto traditional values on Japan in the Meiji period. [**Appreciate historical perspectives**]

9-12 Explain the transformation of Japan from a hereditary social system to a middle-class society. [**Examine the influence of ideas**]

9-12 Explain changes in Japan's relations with China and the Western powers from the 1850s to the 1890s. [**Reconstruct patterns of historical succession and duration**]

| STANDARD 4 | Patterns of nationalism, state-building, and social reform in Europe and the Americas, 1830-1914. |

4A The student understands how modern nationalism affected European politics and society.

Therefore, the student is able to:

7-12 Identify major characteristics of 19th-century European nationalism and analyze connections between nationalist ideology and the French Revolution, Romanticism, and liberal reform movements. [**Appreciate historical perspectives**]

9-12 Analyze causes of the revolutions of 1848 and why these revolutions failed to achieve nationalist and democratic objectives. [**Analyze cause-and-effect relationships**]

5-12 Describe the unification of Germany and Italy and analyze why these movements succeeded. [**Analyze multiple causation**]

9-12 Assess the importance of nationalism as a source of tension and conflict in the Austro-Hungarian and Ottoman empires. [**Analyze cause-and-effect relationships**]

4B The student understands the impact of new social movements and ideologies on 19th-century Europe.

Therefore, the student is able to:

5-12 Analyze causes of large-scale migrations from rural areas to cities and how these movements affected the domestic and working lives of men and women. [**Analyze multiple causation**]

7-12 Explain the leading ideas of Karl Marx and analyze the impact of Marxist beliefs and programs on politics, industry, and labor relations in later 19th-century Europe. [**Consider multiple perspectives**]

9-12 Analyze interconnections among labor movements, various forms of socialism, and political or social changes in Europe in the second half of the 19th century. [**Analyze cause-and-effect relationships**]

9-12 Analyze connections between reform movements and industrialization, democratization, and nationalism. [**Analyze multiple causation**]

7-12 Explain the origins of women's suffrage and other movements in Europe and North America and assess their successes up to World War I. [**Marshal evidence of antecedent circumstances**]

9-12 Explain the ways in which Britain, France, and Italy became more broadly liberal and democratic societies in the 19th century. [**Formulate historical questions**]

9-12 Describe the changing legal and social status of European Jews and the rise of new forms of anti-Semitism. [**Reconstruct patterns of historical succession and duration**]

4C **The student understands cultural, intellectual, and educational trends in 19th-century Europe.**

Therefore, the student is able to:

9-12 Explain how expanded educational opportunities and literacy contributed to changes in European society and cultural life. [**Analyze cause-and-effect relationships**]

5-12 Evaluate major movements in literature, music, and the visual arts and ways in which they expressed or shaped social and cultural values of industrial society. [**Draw upon visual and literary sources**]

9-12 Analyze ways in which trends in philosophy and the new social sciences challenged and shaped dominant social values. [**Analyze cause-and-effect relationships**]

7-12 Describe elements of the distinctive working- and middle-class cultures that emerged in industrial Europe. [**Compare and contrast differing values, behaviors, and institutions**]

4D **The student understands the political, economic, and social transformations in the Americas in the 19th century.**

Therefore, the student is able to:

5-12 Assess the successes and failures of democracy in Latin American countries in the decades following independence. [**Formulate historical questions**]

9-12 Explain Latin America's growing dependence on the global market and assess the effects of international trade and investment on the power of landowners and the urban middle class. [**Analyze cause-and-effect relationships**]

9-12 Assess the consequences of economic development, elite domination and the abolition of slavery for peasants, Indian populations, and immigrant laborers in Latin America. [**Interrogate historical data**]

9-12 Analyze how liberal ideology and the expansion of secular education affected legal and political rights for women in various Latin American countries. [**Examine the influence of ideas**]

7-12 Assess the effects of foreign intervention and liberal government policies on social and economic change in Mexico. [**Analyze cause-and-effect relationships**]

7-12 Explain the factors that contributed to nation-building and self-government in Canada. [**Marshal evidence of antecedent circumstances**]

| STANDARD 5 | Patterns of global change in the era of Western military and economic dominance, 1800-1914. |

5A **The student understands connections between major developments in science and technology and the growth of industrial economy and society.**

Therefore, the student is able to:

7-12 Assess the social significance of the work of scientists, including Maxwell, Darwin, and Pasteur. [**Examine the influence of ideas**]

5-12 Explain how new inventions, including the railroad, steamship, telegraph, photography, and internal combustion engine, transformed patterns of global communication, trade, and state power. [**Analyze cause-and-effect relationships**]

5-12 Analyze how new machines, fertilizers, transport systems, commercialization, and other developments affected agricultural production in various parts of the world. [**Employ quantitative analysis**]

7-12 Explain how new forms of generative power contributed to Europe's "second industrial revolution" and compare the role of the state in different countries in directing or encouraging industrialization. [**Analyze multiple causation**]

9-12 Analyze factors that transformed the character of cities in various parts of the world. [**Analyze cause-and-effect relationships**]

5B **The student understands the causes and consequences of European settler colonization in the 19th century.**

Therefore, the student is able to:

5-12 Explain why migrants left Europe in large numbers in the 19th century and identify temperate regions of the world where they established or expanded frontiers of European settlement. [**Draw upon data in historical maps**]

5-12 Compare the consequences of encounters between European migrants and indigenous peoples in such regions as the United States, Canada, South Africa, Australia, and Siberia. [**Compare and contrast differing values and institutions**]

7-12 Analyze geographical, political, economic, and epidemiological factors contributing to the success of European colonial settlement in such regions as Argentina, South Africa, Australia, New Zealand, Algeria, Siberia, Canada, and the United States. [**Analyze multiple causation**]

5C **The student understands the causes of European, American, and Japanese imperial expansion.**

Therefore, the student is able to:

9-12 Explain leading ideas of Social Darwinism and scientific racism in 19th-century Europe and assess the importance of these ideas in activating European imperial expansion in Africa and Asia. [**Identify issues and problems in the past**]

5-12 Describe advances in transportation, medicine, and weapons technology in Europe in the later 19th century and assess the importance of these factors in the success of imperial expansion. [**Analyze multiple causation**]

7-12 Analyze the motives that impelled several European powers to undertake imperial expansion against peoples of Africa, Southeast Asia, and China. [**Interrogate historical data**]

7-12 Relate the Spanish-American War to United States participation in Western imperial expansion in the late 19th century. [**Analyze cause-and-effect relationships**]

9-12 Assess the effects of the Sino-Japanese and Russo-Japanese wars and colonization of Korea on the world-power status of Japan. [**Analyze cause-and-effect relationships**]

5D **The student understands transformations in South, Southeast, and East Asia in the era of the "new imperialism."**

Therefore, the student is able to:

7-12 Analyze changes in Indian society and economy under British rule. [**Interrogate historical data**]

7-12 Explain the social, economic, and intellectual sources of Indian nationalism and analyze reactions of the British government to it. [**Analyze cause-and-effect relationships**]

9-12 Compare French and British colonial expansion in mainland Southeast Asia and analyze Thailand's success in avoiding colonization. [**Compare and contrast differing values, behaviors, and institutions**]

7-12 Analyze how Chinese began to reform government and society after 1895 and why revolution broke out in 1911. [**Analyze multiple causation**]

5-12 Analyze Japan's rapid industrialization, technological advancement, and national integration in the late 19th and early 20th centuries. [**Formulate historical questions**]

5E **The student understands the varying responses of African peoples to world economic developments and European imperialism.**

Therefore, the student is able to:

7-12 Analyze how the termination of the Atlantic slave trade and increased output of European manufactured goods affected economies of West and Central Africa. [**Reconstruct patterns of historical succession and duration**]

9-12 Explain the impact of religious and political revolutions in the West African Sudan on state-building, Islamization, and European imperial conquest. [**Examine the influence of ideas**]

7-12 Explain the rise of Zanzibar and other commercial empires in East Africa in the context of international trade in ivory, cloves, and slaves. [**Appreciate historical perspectives**]

5-12 Describe the rise of the Zulu empire and analyze its effects on African societies and European colonial settlement. [**Formulate historical questions**]

5-12 Assess the effects of the discovery of diamonds and gold in South Africa on political and race relations among British colonial authorities, Afrikaners, and Africans. [**Analyze cause-and-effect relationships**]

9-12 Analyze the sources and effectiveness of military, political, and religious resistance movements against European conquest in such regions as Algeria, Morocco, West Africa, the Sudan, Ethiopia, and South Africa. [**Analyze cause-and-effect relationships**]

5-12 Explain major changes in the political geography of northern and Sub-Saharan Africa between 1880 and 1914. [**Draw upon the data in historical maps**]

STANDARD 6	Major global trends from 1750-1914.

6   **The student understands major global trends from 1750 to 1914.**

Therefore, the student is able to:

5-12 Describe major shifts in world population and urbanization in this era and analyze how such factors as industrialization, migration, changing diets, and scientific and medical advances affected worldwide demographic trends. [**Interrogate historical data**]

7-12 Compare industrialization and its social impact in Great Britain, France, Germany, the United States, Russia, Japan, or other countries. [**Compare and contrast differing values, behaviors, and institutions**]

7-12 Describe major patterns of long-distance migration of Europeans, Africans, and Asians and analyze causes and consequences of these movements. [**Analyze cause-and-effect relationships**]

7-12 Explain major changes in world political boundaries during this era and analyze why a relatively few European states achieved such extensive military, political, and economic power in the world. [**Analyze cause-and-effect relationships**]

9-12 Assess the importance of ideas associated with nationalism, republicanism, liberalism, and constitutionalism on 19th-century political life in such states as Great Britain, France, the United States, Germany, Russia, Mexico, Argentina, the Ottoman Empire, China, and Japan. [**Identify issues and problems in the past**]

7-12 Identify regions where Christianity and Islam were growing in this era and analyze causes of 19th-century movements of reform or renewal in Buddhism, Christianity, Hinduism, Islam, and Judaism. [**Interrogate historical data**]

9-12 Identify patterns of social and cultural continuity in various societies and analyze ways in which peoples maintained traditions and resisted external challenges in this era of expanding Western hegemony. [**Reconstruct patterns of historical succession and duration**]

ERA 8

A Half-Century of Crisis and Achievement, 1900-1945

Giving Shape to World History

On a winter's day in 1903 the "Kitty Hawk," Orville and Wilbur Wright's experimental flying machine, lifted off the ground for twelve seconds. In the decades that followed air travel was perfected, and all the physical barriers that had obstructed long-distance communication among human groups virtually disappeared. Oceans, deserts, and mountain ranges no longer mattered much when people living thousands of miles apart were determined to meet, talk, negotiate, or do business. For the first time in history the north polar region became a crossroads of international travel as air pilots sought the shortest routes between countries of the Northern Hemisphere. Radio and, at mid-century, television revolutionized communication in another way. Long-distance messages no longer had to be transported from one point to another by boat or train or even transmitted along wires or cables. Now messages, whether designed to inform, entertain, persuade, or deceive, could be broadcast from a single point to millions of listeners or watchers simultaneously.

These and other technological wonders both expressed and contributed to the growing complexity and unpredictability of human affairs. In some ways peoples of the world became more tightly knit than ever before. Global economic integration moved ahead. Literacy spread more widely. Research and knowledge networks reached round the world. However, in other respects division and conflict multiplied. Economic and territorial rivalries among nations became harsher. Laboratories and factories turned out more lethal weapons and in greater quantities than ever before. People rose up against autocratic governments on every continent. Among the turbulent trends of the era, two developments seem most prominent.

The 20th-Century's Thirty Years War: The powers of destruction that centuries of accumulated technical and scientific skill gave to human beings became horrifyingly apparent in the two global wars of the 20th century. In the Thirty Years War of the 1600s, one of Europe's most destructive contests, more than 4 million people may have died. The wars of 1914-1945, by contrast, took 45 million lives. Since World War I sowed copious seeds of the second conflict, the complex links of cause and effect over the entire period make a compelling subject for the world history student. Though both wars engulfed Europe, the globe is the proper context for understanding them. Air power, especially in World War II, meant that no country's borders were safe, whatever the distances involved. Campaigns were fought from the mid-Pacific to West Africa and from Siberia to the North Atlantic. Combatants came from many lands, including thousands from European colonial possessions. The century's first five decades were not, however, all violence and gloom. In the midst of war and world depression heroism and ingenuity abounded. Age-old diseases were conquered or brought under control. Democracy endured in many states despite recurrent crises, and governments responded with remarkable efficiency to the demands of war-time management and welfare.

Revolution and Protest: Human aspirations toward democratic government, national independence, and social justice were first expressed on a large scale in human affairs in the 1750-1914 era. These aspirations continued to inspire revolutions throughout the first half of the 20th century. The most dramatic political changes occurred in Russia, China, Mexico, and Turkey. In all these places jarring shifts and disturbances in economic life, both local and international, were at the root of the political crises. In all of them, moreover, contests quickly developed between the advocates of liberal, parliamentary democracy and those who championed an authoritarian or single-party state as the most efficient instrument of political and economic transformation. Apart from revolutions, relatively peaceful movements of protest and dissent forced a broadening of the democratic base, including voting rights for women, in a number of countries. The European colonial empires saw few violent risings between 1900 and 1945. There was, however, no colonial "golden age." Resistance, protest, and calls for reform, drawing heavily on the liberal and nationalist ideals that the Western powers proclaimed, dogged imperial regimes all across Africa and Asia.

Why Study This Era?

▸ Exploration of the first half of the 20th century is of special importance if students are to understand the responsibilities they face at the close of the millennium. The two world wars were destructive beyond anything human society had every experienced. If students are to grasp both the toll of such violence and the price that has sometimes been paid in the quest for peace, they must understand the causes and costs of these world-altering struggles.

▸ In this era the ideologies of communism and fascism, both rooted in the 19th century, were put into practice on a large scale in Russia, Italy, Germany, and Japan. Both movements challenged liberal democratic traditions and involved elaborate forms of authoritarian repression. The fascist cause was discredited in 1945, communism by the early 1990s. Even so, assessing the progress of our own democratic values and institutions in this century requires parallel study of these two alternative political visions. What did they promise? How did they work as social and economic experiments? In what conditions might they find new adherents in the future?

▸ Active citizens must continually re-examine the role of the United States in contemporary world affairs. Between 1900 and 1945 this country rose to international leadership; at the end of the period it stood astride the globe. How did we attain such a position? How has it changed since mid-century? Any informed judgment of our foreign policies and programs requires an understanding of our place among nations since the beginning of the century.

▸ In both scientific and cultural life this era ushered in the "modern." The scientific theories as well as aesthetic and literary movements that humanity found so exhilarating and disturbing in the first half of the century continue to have an immense impact on how we see the world around us.

Overview

Standard 1: Reform, revolution, and social change in the world economy of the early century

Standard 2: The causes and global consequences of World War I

Standard 3: The search for peace and stability in the 1920s and 1930s

Standard 4: The causes and global consequences of World War II

Standard 5: Major global trends from 1900 to the end of World War II

STANDARD 1	Reform, revolution, and social change in the world economy of the early century.

1A **The student understands the world industrial economy emerging in the early 20th century.**

Therefore, the student is able to:

7-12 Compare the industrial power of Great Britain, France, Germany, Japan, and the United States in the early 20th century. [**Utilize visual and mathematical data**]

5-12 Analyze the impact of industrial development on the culture and working lives of middle- and working-class people in Europe, Japan, and the United States. [**Analyze cause-and-effect relationships**]

7-12 Explain leading ideas of liberalism, social reformism, conservatism, and socialism as competing ideologies in the early 20th-century world. [**Examine the influence of ideas**]

9-12 Explain how entrepreneurs, scientists, technicians, and urban workers in Africa, Asia, and Latin America participated in world trade and industrialization. [**Employ quantitative analysis**]

9-12 Analyze why European colonial territories and Latin American countries continued to maintain largely agricultural and mining economies in the early 20th century. [**Identify issues and problems in the past**]

1B **The student understands the causes and consequences of important resistance and revolutionary movements of the early 20th century.**

Therefore, the student is able to:

9-12 Analyze the degree to which the South African (Anglo-Boer) War was an example of "total war." [**Interrogate historical data**]

7-12 Explain the causes of the Russian rebellion of 1905 and assess its impact on reform in the succeeding decade. [**Analyze cause-and-effect relationships**]

9-12 Analyze the efforts of the revolutionary government of the Young Turks to reform Ottoman government and society. [**Interrogate historical data**]

5-12 Analyze the significance of the Mexican Revolution as the first 20th-century movement in which peasants played a prominent role. [**Appreciate historical perspectives**]

7-12 Assess the promise and failure of China's 1911 republican revolution to address the country's political, economic, and social problems. [**Compare and contrast differing values and institutions**]

STANDARD 2   The causes and global consequences of World War I.

2A   The student understands the causes of World War I.

Therefore, the student is able to:

7-12 Analyze the relative importance of economic and political rivalries, ethnic and ideological conflicts, militarism, and imperialism as underlying causes of the war. [**Analyze multiple causation**]

9-12 Analyze the degree to which class and other social conflicts in Europe contributed to the outbreak of war. [**Analyze multiple causation**]

7-12 Evaluate ways in which popular faith in science, technology, and material progress affected attitudes toward war among European states. [**Formulate historical questions**]

5-12 Analyze the precipitating causes of the war and the factors that produced military stalemate. [**Analyze cause-and-effect relationships**]

2B   The student understands the global scope, outcome, and human costs of the war.

Therefore, the student is able to:

5-12 Describe the major turning points of the war and the principal theaters of conflict in Europe, the Middle East, Sub-Saharan Africa, East Asia, and the South Pacific. [**Interrogate historical data**]

9-12 Analyze the role of nationalism and propaganda in mobilizing civilian populations in support of "total war." [**Examine the influence of ideas**]

5-12 Explain how massive industrial production and innovations in military technology affected strategy, tactics, and the scale and duration of the war. [**Analyze cause-and-effect relationships**]

9-12 Explain how colonial peoples contributed to the war effort of both the Allies and the Central Powers by providing military forces and supplies. [**Evaluate the implementation of a decision**]

7-12 Analyze how the Russian Revolution and the entry of the United States affected the course and outcome of the war. [**Analyze cause-and-effect relationships**]

5-12 Assess the short-term demographic, social, economic, and environmental consequences of the war's unprecedented violence and destruction. [**Formulate historical questions**]

2C **The student understands the causes and consequences of the Russian Revolution of 1917.**

Therefore, the student is able to:

5-12 Explain the causes of the Russian Revolution of 1917 and analyze why the revolutionary government progressed from moderate to radical. [**Analyze multiple causation**]

9-12 Explain Leninist political ideology and how the Bolsheviks adapted Marxist ideas to conditions peculiar to Russia. [**Interrogate historical data**]

7-12 Assess the effects of the New Economic Policy on Soviet society, economy, and government. [**Analyze cause-and-effect relationships**]

5-12 Describe the rise of Joseph Stalin to power in the Soviet Union and analyze ways in which collectivization and the first Five-Year Plan disrupted and transformed Soviet society in the 1920s and 1930s. [**Evaluate the implementation of a decision**]

9-12 Analyze the challenges that revolutionary Russia posed to Western governments and explain the impact of the Bolshevik victory on world labor movements. [**Interrogate historical data**]

STANDARD 3 **The search for peace and stability in the 1920s and 1930s.**

3A **The student understands postwar efforts to achieve lasting peace and social and economic recovery.**

Therefore, the student is able to:

5-12 Describe the conflicting aims and aspirations of the conferees at Versailles and analyze the responses of major powers to the terms of the settlement. [**Consider multiple perspectives**]

9-12 Explain how the collapse of the German, Hapsburg, and Ottoman empires and the creation of new states affected international relations in Europe and the Middle East. [**Analyze cause-and-effect relationships**]

5-12 Explain how the League of Nations was founded and assess its promise and limitations as a vehicle for achieving lasting peace. [**Analyze cause-and-effect relationships**]

7-12 Analyze the objectives and achievements of women's political movements in the context of World War I and its aftermath. [**Analyze cause-and-effect relationships**]

9-12 Analyze how the governments of Britain, France, Germany, and Italy responded to the economic and political challenges of the postwar decade. [**Interrogate historical data**]

7-12 Assess the effects of United States isolationist policies on world politics and international relations in the 1920s. [**Evaluate the implementation of a decision**]

3B   **The student understands economic, social, and political transformations in Africa, Asia, and Latin America in the 1920s and 1930s.**

Therefore, the student is able to:

7-12   Analyze the struggle between the Kuomintang and the Communist Party for dominance in China in the context of political fragmentation, economic transformation, and Japanese and European imperialism. [**Interrogate historical data**]

7-12   Analyze how militarism and fascism succeeded in derailing parliamentary democracy in Japan. [**Interrogate historical data**]

5-12   Explain how the mandate system altered patterns of European colonial rule in Africa and the Middle East. [**Evaluate the implementation of a decision**]

7-12   Explain aims and policies of European colonial regimes in India, Africa, and Southeast Asia and assess the impact of colonial policies on indigenous societies and economies. [**Analyze cause-and-effect relationships**]

9-12   Analyze how social and economic conditions of colonial rule, as well as ideals of liberal democracy and national autonomy, contributed to the rise of nationalist movements in India, Africa, and Southeast Asia. [**Analyze cause-and-effect relationships**]

5-12   Analyze how the World War I settlement contributed to the rise of both pan-Arabism and nationalist struggles for independence in the Middle East. [**Formulate historical questions**]

9-12   Assess the challenges to democratic government in Latin America in the context of class divisions, economic dependency, and United States intervention. [**Analyze cause-and-effect relationships**]

3C   **The student understands the interplay between scientific or technological innovations and new patterns of social and cultural life between 1900 and 1940.**

Therefore, the student is able to:

7-12   Explain the impact of the work of Einstein, Freud, Curie, and other scientists on traditional views of nature, the cosmos, and the psyche. [**Explain the importance of the individual**]

9-12   Describe major medical successes in the treatment of infectious diseases and analyze the causes and social costs of the world influenza pandemic of 1918-1919. [**Employ quantitative data**]

5-12   Explain ways in which the airplane, automobile, and modern railway affected world commerce, international migration, and work and leisure habits. [**Interrogate historical data**]

7-12   Analyze the social and cultural dimensions of mass consumption of goods such as automobiles, bicycles, refrigerators, radios, and synthetic fabrics in various parts of the world. [**Support interpretations with historical evidence**]

9-12 Analyze ways in which new forms of communication affected the relationship of government to citizens and bolstered the power of new authoritarian regimes. [**Formulate historical questions**]

3D **The student understands the interplay of new artistic and literary movements with changes in social and cultural life in various parts of the world in the post-war decades.**

Therefore, the student is able to:

7-12 Evaluate the impact of World War I and its aftermath on literature, art, and intellectual life in Europe and the United States. [**Draw upon visual and literary sources**]

9-12 Evaluate the meaning and social impact of innovative movements in literature, architecture and the fine arts, such as Cubism, Surrealism, Expressionism, Socialist Realism, and jazz. [**Draw upon visual, literary, and musical sources**]

7-12 Evaluate the impact of innovative movements in Western art and literature on other regions of the world and the influence of African and Asian art forms on Europe. [**Draw comparisons across regions**]

5-12 Analyze how new media—newspapers, magazines, commercial advertising, film, and radio—contributed to the rise of mass culture around the world. [**Obtain historical data from a variety of sources**]

3E **The student understands the causes and global consequences of the Great Depression.**

Therefore, the student is able to:

9-12 Analyze the financial, economic, and social causes of the Depression and why it spread to most parts of the world. [**Analyze multiple causation**]

5-12 Assess the human costs of the Depression, and compare its impact on economy and society in different countries and economic regions of the world. [**Compare and contrast differing values, behaviors, and institutions**]

9-12 Analyze ways in which the Depression affected colonial peoples of Africa and Asia and how it contributed to the growth of nationalist movements. [**Analyze cause-and-effect relationships**]

7-12 Analyze how the Depression contributed to the growth of socialist and communist movements and how it affected capitalist economic theory and practice in leading industrial powers in Western countries. [**Analyze cause-and-effect relationships**]

5-12 Describe how governments, businesses, social groups, families, and individuals endeavored to cope with the hardships of world depression. [**Employ quantitative analyses**]

| STANDARD 4 | The causes and global consequences of World War II. |

4A **The student understands the causes of World War II.**

Therefore, the student is able to:

5-12 Explain the ideologies of fascism and Nazism and analyze how fascist and authoritarian regimes seized power and gained mass support in Italy, Germany, Spain, and Japan. [**Analyze multiple causation**]

7-12 Analyze the relative importance of the legacy of World War I, the depression, ethnic and ideological conflicts, imperialism, and traditional political or economic rivalries as underlying causes of World War II. [**Analyze multiple causation**]

5-12 Explain German, Italian, and Japanese military conquests and drives for empire in the 1930s. [**Evaluate major debates among historians**]

7-12 Analyze the consequences of Britain, France, the United States, and other Western democracies' failure to effectively oppose fascist aggression. [**Evaluate major debates among historians**]

7-12 Analyze the precipitating causes of the war and the reasons for early German and Japanese victories. [**Analyze multiple causation**]

9-12 Analyze the motives and consequences of the Soviet nonaggression pacts with Germany and Japan. [**Analyze cause-and-effect relationships**]

4B **The student understands the global scope, outcome, and human costs of the war.**

Therefore, the student is able to:

5-12 Explain the major turning points of the war, and describe the principal theaters of conflict in Western Europe, Eastern Europe, the Soviet Union, North Africa, Asia, and the Pacific. [**Interrogate historical data**]

5-12 Assess how the political and diplomatic leadership of such individuals as Churchill, Roosevelt, Hitler, Mussolini, and Stalin affected the outcome of the war. [**Explain the importance of the individual**]

5-12 Analyze how and why the Nazi regime perpetrated a "war against the Jews" and describe the devastation suffered by Jews and other groups in the Nazi Holocaust. [**Analyze cause-and-effect relationships**]

9-12 Compare World Wars I and II in terms of the impact of industrial production, political goals, national mobilization, technological innovations, and scientific research on strategies, tactics, and levels of destruction. [**Marshal evidence of antecedent circumstances**]

9-12 Assess the consequences of World War II as a total war. [**Formulate historical questions**]

| STANDARD 5 | Major global trends from 1900 to the end of World War II. |

5 **The student understands major global trends from 1900 to the end of World War II.**

Therefore, the student is able to:

5-12 Describe major shifts in world geopolitics between 1900 and 1945 and explain the growing role of the United States in international affairs. [**Analyze cause-and-effect relationships**]

7-12 Assess the nature and extent of Western military, political, and economic power in the world in 1945 compared with 1900. [**Interrogate historical data**]

7-12 Compare the ideologies, policies, and governing methods of 20th-century totalitarian regimes with those of contemporary democracies and absolutist states of earlier centuries. [**Draw comparisons across eras**]

9-12 Assess the degree to which revolutionary movements in countries such as Mexico, Russia, and China either drew upon or rejected liberal, republican, and constitutional ideals of 18th-and 19th century revolutions. [**Identify relevant historical antecedents**]

9-12 Analyze why mass consumer economies developed in some industrialized countries of the world but not in others. [**Employ quantitative analysis**]

5-12 Explain how new technologies and scientific breakthroughs both benefitted and imperiled humankind. [**Formulate historical questions**]

7-12 Analyze ways in which secular ideologies such as nationalism, fascism, communism, and materialism challenged or were challenged by established religions and ethical systems. [**Compare and contrast different sets of ideas, values, and institutions**]

7-12 Assess the relative importance of such factors as world war, depression, nationalist ideology, labor organizations, communism, and liberal democratic ideals in the emergence of movements for national self-rule or sovereignty in Africa and Asia. [**Formulate historical questions**]

7-12 Identify patterns of social and cultural continuity in various societies, and analyze ways in which peoples maintained traditions, sustained basic loyalties, and resisted external challenges in this era of recurrent world crises. [**Explain historical continuity and change**]

ERA 9

The 20th Century Since 1945: Promises and Paradoxes

Giving Shape to World History

The closer we get to the present the more difficult it becomes to distinguish between the large forces of change and the small. Surveying the long sweep of history from early hominid times to the end of World War II, we might reach at least partial consensus about what is important to the development of the whole human community and what is not. The multifarious trends of the past half-century, however, are for the most part still working themselves out. Therefore, we cannot know what history students one or two hundred years from now will think was worth remembering about the decades after World War II. Clearly, the era has been one of tensions, paradoxes, and contradictory trends. Some of these countercurrents provide students with a framework for investigation and analysis.

Democracy and Tyranny: In the three decades following World War II, a multitude of new sovereign states appeared around the world. The breakup of the Soviet Union that began in 1990 introduced fifteen more. Triumphant nationalism, in short, has radically transformed the globe's political landscape. Even so, peoples on every continent have had to struggle persistently for democracy and justice against the powerful counterforces of authoritarianism, neo-colonialism, warlordism, and stolid bureaucracy. Many of the newer independent states have also faced daunting challenges in raising their peoples' standard of living while at the same time participating in a global economic system where industrialized countries have had a distinct advantage. The political, and in some places economic, reform movements that bloomed in Africa, Eurasia, and Latin America in the 1980s are evidence of the vitality of civic aspirations that originated more than two centuries ago.

War and Peace: World War II ended amid anxious hopes for genuine world peace. In 1945, however, the Cold War was already underway. For forty years recurrent international crises and the doubtful consolations of mutually assured destruction dominated world affairs. The European colonial empires were dismantled and power transferred to new nationalist leaders with less violence or acrimony than anyone might have expected—with some exceptions. Nationalists waged protracted anti-colonial wars in Vietnam, Algeria, Angola, and Mozambique. When the Soviet Union collapsed, the threat of catastrophe receded and the world sighed in relief. On the other hand, local wars and terrorist assaults multiplied as ancient enemies settled old scores and ethnic or nationalist feelings rose to the surface. Amid the ruthless confrontations of the second half of the century, people of good will have continued to seek peace. The achievements and limitations of the post-World War II settlements, the United Nations, the European Economic Community, Middle East negotiations, and numerous other forms of international cooperation are all worthy of serious study for the lessons they may offer the coming generation.

Global Links and Communal Identity: The transformations that the world experienced in the previous three eras appear modest in comparison with the bewildering pace and complexity of change in the late 20th century. The revolution of global communication has potentially put everyone in touch with everyone else. Business travelers, scientists, labor migrants, and refugees move incessantly from country to country. Currency transfers ricochet from bank to bank. The young men and women of Bangkok, Moscow, and Wichita Falls watch the same movies and sport the same brand of jeans. In economy, politics, and culture the human community is in a continuous process of restructuring itself. Global interdependence, however, has a flip side. As the gales of change blow, people seek communal bonds and identities more urgently than ever. Communalism has frequently led to fear and suspicion of the "other." Even so, the institutions and values that communities share protect them in some measure from the shocks of the new and unforeseen. The social and cultural bonds of family, village, ethnic community, religion, and nation provide a framework for estimating how others will think and behave and for calculating with some confidence the pattern of affairs from day to day.

Countercurrents in the Quality of Life: The early 20th century promised, at least in the industrialized countries, a new age of progress through science, technology, and rational policy-making. Fifty years and two world wars later, humanity was less optimistic about its future. Art and literature after 1945 starkly reported the era's skepticism and angst. Science, medicine, and techniques of human organization continued to benefit society in wondrous ways. A truly global middle class emerged, and it enjoyed rising prosperity for several decades. Several countries, notably along the eastern Pacific rim, became economic powers to be reckoned with. On the other hand, the world population explosion, persistent poverty, environmental degradation, and epidemic disease have defied the best efforts of statesmanship, civic action, and scientific imagination. Amid the distresses and dangers of the era, people have sought not only communal ties but also moral and metaphysical certainties. Spiritual quests and ethical questionings have been a vital part of the cultural history of the past half-century.

Why Study This Era?

▶ The economic and social forces moving in our contemporary world will make sense to students only in relation to the rush of events since 1945. Historical perspectives on the Cold War, the breakup of empires, the population explosion, the rise of the Pacific rim, and the other sweeping developments of the era are indispensable for unraveling the causes and perhaps even discerning the likely consequences of events now unfolding. Students in school today are going to be responsible for addressing the promises and paradoxes of the age. They will not be able to do this by reading headlines or picking bits of "background" from the past. They must gain some sense of the whole flow of developments and build a mental architecture for understanding the history of the world.

Overview

Standard 1: How post-World War II reconstruction occurred, new international power relations took shape, and colonial empires broke up

Standard 2: The search for community, stability, and peace in an interdependent world

Standard 3: Major global trends since World War II

STANDARD 1	How post-World War II reconstruction occurred, new international power relations took shape, and colonial empires broke up.

1A **The student understands major political and economic changes that accompanied post-war recovery.**

Therefore, the student is able to:

7-12 Explain how the Western European countries and Japan achieved rapid economic recovery after World War II. [**Employ quantitative data**]

7-12 Analyze connections between the political stabilization of Western European societies and the Marshall Plan, the European Economic Community, government planning, and the growth of welfare states. [**Analyze cause-and-effect relationships**]

5-12 Compare the United States' commanding economic position and international leadership after World War II with its international policies following World War I. [**Interrogate historical data**]

9-12 Explain why fascism was discredited after World War II and how popular democratic institutions were established in such countries as Italy, the German Federal Republic, Greece, India, Spain, and Portugal between 1945 and 1975. [**Marshal evidence of antecedent circumstances**]

5-12 Explain why the United Nations was founded and assess its successes and failures up to the 1970s. [**Marshal evidence of antecedent circumstances**]

1B **The student understands why global power shifts took place and the Cold War broke out in the aftermath of World War II.**

Therefore, the student is able to:

5-12 Explain how political, economic, and military conditions prevailing in the mid-1940s led to the Cold War. [**Analyze cause-and-effect relationships**]

7-12 Analyze major differences in the political ideologies and values of the Western democracies and the Soviet bloc. [**Compare and contrast different ideas, values, and institutions**]

7-12   Compare the impact of Soviet domination on Eastern Europe with changes that occurred in German and Japanese society under Allied occupation. [**Compare and contrast differing values, behaviors, and institutions**]

7-12   Explain how the Communist Party rose to power in China between 1936 and 1949 and assess the benefits and costs of Communist policies under Mao Zedong, including the Great Leap Forward and the Cultural Revolution. [**Analyze cause-and-effect relationships**]

5-12   Explain the causes and international and local consequences of major Cold War crises, such as the Berlin blockade, the Korean War, the Polish workers' protest, the Hungarian revolt, the Suez crisis, the Cuban missile crisis, the Indonesian civil war, and the Soviet invasion of Czechoslovakia. [**Formulate historical questions**]

9-12   Analyze how political, diplomatic, and economic conflict and competition between the United States and the Soviet Union affected developments in such countries as Egypt, Iran, the Congo, Vietnam, Chile, and Guatemala. [**Analyze multiple causation**]

7-12   Analyze interconnections between superpower rivalries and the development of new military, nuclear, and space technology. [**Analyze cause-and-effect relationships**]

9-12   Assess the impact of the Cold War on art, literature, and popular culture around the world. [**Obtain historical data from a variety of sources**]

1C   The student understands how African, Asian, and Caribbean peoples achieved independence from European colonial rule.

Therefore, the student is able to:

7-12   Assess the impact of Indian nationalism on other movements in Africa and Asia and analyze why the subcontinent was partitioned into India and Pakistan. [**Analyze cause-and-effect relationships**]

7-12   Analyze the impact of World War II and postwar global politics on the rise of mass nationalist movements in Africa and Southeast Asia. [**Analyze cause-and-effect relationships**]

9-12   Analyze connections between the rise of independence movements in Africa and Southeast Asia and social transformations such as demographic changes, urbanization, and the emergence of Western-educated elites. [**Analyze cause-and-effect relationships**]

7-12   Analyze why some African and Asian countries achieved independence through constitutional devolution of power and others as a result of armed revolution. [**Compare and contrast differing values, behaviors, and institutions**]

5-12   Explain how international conditions affected the creation of Israel and analyze why persistent conflict developed between Israel and both Arab Palestinians and neighboring states. [**Interrogate historical data**]

9-12   Describe economic and social problems that new states faced in the 1960s and 1970s and analyze why military regimes or one-party states replaced parliamentary-style governments throughout much of Africa. [**Reconstruct patterns of historical succession and duration**]

STANDARD 2	The search for community, stability, and peace in an interdependent world.

2A   **The student understands how population explosion and environmental change have altered conditions of life around the world.**

Therefore, the student is able to:

7-12   Analyze causes of the world's accelerating population growth rate and connections between population growth and economic and social development in many countries. [**Analyze multiple causation**]

7-12   Describe the global proliferation of cities and the rise of the megalopolis and assess the impact of urbanization on family life, standards of living, class relations, and ethnic identity. [**Analyze cause-and-effect relationships**]

7-12   Assess why scientific, technological, and medical advances have improved living standards for many yet hunger, poverty, and epidemic disease have persisted. [**Evaluate major debates among historians**]

5-12   Analyze how population growth, urbanization, industrialization, warfare, and the global market economy have contributed to environmental alterations. [**Analyze cause-and-effect relationships**]

5-12   Assess the effectiveness of efforts by governments and citizens' movements to protect the global natural environment. [**Obtain historical data**]

2B   **The student understands how increasing economic interdependence has transformed human society.**

Therefore, the student is able to:

5-12   Analyze how global communications and changing international labor demands have shaped new patterns of world migration since World War II. [**Analyze cause-and-effect relationships**]

5-12   Explain the effects of the European Economic Community and its growth on economic productivity and political integration in Europe. [**Interrogate historical data**]

9-12   Compare systems of economic management in communist and capitalist countries and analyze the global economic impact of multinational corporations. [**Compare and contrast differing institutions**]

7-12   Analyze why economic disparities between industrialized and developing countries have persisted or increased and how both neo-colonialism and authoritarian political leadership have affected development in African and Asian countries. [**Formulate historical questions**]

5-12   Explain the emergence of the Pacific Rim economy and analyze how such countries as South Korea or Singapore have achieved economic growth in recent decades. [**Analyze cause-and-effect relationships**]

7-12   Analyze the continuing growth of mass consumption of commodities and resources since World War II. [**Employ quantitative data**]

9-12   Analyze the importance of such factors as black markets, speculation, and trade in illegal products for both national and global markets. [**Obtain historical data from a variety of sources**]

9-12   Analyze how the oil crisis and its aftermath in the early 1970s revealed the extent and complexity of global economic interdependence. [**Interrogate historical data**]

2C   The student understands how liberal democracy, market economies, and human rights movements have reshaped political and social life.

Therefore, the student is able to:

5-12   Assess the progress of human and civil rights around the world since the 1948 U.N. Declaration of Human Rights. [**Formulate a position or course of action on an issue**]

5-12   Analyze how feminist movements and social conditions have affected the lives of women in different parts of the world and compare women's progress toward - social equality, economic opportunity, and political rights in various countries. [**Draw comparisons across regions**]

7-12   Explain why Cold War tensions eased in the 1970s and analyze how such developments as the Helsinki Accords, the Soviet invasion of Afghanistan, and Reagan-Gorbachev "summit diplomacy" affected progress toward detente. [**Interrogate historical data**]

7-12   Explain why the Soviet and other communist governments collapsed and the Soviet Union splintered into numerous states in the 1980s and early 1990s. [**Marshal evidence of antecedent circumstances**]

9-12   Assess the strengths of democratic institutions and civic culture in countries such as Britain, France, Germany, Canada, the United States, Japan, India, and Mexico and analyze potential challenges to civil society in democratic states. [**Interrogate historical data**]

9-12   Assess the success of democratic reform movements in challenging authoritarian governments in Africa, Asia, and Latin America. [**Formulate a position or course of action on an issue**]

5-12   Explain the dismantling of the apartheid system in South Africa and the winning of political rights by the black majority. [**Explain historical continuity and change**]

2D   The student understands major sources of tension and conflict in the contemporary world and efforts that have been made to address them.

Therefore, the student is able to:

7-12   Analyze causes and consequences of continuing urban protest and reformist economic policies in post-Mao China in the context of state authoritarianism. [**Analyze cause-and-effect relationships**]

7-12   Explain political objectives of militant religious movements in various countries and analyze social and economic factors contributing to the growth of these movements. [**Examine the influence of ideas**]

9-12   Analyze why terrorist movements have proliferated and the extent of their impact on politics and society in various countries. [**Evaluate the implementation of a decision**]

9-12   Assess the impact of population pressure, poverty, and environmental degradation on the breakdown of state authority in various countries in the 1980s and 1990s. [**Analyze multiple causation**]

7-12   Analyze the causes, consequences, and moral implications for the world community of mass killings or famines in such places as Cambodia, Somalia, Rwanda, and Bosnia-Herzegovina. [**Marshal evidence of antecedent circumstances**]

5-12   Assess the progress that has been made since the 1970s in resolving conflict between Israel and neighboring states. [**Analyze multiple causation**]

2E   **The student understands major worldwide scientific and technological trends of the second half of the 20th century.**

Therefore, the student is able to:

5-12   Describe worldwide implications of the revolution in nuclear, electronic, and computer technology. [**Formulate historical questions**]

9-12   Analyze interconnections between space exploration and developments since the 1950s in scientific research, agricultural productivity, consumer culture, intelligence gathering, and other aspects of contemporary life. [**Analyze cause-and-effect relationships**]

5-12   Assess the social and cultural implications of recent medical successes such as development of antibiotics and vaccines and the conquest of smallpox. [**Interrogate historical data**]

9-12   Analyze the changing structure and organization of scientific and technological research, including the role of governments, corporations, international agencies, universities, and scientific communities. [**Employ quantitative data**]

2F   **The student understands worldwide cultural trends of the second half of the 20th century.**

Therefore, the student is able to:

9-12   Evaluate the impact of World War II and its aftermath on literature, art, and intellectual life in Europe and other parts of the world. [**Analyze cause-and-effect relationships**]

9-12   Evaluate the meaning and social impact of innovative movements in literature and the arts such as Existentialism, Abstract Expressionism, or Pop Art. [**Draw upon visual and literary sources**]

5-12   Assess the influence of television, the Internet, and other forms of electronic communication on the creation and diffusion of cultural and political information worldwide. [**Formulate historical questions**]

7-12 Analyze connections among electronic communications, international marketing, and the emergence of popular "global culture" in the late 20th century. [**Obtain historical data from a variety of sources**]

5-12 Describe varieties of religious belief and practice in the contemporary world and analyze how the world's religions have responded to challenges and uncertainties of the late 20th century. [**Analyze the influence of ideas**]

9-12 Describe ways in which art, literature, religion, and traditional customs have expressed or strengthened national or other communal loyalties in recent times. [**Examine the influence of ideas, human interests, and beliefs**]

STANDARD 3   Major global trends since World War II.

3   **The student understands major global trends since World War II.**

Therefore, the student is able to:

7-12 Explain the changing configuration of political boundaries in the world since 1900 and analyze connections between nationalist ideology and the proliferation of sovereign states. [**Marshal evidence of antecedent circumstances**]

7-12 Explain why the Cold War took place and ended and assess its significance as a 20th-century event. [**Analyze multiple causation**]

5-12 Compare causes, consequences, and major patterns of international migrations in the late 20th century with world population movements of the 19th century and the first half of the 20th. [**Draw comparisons across eras and regions**]

9-12 Define "postindustrial society" and assess the usefulness of this concept in comparing the late 20th century with the period from the industrial revolution to 1950. [**Draw comparisons across eras and regions**]

5-12 Assess the degree to which both human rights and democratic ideals and practices have been advanced in the world during the 20th century. [**Formulate historical questions**]

9-12 Analyze causes of economic imbalances and social inequalities among the world's peoples and assess efforts made to close these gaps. [**Employ quantitative analysis**]

7-12 Analyze causes and consequences of the world's shift from bipolar to multipolar centers of economic, political, and military power. [**Analyze cause-and-effect relationships**]

9-12 Analyze connections between globalizing trends in economy, technology, and culture in the late 20th century and dynamic assertions of traditional cultural identity and distinctiveness. [**Analyze cause-and-effect relationships**]

World History Across the Eras

Not all of the events in world history that students should address can be bracketed within one of the nine eras presented in this chapter. The complexities of today's world are in part a consequence of changes that have been in the making for centuries, even millennia. Important historical continuities can be discerned that link one period with another. And even though history may not repeat itself in any precise way, certain historical patterns do recur. Studying one development in world history in the light of an earlier, similar development can sharpen our understanding of both.

This final standard invites teachers and students to give attention to long-term changes and recurring patterns of the past. The range of potential subjects in this category is nearly limitless. What follows is only suggestive of topics that require students to step way back from our spinning planet, as it were, to take in broad vistas and long spans of time.

STANDARD 1	**Long-term changes and recurring patterns in world history.**

Therefore, the student is able to:

7-12 Trace major changes in world population from paleolithic times to the present and explain why these changes occurred, including the effects of major disease pandemics.

5-12 Analyze why humans have built cities and how the character, function, and number of cities have changed over time.

9-12 Assess the usefulness of the concept that the revolutions of tool-making, agriculture, and industrialization constituted the three most important turning points in human history.

5-12 Trace major patterns of long-distance trade from ancient times to the present and analyze ways in which trade has contributed to economic and cultural change in particular societies or civilizations.

7-12 Analyze the origins, development, and characteristics of capitalism and compare capitalist systems with other systems for organizing production, labor, and trade.

5-12 Analyze how ideals and institutions of freedom, equality, justice, and citizenship have changed over time and from one society to another.

5-12 Compare the economic and social importance of slavery and other forms of coerced labor in various societies from ancient times to the present.

7-12 Analyze the development of the nation-state and how nation-states differ from empires or other forms of political organization.

9-12 Analyze the circumstances under which European countries came to exercise temporary military and economic dominance in the world in the late 19th and 20th centuries.

7-12 Compare political revolutionary movements of the past three centuries in terms of ideologies, organization, and successes or failures.

5-12 Analyze ways in which human action has contributed to long-term changes in the natural environment in particular regions or worldwide.

A P P E N D I X

Contributors and Participating Organizations

Organizational Structure of the National History Standards Project

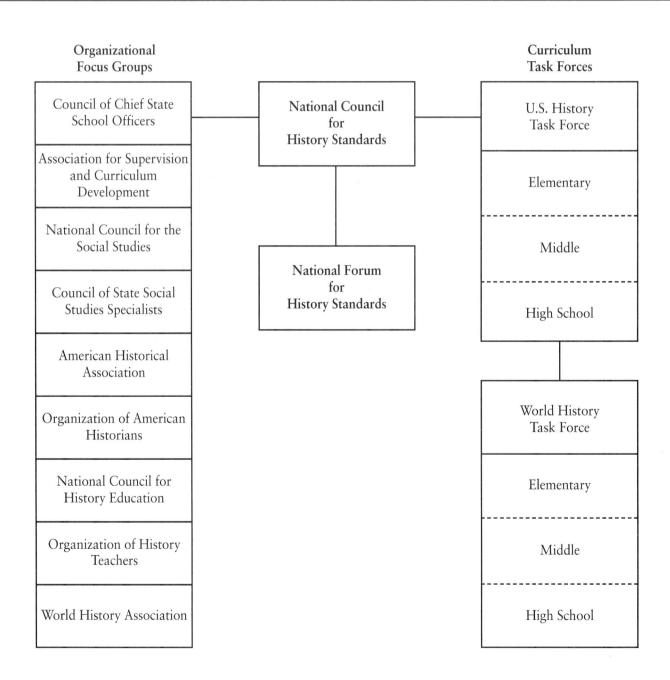

Participating Organizations

American Association of School Librarians

American Association for State and Local History

American Federation of Teachers

American Historical Association

Association for the Study of Afro-American Life and History

Association for Supervision and Curriculum Development

The Atlantic Council of the United States

Center for Civic Education

Council for American Private Education

Council for Basic Education

Council of Chief State School Officers

Council of the Great City Schools

Council of State Social Studies Specialists

League of United Latin American Citizens

Lutheran Schools, The Lutheran Church-Missouri Synod

National Alliance of Black School Educators

National Association for Asian and Pacific American Education

National Association of Elementary School Principals

National Association of Secondary School Principals

National Association of State Boards of Education

National Catholic Educational Association

National Congress of Parents and Teachers

National Council for Geographic Education

National Council for History Education

National Council on Economic Education

The National Council for the Social Studies

National Education Association

Native American Heritage Commission

Organization of American Historians

Organization of History Teachers

Quality Education for Minorities Network

Social Studies Educational Consortium

World History Association

Organizational Rosters

National Council for History Standards

Officers

Charlotte Crabtree, Co-chair
Professor of Education Emeritus
University of California, Los Angeles

Gary B. Nash, Co-chair
Professor of History
University of California, Los Angeles

Linda Symcox, Coordinator
Associate Director
National Center for History in the Schools
University of California, Los Angeles

Members

Charlotte Anderson, President
National Council for Social Studies, 1992-93

Joyce Appleby, President
Organization of American Historians, 1992-1993
Professor of History
University of California, Los Angeles

Samuel Banks, Executive Director
Division of Compensatory and Funded Programs
Baltimore City Public Schools

David Battini, Teacher
Durham High School
Cairo, New York

David Baumbach, Teacher
Woolsair Elementary Gifted Center
Pittsburgh, Pennsylvania

Earl Bell, President
Organization of History Teachers
Teacher, The Laboratory Schools
University of Chicago

Mary Bicouvaris
Associate Professor of Education
Christopher Newport University

Diane Brooks, President
Council of State Social Studies Specialists, 1993
Manager, California Department of Education

Pedro Castillo, Professor of History
University of California, Santa Cruz

Ainslie T. Embree, Professor of History Emeritus
Columbia University

Elizabeth Fox-Genovese, Professor of History
Emory University

Carol Gluck, Professor of History
Columbia University

Darlene Clark Hine, Professor of History
Michigan State University

Bill Honig, President,
Council of Chief State School Officers, 1992
Distinguished Visiting Professor of Education
San Francisco State University

Akira Iriye, Professor of History
Harvard University

Barbara Talbert Jackson, President
Association for Supervision and
Curriculum Development, 1993-94

Kenneth Jackson, Professor of History
Columbia University

Morton Keller, Professor of History
Brandeis University

William Leuchtenburg, President
Americal Historical Association, 1991
Professor of History
University of North Carolina, Chapel Hill

Bernard Lewis, Professor of History
Princeton University

William McNeill, Professor of History Emeritus
University of Chicago

Alan D. Morgan, President,
Council of Chief State School Officers, 1993
State Superintendent of
Public Instruction, New Mexico

Stephanie Pace-Marshall, President
Association for Supervision and Curriculum
Development, 1992-93

John J. Patrick, Director,
Social Studies Development Center and
Professor of Education
Indiana University

Theodore K. Rabb, Chairman,
National Council for History Education
Professor of History
Princeton University

C. Frederick Risinger, Associate Director
Social Studies Development Center and
Professor of Education
Indiana University

Denny Schillings, President
National Council for the Social Studies, 1993-94
Teacher, Homewood-Flossmoor High School
Flossmoor, Illinois

Gilbert T. Sewall, Director
American Textbook Council

Warren Solomon, Curriculum Consultant for
Social Studies
Missouri Department of Elementary and
Secondary Education

Michael R. Winston, Vice President Emeritus
Howard University and
President, Alfred Harcourt Foundation

K-4 Curriculum Task Force

David Baumbach, Teacher
Woolsair Elementary Gifted Center
Pittsburgh, Pennsylvania

Charlotte Crabtree, Professor of Education Emeritus
University of California, Los Angeles

Helen Debelak, Teacher
Birchwood Elementary and Junior High School
Cleveland, Ohio

John M. Fisher, Teacher
Fifth Avenue Elementary School
Columbus, Ohio

Marilyn McKnight, Teacher
Forest Home School
Milwaukee, Wisconsin

Lori Lee Morton, Teacher
Riverside Elementary Schools
Alexandria, Virginia

Minna Novick, Curriculum Consultant
Chicago, Illinois

Joan Parrish-Major, Teacher
University Elementary School
University of California, Los Angeles

Sara Shoob, Vice Principal
Cub Run Elementary School
Centreville, Virginia

Linda Symcox, Associate Director
National Center for History in the Schools
University of California, Los Angeles

U.S. Curriculum Task Force

Kirk S. Ankeney, Teacher
Scripps Ranch High School
San Diego, California

Earl Bell, Teacher
The Laboratory Schools
University of Chicago

Charlotte Crabtree, Professor of Education Emeritus
University of California, Los Angeles

Mark W. Gale, Teacher
Coupeville Junior/Senior High School
Coupeville, Washington

Melvin Garrison, Teacher
Kearny High School
Philadelphia, Pennsylvania

Stan Miesner, Teacher
Reed Junior High School
Springfield, Missouri

Lawrence A. Miller, Head
Social Studies Department
Baltimore City College High School
Baltimore, Maryland

Lori Lee Morton, Teacher
Riverside Elementary Schools
Alexandria, Virginia

Gary B. Nash, Professor of History
University of California, Los Angeles

Minna Novick, Curriculum Consultant
Chicago, Illinois

John J. Patrick, Professor of Education
Indiana University

Daniel A. Preston, Teacher
Umatilla High School
Umatilla, Florida

John Pyne, Humanities Supervisor
West Milford High School
West Milford, New Jersey

Angeline Rinaldo, Teacher
Eaglecrest High School
Aurora, Colorado

William C. Schultheis, Teacher
Lake Clifton/Eastern High School
Baltimore, Maryland

Gloria Sesso, Teacher
Half Hollow High School East
Dix Hills, New York

Linda Symcox, Associate Director
National Center for History in the Schools
University of California, Los Angeles

Helen Treacy, Teacher
Kettering High School
Detroit, Michigan

David Vigilante, Teacher Emeritus
Gompers Secondary School
San Diego, California

World History Curriculum Committee

Joan Arno, Teacher
George Washington High School
Philadelphia, Pennsylvania

David Baumbach, Teacher
Woolsair Elementary Gifted Center
Pittsburgh, Pennsylvania

Richard Bulliet, Professor of History
Columbia University

Ainslee T. Embree, Professor of History Emeritus
Columbia University

Carol Gluck, Professor of History
Columbia University

Akira Iriye, Professor of History
Harvard University

Henry G. Kiernan, Director of Curriculum
West Morris Regional High School District
Chester, New Jersey

Colin Palmer, Professor of History
University of North Carolina, Chapel Hill

Theodore K. Rabb, Professor of History
Princeton University

Richard Saller, Professor of History
University of Chicago

Michael R. Winston, Vice President Emeritus
Howard University, and
President, Alfred Harcourt Foundation

World History Curriculum Task Force

Joann Alberghini, Teacher
Lake View Junior High School
Santa Maria, California

John Arevalo, Teacher
Harlandale High School
San Antonio, Texas

Joan Arno, Teacher,
George Washington High School
Philadelphia, Pennsylvania

David Baumbach, Teacher
Woolsair Elementary Gifted Center
Pittsburgh, Pennsylvania

Edward Berenson, Professor of History
University of California, Los Angeles

Margaret Binnaker, Teacher
St. Andrews-Swanee School
St. Andrews, Tennessee

Jacqueline Brown-Frierson, Teacher
Lemmel Middle School
Baltimore, Maryland

Richard Bulliet, Professor of History
Columbia University

Stanley Burstein, Professor of History
California State University, Los Angeles

Anne Chapman, Academic Dean
Western Reserve Academy
Hudson, Ohio

Peter Cheoros, Teacher
Lynwood High School
Lynwood, California

Charlotte Crabtree, Professor of Education Emeritus
University of California, Los Angeles

Sammy Crawford, Teacher
Soldotna High School
Soldotna, Alaska

Ross Dunn, Professor of History
San Diego State University

Benjamin Elman, Professor of History
University of California, Los Angeles

Jean Fleet, Teacher
Riverside University High School
Milwaukee, Wisconsin

Jana Flores, Teacher
Pine Grove Elementary School
Santa Maria, California

Michele Forman, Teacher
Middlebury High School
Middlebury, Vermont

Charles Frazee, Professor of History Emeritus
California State University, Fullerton

Marilynn Jo Hitchens, Teacher
Wheat Ridge High School
Denver, Colorado

Jean Johnson
Friends Seminary
New York, New York

Henry G. Kiernan, Director of Curriculum
West Morris Regional High School District
Chester, New Jersey

Carrie McIver, Teacher
Santee Summit High School
Santee, California

Susan Meisler, Teacher
Vernon Center Middle School
Vernon, Connecticut

Gary B. Nash, Professor of History
University of California, Los Angeles

Joe Palumbo, Administrative Assistant
Long Beach Unified School District
Long Beach, California

Sue Rosenthal, Teacher
High School for Creative and Performing Arts
Philadelphia, Pennsylvania

Heidi Roupp, Teacher
Aspen High School
Aspen, Colorado

Irene Segade, Teacher
San Diego High School
San Diego, California

Geoffrey Symcox, Professor of History
University of California, Los Angeles

Linda Symcox, Associate Director
National Center for History in the Schools
University of California, Los Angeles

David Vigilante, Teacher Emeritus
Gompers Secondary School
San Diego, California

Scott Waugh, Professor of History
University of California, Los Angeles

Julia Stewart Werner, Teacher
Nicolet High School
Glendale, Wisconsin

Donald Woodruff, Headmaster
Fredericksburg Academy
Fredericksburg, Virginia

National Center for History in the Schools Advisory Board

Joyce Appleby
Department of History
University of California, Los Angeles

Robert Bain
Beachwood High School
Cleveland Heights, Ohio

Jerry H. Bentley
Department of History
University of Hawaii

Daniel Berman
Fox Lane High School
Bedford, New York

Linda Black
Langham High School
Houston, Texas

Douglas Greenberg, President
Chicago Historical Society
Chicago, Illinois

Melinda Hennessey
The Bishop's School
La Jolla, California

Linda Heywood
Department of History
Howard University
Washington, D.C.

David Hollinger
Department of History
University of California, Berkeley

Evelyn Hu-DeHart
Ethnic Studies and Asian American History
University of Colorado

Donna Rogers-Beard
Clayton High School
Clayton, Missouri

Gloria Sesso
Half Hollow High School East
Dix Hills, New York

Donald Woodruff
Baltimore, Maryland

Judith P. Zinsser
Department of History
Miami University

National Forum for History Standards

Sara Shoob
National Association of Elementary School Principals

Kathy Belter
National Congress of Parents and Teachers

Nguyen Minh Chau
National Association for Asian and
Pacific American Education

Cesar Collantes
League of United Latin American Citizens

Mark Curtis
The Atlantic Council of the United States

Glen Cutlip
National Education Association

Graham Down
Council for Basic Education

Chester Finn
Educational Excellence Network

Mary Futrell
Quality Education for Minorities Network

Keith Geiger
National Education Association

Ivan Gluckman
National Association of Secondary School Principals

Ruth Granados
Council of the Great City Schools

Joyce McCray
Council for American Private Education

Sr. Catherine T. McNamee
National Catholic Educational Association

Patricia Gordon Michael
American Association for State and Local History

Mabel Lake Murray
National Alliance of Black School Educators

Cynthia Neverdon-Morton
Association for the Study of Afro-American
Life and History

George Nielsen
Lutheran Schools
The Lutheran Church-Missouri Synod

Charles N. Quigley
Center for Civic Education

Christopher Salter
National Council for Geographic Education

Adelaide Sanford
National Association of State Boards of Education

Ruth Toor
American Association of School Librarians

Clifford Trafzer
Native American Heritage Commission

Hai T. Tran
National Association for Asian and
Pacific American Education

Ruth Wattenberg
American Federation of Teachers

Council of Chief State School Officers
Focus Group

Sue Bennet
California Department of Education

Pasquale DeVito
Rhode Island Department of Education

Patricia Dye, History/Social Studies Consultant
Plymouth, Massachusetts

Mary Fortney
Indiana Department of Education

Constance Miller Manter
Maine Department of Education

Alan D. Morgan
New Mexico State Superintendent of Public Instruction

Wayne Neuburger
Oregon Department of Education

Charles Peters
Oakland Schools, Waterford, Michigan

Thomas Sobol
New York Commissioner of Education

Robert H. Summerville
Alabama Department of Education

Staff

Fred Czarra, Consultant in International Education,
Social Studies and Interdisciplinary Learning

Ed Roeber, Director of the State Collaborative on
Assessment and Student Standards

Ramsay Selden, Director, State Education
Assessment Center

Association for Supervision and Curriculum Development
Focus Group

Glen Blankenship, Social Studies Coordinator
Georgia State Department of Education
Atlanta, Georgia

Joyce Coffey, Teacher
Dunbar Senior High School
District Heights, Maryland

Sherrill Curtiss, Teacher
Chairman, Dept. of History/Social Studies
Providence Senior High School
Charlotte, North Carolina

Geno Flores, Teacher
Arroyo Grande High School
Arroyo Grande, California

Alan Hall, Teacher
Chairman, Social Studies Department
Yarmouth High School
Yarmouth, Massachussetts

Erich Martel, Teacher
Wilson Senior High School
Washington, D.C.

Marilyn McKnight, Teacher
Forest Home School
Milwaukee, Wisconsin

Mike Radow, Teacher
Tops Middle School
Seattle, Washington

Karen Steinbrink, Assistant Executive Director
Bucks County Intermediate Unit
Doylestown, Pennsylvania

Staff

Diane Berreth, Deputy Executive Director

Brian Curry, Policy Analyst

National Council for the Social Studies
Focus Group

Linda Levstick, Professor of Education
University of Kentucky

Janna Bremer, Teacher
King Philip Regional High School
Foxborough, Massachusetts

Jean Craven, District Coordinator/Curriculum Devel.
Albuquerque Public School District
Albuquerque, New Mexico

Mathew Downey, Professor of Education
University of California, Berkeley

Rachel Hicks, Teacher
Jefferson Junior High School
Washington, D.C.

Jack Larner, Coordinator of Secondary
Social Studies, Department of History
Indiana University of Pennsylvania

Tarry Lindquist, Teacher
Lakeridge Elementary
Mercer Island, Washington

Denny Schillings, Teacher
Homewood-Flossmoor High School
Flossmoor, Illinois

Judith S. Wooster, Assistant Superintendent
Bethlehem Central Schools
Del Mar, New York

Ruben Zepeda, Teacher
Grant High School
Van Nuys, California

Council of State Social Studies Specialists
Focus Group

Norman Abramowitz, New York
Margaret (Peggy) Altoff, Maryland
Wendy Bonaiuto, South Dakota
Patricia Boyd, Nevada
Diane Brooks, California
Harvey R. Carmichael, Virginia
John M. Chapman, Michigan
Nijel Clayton, Kentucky
Pat Concannon, New Mexico
Edward T. Costa, Rhode Island
Thomas Dunthorn, Florida
Patricia Dye, Massachusetts
John D. Ellington, North Carolina
Curt Eriksmoen, North Dakota
Mary Fortney, Indiana
Rita Geiger, Oklahoma
Daniel W. Gregg, Connecticut

Carter B. Hart, Jr., New Hampshire
H. Michael Hartoonian, Wisconsin
Lewis E. Huffman, Delaware
Barbara Jones, West Virginia
Sharon Kaohi, Hawaii
Mary Jean Katz, Oregon
Marianne Kenney, Colorado
Judith Kishman, Wyoming
Frank Klajda, Arizona
John LeFeber, Nebraska
Richard Leighty, Kansas
Constance Miller Manter, Maine
Nancy N. Matthew, Utah
Nanette McGee, Georgia
Marjorie Menzi, Alaska
William Miller, Louisiana
Kent J. Minor, Ohio

John A. Nelson, Vermont
Bruce Opie, Tennessee
Linda Vrooman Peterson, Montana
Barbara Patty, Arkansas
Ann Pictor, Illinois
Joan Prewitt, Mississippi
Orville Reddington, Idaho
Michael Ryan, New Jersey
Warren Solomon, Missouri
Larry Strickland, Washington
Robert H. Summerville, Alabama
Cordell Svegalis, Iowa
Elvin E. Tyrone, Texas
Margaret B. Walden, South Carolina
Roger Wangen, Minnesota
James J. Wetzler, Pennsylvania

Organization of American Historians
Focus Group

Joyce Appleby, Professor of History
University of California, Los Angeles

Earl Bell, Teacher
The Laboratory Schools
University of Chicago

Alan Brinkley, Professor of History
Columbia University

George Burson, Teacher
Aspen High School
Aspen, Colorado

Albert Camarillo, Professor of History
Stanford University

William H. Chafe, Professor of History
Duke University

Christine L. Compston, Director
History Teaching Alliance
National History Education Network

Terrie Epstein, Professor of Education
University of Michigan

Eric Foner, Professor of History
Columbia University

Mary A. Giunta
National Historical Publications and Records
Commission

Scott L. Greenwell, Principal
North Layton Junior High
Layton, Utah

David C. Hammack, Professor of History
Case Western Reserve University

Louis Harlan, Professor of History
University of Maryland, College Park

George Henry, Jr., Teacher
Highland High School
Salt Lake City, Utah

Marilynn Jo Hitchens, Teacher
Wheat Ridge High School
Denver, Colorado

Michael Kammen, Professor of History
Cornell University

Harvey J. Kaye, Rosenberg Professor of
Social Change and Development
University of Wisconsin, Green Bay

Kathleen C. Kean, Teacher
Nicolet High School
Glendale, Wisconsin

Lawrence W. Levine, Professor of History
University of California, Berkeley

William J. McCracken, Teacher
Pine View School
Sarasota, Florida

Lynette K. Oshima, Professor of Education
University of New Mexico

Pamela Petty, Teacher
Apollo High School
Glendale, Arizona

John Pyne, Humanities Supervisor
West Milford High School
West Milford, New Jersey

Eric Rothschild, Teacher
Scarsdale High School
Scarsdale, New York

Peter Seixas, Professor of Social and
Educational Studies
University of British Columbia

Gloria Sesso, Teacher
Half Hollow High School East
Dix Hills, New York

George Stevens, Professor
Dutchess Community College
Poughkeepsie, New York

Organization of American Historians Focus Group (continued)

Steven Teel, Teacher
Berkeley High School
Hercules, California

Sandra F. VanBurkleo, Professor of History
Wayne State University

David Vigilante, Teacher Emeritus
Gompers Secondary School
San Diego, California

Bertram Wyatt-Brown, Professor of History
University of Florida

Deborah White, Professor of History
Rutgers University

Mitch Yamasaki, Teacher
Chaminade University of Honolulu
Kaneohe, Hawaii

Charles Anthony Zappia, Professor of History
San Diego Mesa College

Staff

Arnita A. Jones, OAH Executive Director

American Historical Association
U.S. History Focus Group

Albert Camarillo, Professor of History
Stanford University

Terrie Epstein, Professor of Education
University of Michigan

Ned Farman, Teacher
Westtown School
Westtown, Pennsylvania

Elizabeth Faue, Professor of History
Wayne State University

Donald L. Fixico, Professor of History
Western Michigan University

James R. Grossman, Director
Family and Community History Center
Newberry Library
Chicago, Illinois

Louis Harlan, Professor of History
University of Maryland, College Park

James O. Horton, Professor of History
George Washington University

Thomas C. Holt, Professor of History
University of Chicago

David Katzman, Professor of History
University of Kansas

Lori Lee Morton, Teacher
Riverside Elementary School
Alexandria, Virginia

Howard Shorr, Teacher
Columbia River High School
Vancouver, Washington

Kathleen Anderson Steeves, Professor of
Teacher Preparation
George Washington University

Staff

James B. Gardner, Acting Executive Director

Noralee Frankel, Assistant Director on Women and
Minorities

Robert B. Townsend, Managing Editor

American Historical Association
World History Focus Group

Peter N. Stearns, Professor of History
Carnegie Mellon University

Robert A. Blackey, Professor of History
California State University, San Bernardino

John H. Coatsworth, Professor of History
Harvard University

Ross E. Dunn, Professor of History
San Diego State University

Robert Gutierrez, Teacher
Miami Sunset Senior High School

Joseph C. Miller, Professor of History
University of Virginia

Colin Palmer, Professor of History
University of North Carolina, Chapel Hill

Howard Spodek, Professor of History
Temple University

Julia Stewart Werner, Teacher
Nicolet High School
Glendale, Wisconsin

Judith P. Zinsser, Assistant Professor of History
Miami University

Staff

James B. Gardner, Acting Executive Director

Noralee Frankel, Assistant Director on Women and
Minorities

Robert B. Townsend, Managing Editor

National Council for History Education
U.S. History Focus Group

Douglas Greenberg, Chair, 1994
Director, Chicago Historical Society

James Bruggeman, Principal
Irving Elementary School
Bozeman, Montana

Miriam U. Chrisman, Professor of History Emeritus
University of Massachusetts

Robert D. Cross, Professor of History
University of Virginia

Carl N. Degler, Professor of History
Stanford University

Paul H. Fagette, Jr., Professor of History
Arkansas State University

Betty B. Franks, Social Studies Dept. Chairperson
Maple Heights High School
Maple Heights, Ohio

David Alyn Gordon, Teacher
Tempe School District
Tempe, Arizona

Ann N. Greene, Teacher
National Cathedral School for Girls
Washington, D.C.

Larry A. Greene, Chairman
Department of History
Seton Hall University

Michael S. Henry, Teacher
Bowie High School
Bowie, Maryland

Byron Hollinshead, Chair, 1993
Publisher/Chairman
American Historical Publications
New York, New York

Diane N. Johnson, Teacher
Anne Arundel County Schools
Arnold, Maryland

Henry G. Kiernan, Director of Curriculum
West Morris Regional High School District
Chester, New Jersey

Melissa Kirkpatrick, Information and
Research Consultant
Cassandra Associates
Reston, Virginia

National Council for History Education U.S. History Focus Group (continued)

Josef W. Konvitz, Chair, 1992
Professor of History
Michigan State University

Donald Lankiewicz, Education Consultant
Windermere, Florida

Joel Latman, Teacher
Montville High School
Oakdale, Connecticut

Kurt E. Leichtle, Professor of History
University of Wisconsin, River Falls

Arthur S. Link, Professor of History Emeritus
Princeton University

Arna M. Margolis, Head, History Department
The Bryn Mawr School
Bryn Mawr, Maryland

Susan Mertz, Education Consultant
IMPACT!
Summerville, South Carolina

Edmund S. Morgan, Professor of History Emeritus
Yale University

Mary Beth Norton, Professor of History
Cornell University

Paul H. Pangrace, Teacher
Garrett Morgan School of Science
Cleveland, Ohio

Theodore C. Parker
Writer/Education Specialist
Camarillo, California

Kathryn Kish Sklar, Professor of History
University of Binghamton

Peg Killam Smith, Teacher
Seton Keough High School
Arnold, Maryland

Sheldon Stern, Historian
John F. Kennedy Library
Boston, Massachusetts

Jo Sullivan, Principal
Federal Street School
Salem, Massachusetts

Robert H. Summerville, Social Studies Specialist
Alabama Department of Education

Susan Taylor, Teacher,
Withrow School
Cincinnati, Ohio

William L. Taylor, Professor of Social Science
Plymouth State College

Stephan Thernstrom, Professor of History
Harvard University

Carl Ubbelohde, Professor Emeritus
Case Western Reserve University

W. Jeffrey Welsh, Professor of History
Bowling Green State University, Firelands

James Wilkinson, Director
Derek Bok Center
Harvard University

Peter H. Wood, Professor of History
Duke University

Staff

Elaine Reed, Executive Secretary

National Council for History Education
World History Focus Group

Thomas N. Bisson
Professor of History
Harvard University

Philip Curtin, Chair, 1994
Professor of History
The Johns Hopkins University

Jerry H. Bentley, Editor
Journal of World History
University of Hawaii

Mary Bicouvaris
Associate Professor of Education
Christopher Newport University

Marjorie Bingham
St. Louis Park High School
Minnetonka, Minnesota

Hank Bitten, Teacher
Ramapo High School
Franklin Lakes, New Jersey

Jane Christie, Assistant Director for Education
Connecticut Humanities Council
Middletown, Connecticut

Marie Cleary, Five College Associate
Five Colleges, Inc.
Amherst, Massachusetts

Timothy Connell, Teacher
Laurel School
Shaker Heights, Ohio

James A. Diskant, Researcher
Primary Source, Inc.
Cambridge, Massachusetts

Susan Douglass, Humanities Coordinator
Tottenville High School
Staten Island, New York

Paul Filio, Curriculum Specialist
Cincinnati Public Schools
Cincinnati, Ohio

Darlene E. Fisher, Teacher
New Trier High School
Evanston, Illinois

Claudette Hagar, Teacher
Hawaii Preparatory Academy
Kamuela, Hawaii

Blythe Hinitz, Professor of Education
Trenton State College
Trenton, New Jersey

John D. Hoge, Professor of Education
University of Georgia

David Huston, Teacher
Laurel School
Cleveland Heights, Ohio

Patricia M. Keppler, Teacher
Milford High School
Milford, Massachusetts

Henry G. Kiernan, Director of Curriculum
West Morris Regional High School District
Chester, New Jersey

Josef W. Konvitz, Chair, 1992
Professor of History
Michigan State University

Frederick W. Pfister, Teacher
Cranbrook Kingswood School
Bloomfield Hills, Michigan

Theodore K. Rabb, Professor of History
Princeton University

Gary Regnerus, Teacher
Unity Christian High School
Orange City, Iowa

Linda K. Salvucci
Department of History
Trinity University

Robert J. Sinner, Academic Dean
The Montclair Kimberley Academy
Montclair, New Jersey

Richard E. Smith, Teacher
East Corinth Elementary School
Corinth, Mississippi

Lawrence A. Spalla, Teacher
Trinity High School
Washington, Pennsylvania

Michael F. Stanislawski, Professor of History
Columbia University

Sandra Stewart, Teacher
Hawaii Preparatory Academy
Kamuela, Hawaii

Organization of History Teachers
U.S. History Focus Group

John Tyler, Chair
Groton School
Groton, Massachusetts

Earl P. Bell, Teacher
The Laboratory Schools
University of Chicago

Ron Briley, Teacher
Sandia Preparatory School
Albuquerque, New Mexico

Ron Buchheim, Teacher
Dana Hills High School
Dana Point, California

Tom English, Teacher
The George School
Newtown, Pennsylvania

Marianne Gieger, Teacher
Sousa Elementary School
Port Washington, New York

Joe Gotchy, Teacher
Thomas Jefferson High School
West Milford, New Jersey

Paul Horton, Teacher
The Laboratory Schools
University of Chicago

Doris Meadows, Teacher
Wilson Magnet School
Rochester, New York

John Pyne, Humanities Supervisor
West Milford High School
West Milford, New Jersey

Robert Rodey, Teacher
Marion Catholic High School
Chicago Heights, Illinois

Gloria Sesso, Teacher
Half Hollow High School East
Dix Hills, New York

Peggy Smith, Teacher
St. Mary's High School
Annapolis, Maryland

Richard Swanson, Teacher
The McCallie School
Chattanooga, Tennessee

World History Association
Focus Group

John Mears, Chair
Professor of History
Southern Methodist University

Roger Beck, Professor of History
Eastern Illinois University

Jerry Bentley, Professor of History
University of Hawaii

Timothy Connell, Teacher
Laurel School
Shaker Heights, Ohio

Darlene Fisher, Teacher
New Trier Township High School
Winnetka, Illinois

Steve Gosch, Professor of History
University of Wisconsin, Eau Claire

William B. Jones, Professor of History
Southwestern University

Donald Johnson, Professor of History
New York University

Jeannine Marston, Teacher
Castellaeja School
Palo Alto, California

Patricia O'Neill
Department of History
Central Oregon Community College
Bend, Oregon

Kevin Reilly
Department of History
Raritan Valley Community College

Sue Robertson, Teacher
Mills E. Godwin High School
Richmond, Virginia

Heidi Roupp, Teacher
Aspen High School
Aspen, Colorado

Lynda Shaffer, Professor of History
Tufts University

Council for Basic Education Review Panels
World History Panel

Steven Muller, Chair
President Emeritus
The Johns Hopkins University

Hilary Ainger
Head of Humanities
U.N. International School

Robert Bain
Social Studies Teacher
Beachwood High School
Cleveland Heights, Ohio

Allison Blakely
Professor of European and Comparative History
Howard University

A. Lee Blitch
Regional Vice President-Southwest
AT&T
Dallas, Texas

Philip D. Curtin
Herbert Baxter Adams Professor of History
The Johns Hopkins University

Prasenjit Duara
Professor of History
University of Chicago

Michael F. Jimenez
Assistant Professor of History
University of Pittsburgh

Ramsay MacMullen
Professor of History (Emeritus)
Yale University

Marjorie Malley
Independent Scholar
Bartlesville, Oklahoma

Joan Wallach Scott
Professor of Social Science
Institute for Advanced Study
Princeton University

John Obert Voll
Professor of History
Georgetown University

Council for Basic Education Review Panels
U.S. History Panel

The Honorable Albert Quie, Chair
Governor, State of Minnesota, 1979-83
Member of U.S. Congress, 1958-1978

Cary Carson
Vice President for Research
Colonial Williamsburg Foundation

Evelyn Brooks Higginbotham
Professor of Afro-American Studies and
African-American Religion
Harvard University

David Hollinger
Professor of History
University of California, Berkeley

Jeanette LaFors
Social Studies Teacher
Carlmont High School
Belmont, California

Diane Ravitch
Senior Research Scholar and
Adjunct Professor of Education
New York University

Rex Shepard
Supervisor, Office of Social Studies
Baltimore Co. Public Schools

Stephan Thernstrom
Professor of History
Harvard University

Reed Ueda
Associate Professor of History
Tufts University

Maris A. Vinovskis
Professor of History
University of Michigan